# THE KITE THAT COULDN'T FLY

## And Other May Avenue Stories

## MICHAEL J. MENARD

burning soul press

**The Kite That Couldn't Fly**

And Other May Avenue Stories

**Copyright © 2024 by Michael J. Menard**

**All rights reserved.**

Cover Art Credit: Svetlana Hristova

Chapter Illustration Credit: Svetlana Hristova

Author Photo Credit: Joaquin Films Co.

ISBNs:

Paperback: 978-1-950476-92-3

Hardcover: 978-1-950476-93-0

Ebook: 978-1-950476-91-6

*This book is dedicated to my mother, Arletta Menard—our teacher and kite maker.*

# PRAISE FOR THE KITE THAT COULDN'T FLY

*"What a truly superb and beautiful book! Michael Menard is a master storyteller, whose tales brought me from laughter one moment to tears another.* The Kite That Couldn't Fly *is chock full of wisdom, humor, and insights about why we thrive and why we stumble. It shows how unconditional love, hope, faith, and a strong spine over-come the most difficult circumstances. I'm grateful for the pleasure of reading it and know it will be an inspiration and uplift to all who read it."*

— GLENN R. SCHIRALDI, PH.D., LT. COLONEL, AUTHOR, *THE ADVERSE CHILDHOOD EXPERIENCES RECOVERY WORKBOOK*

*"An amazing journey from violence and poverty into triumph! The stories are compelling and touching but it's more than a story. This book can help heal the wounds we carry from childhood. I couldn't put it down."*

— DAVE FARROW, INTERNATIONAL BESTSELLING AUTHOR

*"Menard has written a midwestern version of Frank McCourt's* Angela's Ashes *and even the malignant nuns make a cameo. It's the storytelling and the unique structure of the book that makes* The Kite That Couldn't Fly *so compelling."*

— JAMES MURRAY, PHD

"This book is a must read for most everyone. Some to better understand their own childhood challenges, and some to better understand their own humanity. Some greatness takes years. Harlan Sanders started KFC at age 65. Laura Ingalls Wilder wrote Little House on the Prairie at 65. Grandma Moses started painting at 76.

Michael Menard has already achieved great success as a world class inventor, entrepreneur, business leader, and father. At age 73, Michael's book The Kite That Couldn't Fly may be his greatest contribution to the planet."

— DAVID E. NELSON, BESTSELLING AUTHOR,
THE 9 DIMENSIONS OF CONSCIOUS SUCCESS


"I have been working in the clinical field for 25 years with a focus on chronic depression and the trauma that typically precedes it. Michael Menard's book, The Kite That Couldn't Fly is not only entertaining but packed full of hope and resilience. The toxic stress from childhood trauma creates mental and physical health hazards that affects over 150 million adults today in the USA alone, and over a billion people on our planet. Michael tells his stories with vulnerability and raw openness; stories that open eyes, minds and doors to those suffering from generations of childhood trauma. Rarely is there a book that comes along that is not only a great read, but also reveals beacons of hope and healing."

— LEE LONG, EDD, LPC-S, DIRECTOR OF
RESTORATION COUNSELING

# CONTENTS

"There is no greater agony than bearing an untold
story inside you."

– Maya Angelou

# FOREWORD

## Kristin Trudeau

As part of my private practice, I offer potential clients a free, fifteen-minute consultation to help determine if I would be the best fit as a therapist for them. It was during one such consultation that I met Mike. Within forty-five seconds, I knew he would not be my typical client; within two minutes, I knew we were headed down a path I had never taken. Mike made it clear to me that he was not looking to become a client, wasn't looking to get anything "fixed," and had no interest in "psychoanalysis." Mike ensured I knew early on that he had a very high level of well-being and was most likely the happiest guy I would ever know. As it turns out, Mike was right.

I was one of many therapists, psychologists, and psychiatrists Mike had interviewed. He wasn't seeking therapy; he was looking for a consultant. For what? Neither of us were quite sure. But for a reason, he picked me.

In our first consultative appointment, the mystery began to clear up. Mike was looking for a mental health professional to talk through the latest book he was writing, a collection of non-fiction stories that he believed were just too good to be true. He wanted me to offer a reflection after each of his stories.

Mike began by sharing an overview of his adult life. Mike is a humble guy who struggled while sharing his long list of life's achievements. They were astounding accomplishments; he is a success by all measures. It was important to Mike that I understood that he was successful—Mike was searching to understand the "why" behind his own, and some of his siblings', success. He questioned whether they had been successful despite, or because of, their childhood.

Then Mike introduced me to the stories of 118 South May Avenue, the address where he grew up. As he shared his stories, I felt like I was watching a movie. A gifted storyteller, Mike gave me a front-row seat to his thoughts, feelings, and childhood trauma that were unlike anything I had heard before. We have all been through some tough stuff, but Mike's experiences were off the charts.

Meeting Mike has been life-changing—and I know I'm not the only one who can say that. His stories, so full of vulnerability and wisdom, travel directly from his heart and pierce your own. Key lessons and takeaways from these stories can be transformative. Why? Because Mike's experiences and May Avenue Stories are inspirational. They tell us all, "You are not alone." That's what this book is all about. This isn't a self-help book filled with advice and guidance; no "how-to" book here. Instead, in the pages that follow, you will walk the path of a boy who has been through the darkness of childhood trauma and back.

This is not simply another life story about struggle, hurt, and pain. This story is about the human spirit and its capacity for resilience, hope, and healing, and the critical reminder that gratitude is a choice. This book is about all of us who have experienced trauma or adversity, who may feel inadequate or broken, and serves as proof and empowerment that our suffering and circumstances do not define us.

The stories that await you range from humorous to unthinkable to unfathomable and offer a raw and courageous glimpse into a journey none of us would choose, yet, in a sense, are all on in one way or another.

Depending on your own trauma and experiences, you may feel triggered by some of the stories. If you need to put the book down and take a break, do that. Take care of yourself. But I implore you to embark on the journey ahead with an open mind and heart and the willingness to believe that your trauma does not define you. There is hope in your own resilience, the ability to heal, and the power of choosing gratitude.

Your journey awaits. I welcome you to lean into *The Kite That Couldn't Fly: and Other May Avenue Stories.*

– KRISTIN TRUDEAU, M.A., LPC-MHSP, LADAC, CFRC

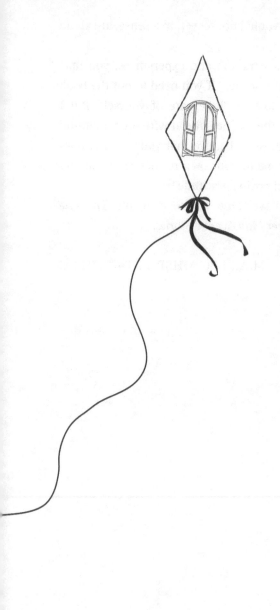

# PREFACE

"We are born into stories, raised in stories, and live and
  die in stories."

– Dan Taylor

We were celebrating Mom and Dad's fortieth wedding
anniversary. All fourteen of their children—four girls and ten
boys—were at the party. Yes, they were all from the same
parents, and no, there were no twins. We made up half of the 200
partygoers with our spouses and children.

In birth order, we each took the stage to offer congratulations
and share one of our favorite childhood stories. Jamie (born in
1949), myself (1951), Polly (1953), David (1954), Mary (1955),
Tim (1956), Bill (1957), Allen (1960), Patrick (1961), Warren
(1962), Maria (1964), Mark (1965), Adam (1966), and Ellen

(1969). We did not compare notes before delivering our stories; surprisingly, there were no duplicates. Not surprisingly, most stories were about our mother. Since we wanted to keep the stories positive, they must be about Mom. You see, my siblings and I grew up with an angel on one shoulder and a devil on the other.

Every story brought tears to the eyes of those in the room. Tears of joy and sadness, but mostly from laughter that hurt your side.

I took notes on all fourteen stories that night. While none of the stories were new to me, I was struck by three things:

Firstly, the richness of the stories. I recall whispering, "You can't make shit up this good." Secondly, the beautiful people my siblings had become. Even in the face of acute adversity, poverty, and the struggle between right and wrong, these fourteen children grew up to be excellent, extraordinary people, happy and successful by any measure. Still, to this day, they remain my best friends and are the sunniest people I know. Finally, each story, while wildly entertaining, delivered a life lesson that Mom and Dad had taught us through either their words or actions.

I began telling what became known as the "May Avenue Stories" to friends and strangers. They evolved into bedtime stories for my five young daughters. I have told them over 2,000 original bedtime stories from the library of May Avenue Stories. Zeke, our May Avenue family pet raccoon, was a main character in many of these bedtime stories.

Over time, I added to the list of my childhood memories. I asked my siblings to share all the stories they could remember from our May Avenue childhood: the good, the bad, and the ugly. I asked them only to include stories they were comfortable with me sharing with others. The list grew, including a few I wanted to forget. Thirty years ago, I began consolidating and categorizing the stories for the book I would someday write.

While recalling and collecting the stories, I doubted myself, questioning the accuracy of my memory. *Were these real happenings or a mix of truth and fixational family lore?* Albus Dumbledore's words helped me: "Of course it is happening inside your head, Harry, but why on earth should that mean that it is not real?"

For decades, I toyed with publishing the May Avenue Stories. I was often told that the stories belonged in a book. As a Christmas gift in 2022, my wife Emilie gave me a subscription to a web-based service that sent me a weekly question. I was to submit responses to the questions each week, then a book would be sent to me at the end of the year. Emilie thought it was time I wrote the May Avenue book. I never used her gift, but her gift and the nudge it symbolized motivated me to knuckle down and write this book.

As validation that these stories were not just in my head, I shared a list of the final story ideas with my siblings. I gave them each story's headline. For example, "Tell me about the fight between Jamie and Micky Cooper." And yes, my memory was confirmed for each story. My siblings also offered additional stories I had forgotten. I received permission to print each story and to "name names." I levy no judgment on those readers who find some stories fictional. I would not believe some of these stories had I not lived them. They are so rich. *You can't make shit up this good.*

When writing the stories that included sadness and what was clearly suffering, I tried convincing myself that they didn't happen. I had a hard time believing and reliving the sadness.

I had previously written two business books; I understood the process—it's straightforward. Most of my work was done, since I'd collected the stories in a journal, or so I thought. It should be simple: no plot and no beginning or end. It wouldn't be a memoir, just a collection of accounts listed in chronological order.

While in the early stages of writing, I glanced at a piece of

Stella's English homework. Stella is my fifth and youngest child and was in the eighth grade at the time. She had written in her notes, "We are a story-needy people—God created us this way." Stella explained she had copied something her teacher, Mrs. Cheney, wrote on the whiteboard. I emailed Mrs. Cheney, told her about the book, and asked her to expand on what she had written on that whiteboard.

Mrs. Cheney responded immediately and with enthusiasm. She replied, "Yes, Mike, I wrote those words on my whiteboard. I believe God has made us so that stories reach, teach, renew, and capture us in ways God's Spirit uses in our lives." I had struck gold. Mrs. Cheney sent me a copy of a speech to reinforce her belief. The speech was titled "The Life-Shaping Power of Story" and was delivered by author and speaker Dan Taylor. Dan's message:

"Human beings are story-shaped creatures. We are born into stories, raised in stories, and live and die in stories. Whenever we have to answer a big question—who am I, why am I here, what should I do, what happens to me when I die?—we tell a story. Story, as does life, engages all of what we are—mind, emotions, spirit, body. It is no surprise, then, that the central record of faith in human history opens with an unmistakable story signature: 'In the beginning...'"

I further researched storytelling and found overwhelming evidence of the importance of storytelling in the human experience. So, the May Avenue Stories are worth telling. I wanted my daughters and grandchildren to know my mom, my dad, Jamie, and the other twelve. We get to know others through stories. The wild, happy, sad, and courageous stories we tell reveal us. My book is a collection of stories that must be told.

On a catch-up call with my daughter Melissa, I shared my decision to write the book I had talked about for many years. She asked, "What is the red thread?" *What?* She explained that every book needs a reason to be written. "What's your message?

What's the purpose of the book? What's the theme that will run through your book like a thread? Why are you writing it?"

I explained that my motivations for publishing the May Avenue Stories were clear and simple: I wanted to capture some history of my childhood, pass it down to my children and grand-children, and entertain readers. Still, I couldn't answer Melissa's question. *Where was the red thread?* I needed to dig deeper.

I needed to admit to myself that I had a hidden motivation to write this book. This book could help answer some of my burn-ing, unasked questions about my siblings and me. How did we survive? No, why had we excelled in life as adults? Why did twelve of the fourteen emerge as extraordinary adults—great spouses and parents, happy, healthy, and successful? Why did Patrick and Adam lose their lives to drug addiction? Was there an alchemy created by mixing a loving, spiritual mother, a hard-as-nails, street-fighting father, and poverty, all while growing up in a tiny house? Was the red thread hidden within the stories? I couldn't answer those questions.

I became convinced that simply sharing a collection of inter-esting stories was not enough. So, I decided to find a mental health expert to help guide the writing of the book and answer those questions, both for my siblings and myself. If credible answers and explanations were unearthed, what are the universal lessons and truths that could be extracted and applied to thousands, maybe even millions, of readers? Perhaps the red thread is hidden in there. The book took a serious turn.

I threw a wide net and captured a list of possible therapists and psychologists. I filtered the list down to twenty mental health professionals. I interviewed fifteen either in person or virtually. It was an exhausting yet rich experience. I was repeat-edly impressed with the brain power and knowledge of these professionals. I selected Kristin, a licensed therapist with exper-tise in childhood trauma, as my subject matter expert.

My initial meeting with Kristin left me wishing I had a

mental health issue that she could help me fix. She was a great listener as I clumsily explained how I needed her help deciphering why my siblings and I became the adults we are today. She asked penetrating questions. I needed to understand why most of my siblings and I were such positive outliers in the face of adversity. I wanted her to bring clarity and authenticity to the book and reveal universal truths and lessons to help others improve their well-being.

I told Kristin the May Avenue Stories ranged from heartwarming and funny to sad and tragic. Kristin asked me to tell her three stories: two funny and one sad. She listened as I told the rehearsed stories as I had hundreds of times before. I read once that the Beatles had sung "I Want to Hold Your Hand" 10,000 times. The May Avenue Stories had become my hit songs.

Kristin's first response focused on the story about Polly and me making gloves out of mouse skins from mice we had captured, killed, and skinned. With a serious tone, Kristin explained that what I had classified as a fun story wasn't funny at all—it was sad. She said, "Just think about it, Mike: how did that twelve-year-old boy, living in a rodent-infested house, killing and skinning mice, feel?" She raised her eyebrows and held them up until I could conjure an answer. I told her the little boy was happy, having fun, and proud of those gloves. She didn't buy it.

At my second session with Kristin, I shared more stories and explored how she might contribute to the book. While she was listening intently, I felt that there was something she needed to say.

She said with her serious but kind face, "Let me go off subject for a minute. Based on your stories, you and your siblings experienced repetitive childhood trauma. It might take one session or five, but I know you would benefit from therapy." I thought I told her in the beginning that I was not the client.

She explained that this would, at a minimum, improve my ability to write the book. I told her I would think about it (I knew

I wouldn't), and I also told her that I believed I was the healthiest, happiest person she would ever meet. We ended that session with her saying she was willing to write the foreword for the book. I told her I wanted more, but I would accept the offer. Next, she would read the entire manuscript, and then we would have another session.

By our third session, Kristin was fully engaged. After saying a few things about how impressed she was with the book, she explained that as a mother she identified closely with my mom.

What she said next was unexpected and disturbing. Kristin told me that what my siblings and I had experienced was "complex childhood trauma." *What?* Based on the May Avenue Stories, Kristin was confident that not all fourteen siblings excelled and became happy and healthy adults. Patrick and Adam had sad, unhappy endings. She went on to tell me she could not explain how any of my siblings came to be successful and well-adjusted. She said that only I could do that. I left that meeting reeling and believing I would not see her again.

That meeting with Kristin caused me to feel disorganized and chaotic, setting my book on a different trajectory. I began reading books on childhood trauma. I read a book a day for eighteen days straight. I became consumed by the subject and tried to understand what happened to my siblings and me. On that eighteenth day, my wife Emilie stopped me. She said, "Michael, you are digging a hole. You have changed. I feel your sadness and confusion. It's time you stopped digging. You know enough now. Stop reading and start writing. You know what to write."

Yes, I had gone down a hole. I experienced feelings foreign to me: confusion, sadness, depression. I learned that over half of adults have experienced childhood trauma. I was crying for my siblings and for all those who had and are experiencing complex childhood trauma. But I learned so much in those eighteen days. My book needed to be more than a bunch of interesting stories. I followed Emilie's trusted and loving advice. I climbed out of the hole, brushed myself off, and finished my book.

Maybe life is supposed to be hard. While I would never wish suffering on anyone, we could never develop the tools and confidence to overcome hardship and misfortune without it. My siblings and I, and many of you, have experienced tough challenges as children. It could have been neglect, or physical or mental abuse—Adverse Childhood Experiences (ACEs) affect every family, every neighborhood, every community, and every country. ACEs, left unresolved, will change our brain chemistry, biology, and well-being for our entire lifetime. My research has convinced me that ACEs are a massive problem for humankind. Glenn Schiraldi, PhD, wrote in his book *The Adverse Childhood Experiences Recovery Workbook*, "ACEs may well be called the number-one unaddressed public health concern because of the devastation they leave in their wake."

I did not change any of the May Avenue Stories following my brief but deep dive into the subject of childhood trauma. The stories are what they are. I have added some reflections following some of the stories, sharing what I have discovered and learned. Kristin helped by offering reflections from a mental health professional's perspective.

Let me be clear: this book does not advocate for blaming problems on the past. Blaming and judging never work, and in fact, it hurts us. It turns us into victims and causes us to miss opportunities for healing. Don't blame yourself, don't blame your parents, don't blame the offenders—this will just keep you crushed under bitterness and doubt. Instead, I hope this book will help anyone who has experienced childhood trauma understand that you are not alone; there is hope and potential for true healing and reclaiming the glorious life you deserve.

Just as blame is out of bounds, so is using your childhood trauma as an excuse to misbehave. If you are using your childhood trauma as an excuse to do wrong to yourself or others, then you are already aware and, therefore, must begin the journey to healing. Starting that journey could be as simple as opening up to someone you trust and maybe even love.

After my hole digging, I reunited with Kristin. I've done my best to follow her guidance. In addition to telling the May Avenue Stories, I offer reflections as an adult about my siblings and myself. I've attempted to explain how my siblings emerged as amazing women and men, why Patrick and Adam fell through the cracks, and how light can come from darkness. Ultimately, I describe the paradox of childhood trauma as a beautiful, unexpected gift.

This is not a self-help book, but I offer suggestions and lessons that might help readers begin the journey to becoming happier, healthier people, better parents, and more understanding, grateful, and forgiving daughters or sons. I hope you find your red threads running through this book.

As a child living at 118 South May Avenue, I pressed my face against the window and looked out for hours. I was entertained by the nose and lip marks I made on the glass. Now, I'm making those imprints on the outside of the glass, looking back at the memories that shaped our lives.

These are true stories. Please enjoy them. They are stories of beauty, love, and adventure. Stories of danger and loss and heroism and betrayal. But overall, of redemption.

Perhaps maybe my stories will bring you back to your stories, back to your secrets. The powerful combination of awareness and knowledge can expand your perspective and lift you to unimaginable heights.

# 118 SOUTH MAY AVENUE

## An Introduction

118 South May Avenue was located near the west side of Kankakee, Illinois. The neighborhood could easily be called quaint. Homes ranged from small to smaller, built to accommodate GIs returning from World War II. Veterans Affairs loans made homeownership possible for veterans, including my dad. Large elm trees grew in each yard, creating an arch of branches that shaded the yards and the entire street. Soon after we moved in, Dutch elm disease wiped out every tree on our street, turning the look from charming to barrack-like.

Mom and Dad bought our May Avenue home in 1954; one bedroom, one bath, with a low and narrow attic and a basement. Our type of home was called a strawberry box house. Dad finished the attic with drywall and a plywood floor. A long, narrow room with knee walls and a divider wall in the middle; one side for girls, one for boys. Dad converted the one-car garage in the alley into a pigeon coop.

The front entrance had no porch, just a stoop, two steps, and a small, concrete, six-foot square pad. The front door opened into the living room. To the right was a small set of stairs leading to the attic. In the living room was one sofa, and the family radio, which was eventually replaced by a television. A combination kitchen and dining area was four steps toward the back of the home. It was a small kitchen with a refrigerator, stove, sink, and small cabinet counter. To the far right was the doorway to the basement stairs. To the left was space for a dining table that sat six. The bathroom was in the far-right corner, and the far-left corner was the door to the bedroom belonging to Mom, Dad, and the arriving baby. The only closet in the house was between the bathroom and bedroom doors, three feet wide and six feet deep.

The basement was dungeon-like, with stone walls, foundation that wept whenever it rained, and a cracked and chipped concrete floor. It smelled like mildew. A cistern that caught and used rainwater was converted into a coal room. The coal furnace took up most of the area in the basement.

The home at 118 South May Avenue was approximately 900 square feet. With a peak occupancy of fifteen people, that translated to sixty square feet per person; if everyone spread out evenly in the home, the most space they could occupy alone would be eight square feet, about the size of a prison cell.

The home was continually infested with cockroaches and mice. Arriving home after dark with the lights out, in the three steps it took to get to the kitchen and pull a string to turn that light on, you stepped on and killed multiple cockroaches. Our neighbors on both sides regularly set off whole-house insect bombs, requiring the occupants to be gone for eight hours. These insect bombs did not kill the roaches; it relocated them to the closest home: ours. My parents could not afford the bombs, so 118 South May Avenue became a cockroach safehouse.

Growing up in such a small space with many others was far from ordinary. It isn't easy to describe, but I only recall the good aspects of living that way. My mom made it work. She was thankful for our home and was constantly reminding us of the benefits and blessings of being so close to each other.

The following stories have been loosely called the "May

Avenue Stories" and took place between 1954 and 1966. While the book includes all types of stories, you will find three main characters: Mom, Dad, and our eldest brother, Jamie.

The May Avenue Stories took place in the early evolution of the Menard family, with a focus on the first five or so siblings. I want to make sure the readers know all my other siblings are amazing women and men, and all remain to be best friends. Each have their own stories as interesting as those about Jamie, all deserving of their own book. However, the real protagonist throughout these stories is my mother, Arletta Menard.

## ARLETTA MENARD

Mom kept two things on our tiny front porch. One was a concrete goose that she dressed up in holiday garb; the other, a flag that would fly depending on the season or holiday. One year, Mom mentioned to me a month before Christmas that she wanted a flag made with fourteen stars, one for each of her children, so all the multi-colors would fly on her porch. I had one made and gave it to her on Christmas Eve.

I loved to make Mom laugh. She had an easily-triggered, hearty, infectious laugh. She had a keen sense of humor, one of the many gifts she passed down to her children. With the flag, I had one of the stars made of metallic gold cloth. I gave the flag to her in private, and when she opened it and saw that gold star, she erupted into that famous laugh. Mission accomplished.

Years later, I confirmed that she told each of my siblings that the gold star represented them. They all believed her completely. Throughout childhood, she made us feel deep in our hearts that we were her favorite. What a challenge that must have been.

Many words aptly define our mother: extraordinary, faithful, indescribable, selfless, kind, wise, supermom, and indestructible. John Steinbeck stated in *East of Eden*, "I believe a strong woman may be stronger than a man, particularly if she happens to have love in her heart. I guess a loving woman is indestructible."

Mom was born to serve others and her Lord. She was also born to have fourteen children. Of course, many mothers bore many children, although sometimes out of ignorance, with no idea of what it takes to be a great mother to their children. Arletta was an outlier. Mom told us the story about the recurring nightmare she had as a young woman before marriage. She would be in a long dormitory, tied to a chair, and she could not move, hands behind her back. Down each wall were sixteen babies (always sixteen), all needing her, all crying. Some in cribs required changing. Some were hungry and in highchairs. Others sat on the floor, bleeding from minor cuts. It was torture for her.

Even before marrying our dad, our mom wrote in a letter to our dad while he was in the Navy during WWII, declaring, "We will have sixteen children." As one of fourteen, it was comforting to know she wanted all fourteen of us.

Dad worked at the factory, raised and raced his pigeons, and tended to the "must-do" house repairs. Mom did everything else, and I mean *everything*.

At forty-six, my mom miscarried her final pregnancy at home. I was seventeen and took her to the doctor. The doctor scolded her, "Mrs. Menard, you must stop getting pregnant; your body is falling apart." Mom responded, "Only He will decide when I will stop having babies," as she pointed to her God. Mom had sixteen pregnancies, including two miscarriages. When strangers heard she had fourteen children, their natural response was, "God bless you." Mom would reply, "He did—fourteen times."

I wonder how she became such an incredible, extraordinary mother and teacher. *Who taught her? Where did she discover the wisdom and techniques she used? What was the source of her energy?* She taught us faith, mercy, grace, forgiveness, and self-love. She taught her sons about women and her daughters about men. She taught us about sexuality and how respect for each other is the root of a great relationship. She told everyone her strength came from Jesus and her faith in Him. Of all the lessons she taught us, the one that rings in my ears every day is that *God loves a thankful heart.*

## PAUL MENARD

Based on the following stories, one might conclude that my dad was the antagonist, the bad guy. And while I don't help by referring to my dad as the devil on my shoulder, he was neither evil nor a monster. Many stories told here are disturbing and dark. As I wrote them, I didn't want to believe them. His wife, children, grandchildren, and close friends loved him. But honestly, I am still seeking to understand his influence on my siblings and me.

I'm confused and amazed at how we, his children, held and continue to keep our father in such high regard, given his teachings, meanness, and absence. *Is it simply the love of a father? Is it about forgiveness? Was it my mother erasing the harmful impact along his path?*

My siblings are standouts—successful and uniquely fabulous men and women. I see parts of my dad in each of us; what I see in them is all goodness.

Father's Day always prompts happy thoughts and some sadness about my dad. Not only because I miss him but also because I end up reflecting on the sadness and pain he caused me, my brothers, sisters, and our mom. I have forgiven and released him a long time ago.

As forgiveness took hold, I considered him not as someone who had hurt me and deprived my siblings and me of love, attention, or companionship but as someone who himself had been robbed by his father and his mother. My father had wounds that no one ever offered to heal. His father was an alcoholic and mean, and there were some tough years for my dad as a young man, just as there were for his children. Forgiveness is powerful and cathartic for the one offering it, but it should never excuse toxic, abusive behavior or harm done.

Mom was the prevailing teacher, delivering each lesson when we were ready and when it was needed. While Dad regularly needed our forgiveness, he never asked for it. Mom repeatedly told me I needed to forgive my dad for my well-being, not his. She taught me that when I forgave my dad, I wasn't saying, "It didn't matter," or "I probably deserved part of it anyway."

My forgiveness says, "It was wrong; it mattered, and I release you." Then she advised me to ask God to father me and to tell me my true name. Sadly, a few of my siblings still haven't found a way to forgive our dad. They remain prisoners. Forgiveness is letting a person out of jail, and that person is you.

It was 1972. I was newly-married and living in our first apartment. In those days, the TV repair man came to the house. As the repair man wrote the receipt, he asked me if I was related to "Bowser Menard." I knew the name and the man well; I told the repair man "Bowser" was my dad.

"See this nose?" the repair man asked. I noticed his nose when he entered my home. It spread across his face and was squished flat. "Your dad did this with one punch—but I deserved it." He told me how he said something disrespectful to my mom.

Dad had shared bits and pieces about his violent youth, but we mainly learned about him from family and friends. Dad grew up in a boxing and street fighting culture in the 1930s and 1940s. His father was an alcoholic, who regularly beat his children. This hardened my dad, making him "battle-ready" at an early age. In addition to being born a powerful boy, someone had taught my dad boxing and street fighting, which he later taught us. "Bowser" became a fighting legend. At twelve, my grandpa, Henry Menard, took my dad to the bars and matched him up with other men's sons for bare-knuckle fights. The winner's dad got a free beer, and the winner got a root beer. Dad never lost. The bets increased in value over the years, and my dad's opponents grew bigger and older. The fights drew crowds from as far away as Chicago. Before my dad entered the Navy at sixteen, he fought and won against full-grown men. Dad had perfected the one-two—a right hook followed by a left uppercut. The right hook puts you in the hospital, and the left uppercut puts you six feet under. While he didn't finish high school, he entered the Navy with a PhD in violence.

Dad became the best boxer in the Navy at the peak of WWII. In 1944, he fought in the Army-Navy Boxing Championship. I have a picture from the newspaper of that fight. Dad lost that night. He never made excuses. It was Mom who told us that before the fight, Dad received all the shots required to deploy to the Philippines the next day. Mom told me his arms were so swollen from the shots that he could hardly lift his fists.

While in the service, Dad contracted rheumatic fever. The illness damaged three of the four valves in his heart, and he was honorably discharged early with a determination that he was partially disabled. With a weak heart, Dad went on to work in the factory, lifting steel stove tops for twenty-five years.

Once a year, the Roper Stove factory opened its doors to family and friends. The motivation was likely to groom and recruit the next generation of laborers for the factory. I vividly remember walking into the factory with Dad and Jamie. The ceilings were high, with a network of beams and bracing. The floor was concrete and had a film of oil and grit so slippery it felt like I was on ice skates. It was summertime, and it was hot in the factory. When we got to Dad's workstation, I immediately understood why Dad came home depleted and exhausted. Dad was a press operator. There was a tall stack of large steel sheets the size of a stovetop next to his workstation. Now that I was close to the machine Dad used to form the sheets, I discovered a different smell. Dad told me it was hydraulic fluid. Dad lifted a single sheet of steel from the stack and slid it flat into the belly of a large press machine. A machine about the size of a car standing on its nose with an opening about twelve inches tall. It was a hydraulic press that would, once my dad pressed the two safety buttons to ensure his hands were clear of the hole, cycle down atop the sheet of steel, crushing it into the shape of the stovetop while punching the holes for the burners and trimming the four edges. The whole world shook when the top of the press slammed into the bottom plate. The noise was deafening. *How did Dad do this eight hours a day?* Dad's quota was to produce 4,100 tons each eight-hour shift. That translates to lifting 40,000 pounds or twenty tons per week.

Dad was paid based on piecework. The more tops he made, the higher his pay. He didn't get paid by the hour. It was the adage: you eat what you kill. The system ensured the press operators worked themselves to death, lost a limb, and retired. Unions, safety rules, accountability, and OSHA didn't exist.

Dad was the highest-paid press operator in the factory. If he could have, he would have had a patch on his work shirt, making sure everyone in the factory was aware of his superiority. The responsibility to feed sixteen people is a potent motivator. In addition to being superhumanly strong and a hustler, Dad was creative. Like Maurice, Belle's father in *Beauty and the Beast*, he always worked on his next invention in his basement shop. He had many great ideas that he brought to life, but none translated to money and the chance to get out of that factory. I listened and learned. It was no accident that I spent my early career as an inventor, creating products and machinery that led to fifteen US patents.

One of Dad's ideas to increase the number of tops he made in an hour was to tape closed those two safety buttons on each side of the hydraulic press. When he did this and turned the power on, the press came alive like an evil transformer and delivered a thunderous "bang" about every five seconds. Dad doubled his output and pay with the machine on automatic and in continuous motion. The other press operators quickly copied the shortcut. The factory's management was happy—more stoves per day. The press operators were happy—more pay per day. Everyone was happy! Well, almost everyone.

Unsure if it was fatigue, footing, or a mishap, one of the press operators slipped, and his arms fell into the press chamber. The coworker standing to his right saw the imminent danger unfold. The coworker lunged and hit the emergency button, applying a brake to the mammoth press, and brought everything to a screaming halt. The press came to what looked like a slow-motion stop, with the giant press shaper and cutter (called a die) trapping the pressman's arms into the press up to his biceps. The die just barely broke the man's skin, which generated a small trickle of blood on both arms.

All who witnessed the near-catastrophic accident exhaled collectively. As my dad told the story, the exhale was followed by a triumphant cheer. The focus immediately shifted to freeing the pinned pressman. There was a brief discussion.

Then, a voice suggested: "Push the cycle up button, which will raise the die to the top center of the press."

All agreed. The foreman hit the button. Horrifyingly, the die continued downwardly, severing the man's arms with a ka-chunk, smashing them to an eighth of an inch thickness, extruding tissue, bone, and blood in all directions. The factory closed for the day. When the factory reopened the following day, you could hear the automatic bashing from the presses across the factory floor. All the "go" buttons remained taped and on automatic.

A "chip on your shoulder" is a metaphor that means you are habitually negative, combative, or hostile, usually because of a deep resentment or long-held injustice. This term was first used to describe the Royal Navy Dockyards' shipwrights' entitlement to timber offcuts. The shipwrights took home these "chips" on their shoulders. In the eighteenth century, the allotment of wood became too costly for the shipyard, and the officers began to limit the amount of timber a shipwright took home. This led to fights concerning the size of the chips on their shoulders.

Later, an aggressive young man placed a chip on his shoulder in nineteenth-century America and dared another to knock it off. A fight commenced if the challenged man knocked the chip off the other's shoulder. Dad carried a giant redwood on his shoulder. He was always looking for a fight.

Dad had groups of contradictory qualities. He unleashed violence like a monster, yet gently held his grandchild or a baby pigeon. He only completed his sophomore year in high school, but still taught himself advanced trigonometry, which amazed all the factory engineers at Roper Stove. He was a poor man with fourteen children who only had hand-me-down clothes, yet, because of his appearance and idiolect, you could easily mistake him for a Harvard Professor.

In 1971, Dad had a heart attack. One of the valves damaged twenty-five years earlier gave out. I followed the ambulance to the Veterans Hospital in Chicago with Dad. In the emergency room, an intern collected Dad's history.

"And do you have any children?"

Dad replied, "Yes, fourteen."

"Wow! For a minute, I thought you were a professor or an executive."

"How do you know I'm not a professor? You haven't asked me about my work yet."

Dad gave me his famous shit-eating grin and a wink while the red-faced intern buried his face in his clipboard.

After twenty-five years of illness and four open-heart surgeries, Dad chose death over another surgery. Mom told us that Dad had only days left and wanted some last words with his children. I flew from Doylestown, Pennsylvania, to Chicago with my oldest daughters Laura (eighteen) and Jenna (sixteen).

Dad was a kind, loving grandpa to his forty-two grandchildren. Laura and Jenna idolized their grandpa. They knew nothing of his brutality and cold-heartedness.

At his bedside, Dad, for the last time, made Laura and Jenna laugh as he did every time they were together. Always a joke or a trick.

Then he spoke his last words to me, "You've been a good boy. It would be best if you worked on your patience. You are always in a hurry. No need to rush, Mike; you are already there." Then, through tears, he added, "I know I wasn't the best dad, but I was the best I could be." He believed it. I believed it. I hope to say the same to my daughters when my time comes.

## JAMIE MENARD

Release a bunch of helium balloons and watch their paths. Some will ascend immediately at eight feet per second, but not all balloons will rise simultaneously. An outlier might bounce along the ground and drift away from the bunch. And then, for no known reason, maybe an updraft, that outlier shoots up to the heavens, going faster and higher than all the other balloons. Jamie was that outlier. Joanie was Jamie's updraft. She still is.

The firstborn of the fourteen, Jamie, appears in this book often. Many interesting May Avenue Stories are about Jamie, partly because I am Jamie's closest sibling and witnessed most of them. Jamie was, and still is, a larger-than-life man. He is our family's leader, spiritual guide, teacher, and three-ring circus. To know Jamie is to love Jamie.

Like his father, Jamie was a unique mix of extreme characteristics. Jamie was on a path to prison or death. The Jamie we know today is a different man than the subject of the stories here.

Jamie had gifts and demons that revealed themselves at a young age. He still possesses a charm that is disarming. Juxtaposed, he had a rebellious streak and a propensity to engage in physical violence triggered by the slightest impulse. Jamie carried his own giant redwood tree on his shoulder. To this day, Jamie is my protector and shared everything he had with me as a child. He was generous, kind, *and* an inferno; after his First Communion party, he gave me half his gift money, yet put his fist through my first guitar a day later over a small argument.

Jamie hated school. He regularly walked off the schoolyard and arrived home at dinner time. Mom didn't drive, and Dad was always at the factory. The teacher would call Mom; Mom would call Dad. Dad would leave work, drive around until he found Jamie, and take him back to school. An hour later, Jamie would walk away again. It reached the point that Dad couldn't afford to take more time off chasing Jamie.

Jamie's report cards were all F's. I sat and listened to an after-school meeting with Mom and Mrs. Bergman, Jamie's fifth-grade teacher. "He is a charming boy; everyone loves him, but he just won't do his work. I know he is smart, but he won't apply himself."

Two years younger than Jamie, I watched all this very closely. *How much can I get away with? What are Mom and Dad going to do with Jamie?* They tried everything: prayer, threats, whoopings.

Then, Mrs. Bergman had an idea to offer a bribe. My parents told Jamie, "Get straight A's on your next report card, and we'll buy you that BB gun you've been begging for." I was confident no number of A's would win that BB gun for Jamie. There wasn't even enough food for the table. How would Mom and Dad find the money for such an expensive reward?

The day after they made the offer, Jamie had perfect attendance. All homework turned in on time. The following report card was straight A's. Jamie got his BB gun, the envy of his siblings and all the neighbor boys. So now we knew Jamie wasn't slow, wasn't mentally challenged, and had no learning disabilities. However, the next marking period arrived, and all F's. Mom and Dad could not afford to motivate Jamie with future bribes. Jamie's struggle and lack of interest continued until he (barely) graduated from high school.

The Rainbow Inn was a burger, fries, and shake place on Court Street. A drive-up where the waitresses skated to your car and food was served on a tray hanging off the halfway rolled-up car door window. It was the place to be.

On the morning I got my driver's license, I purchased a twenty-five-dollar 1953 Plymouth in the afternoon and had a date by 6 p.m. It was a first date, and she was sweet and innocent. It was a big deal for her parents to allow her on a date with a boy in a car. We were both uneasy, and she was hugging the passenger armrest. Like a pro, I pulled into a space at Rainbow Inn. And then the sky fell in. A car pulled into the space on my right. It was a black flamingo 1957 Chevy. The driver was a woman who looked like Charlene "Cha-Cha" DiGregorio from the movie *Grease*, with a scarf around her neck. Jamie was in the middle, so drunk he could hardly hold his head up. On Jamie's right was another "Cha-Cha."

*What to do? Will he see me? Maybe I can survive this.* "Hey, Mikey Joe! I want you to meet my two dates."

In a panic, my date asked me to take her home.

Jamie was born with an angelic singing voice and has that voice today at age seventy-three. He sang the solos in the church choir. He easily won the lead in all the school's musicals. After one of Jamie's high school musical performances in *The Music Man*, Eve Arden, a famous film actress, went backstage to tell Jamie he belonged on Broadway.

Except for his fight club challengers, everyone loved Jamie. Jamie was a unique and charismatic combination of good and bad. When Joanie entered Jamie's life, all the bad evaporated.

"I don't care; I still love him." This had to be what Joanie thought when she fell in love with Jamie during her senior year of high school.

Most of us carry baggage and try to hide it. There was no way Jamie could keep his baggage a secret from Joanie. It was too late. Jamie was a legend at age eighteen. He was a remorseless street fighter; his first and last loss was the same fight at age twelve. One of his fights resulted in an arrest for attempted murder. He repeatedly smashed his enemy's face into a windshield, and this was after Jamie had won (more on this fight later). Jamie was a player. A charming and beautiful boy, he enchanted the women he met. Until he met Joanie, who was not Jamie's typical type of woman.

The first thing Joanie taught Jamie about was Jesus. We were born and raised Catholic. As a Catholic, you grow up being taught that you are bad, you will never do enough to please God, and that the only way to Jesus is through a priest. Jamie wasn't having any of that. When Joanie and her mom, Teresa, explained the true meaning of Christianity, especially about the blood of Christ erasing all our sins, Jamie got it and was saved. Drunk again, but this time on God's milk, he began preaching to me. It was Jamie who taught me about salvation and eternity. With Joanie and Jesus by his side, Jamie transformed and evolved into the man he is today.

After meeting Joanie, Jamie knew he needed a new path. When Joanie entered Southern Illinois University, Jamie also applied for entrance but was rejected based on poor grades. So, he enrolled in a community college, got straight A's, and was accepted into SIU the following year. Joanie was the new BB gun. He ironically graduated with a bachelor's degree and earned a master's in Education. In his early career, Jamie moved from being a special education teacher to school principal. Following his stint in education, Jamie founded three successful businesses, and, after fifty-three years of marriage, Joanie remains Jamie's updraft.

The May Avenue Stories all took place pre-Joanie. When Jamie hears me tell his stories today, he is embarrassed. It's as if he doesn't remember being that person. But deep down, I still see flashes of pride. I catch a glimpse of that devilish smile that says, "It's okay, Mike," and I know I have his unspoken permission to tell a few more stories.

I consulted with Jamie during the writing of this book. He helped me bridge some gaps and add stories I had forgotten. He also ensured I knew which stories I wasn't allowed to print. Jamie and I will take those stories to our graves.

"Sorrow prepares you for joy. It violently sweeps everything out of your house, so that new joy can find space to enter. It shakes the yellow leaves from the bough of your heart, so that fresh, green leaves can grow in their place. It pulls up the rotten roots, so that new roots hidden beneath have room to grow. Whatever sorrow shakes from your heart, far better things will take their place."

– Rumi

# MAY AVENUE STORIES

# MOUSE SKIN GLOVES

## CHAPTER 1

"Innovation comes out of great human ingenuity and very personal passions."

– Megan Smith

IN 1963, THE CIRCUS arrived by train, and we knew exactly when it would come. Historically, the Barnum and Bailey Circus arrived at the Kankakee train station at the break of dawn on August 1st, give or take a few days.

Three days before the train arrived, a man appeared and plastered circus paper signs on every storefront in town. The day after, that same man put up arrow signs showing the way to the train station for all the truck drivers who would offload the trains.

Jamie and I were always there to greet the circus train at daybreak. Watching the brightly-covered train pull in was the highlight of our year; it almost looked like a cartoon. It was the start of a big day. Ramps were set up to lead the horses and horse-pulled carts off the train cars. The first to be set up and ready to go were the concession carts.

The parade would start around 10 a.m. from the train station along Washington Avenue and continue to the Kankakee County Fairgrounds, about five miles away. Everyone from town would be there. We followed the parade to the city limits and then returned home.

Mom always said, "Children need to see the circus." I don't know how she came up with the money each year to afford the outing, but we knew we would be going to the circus. It was a big treat. Not only was it "The Greatest Show on Earth" but going to the circus also meant getting roasted peanuts in the shell, cotton candy, and lemonade. The day's biggest prize was arriving home with either a chameleon on a string held onto our shirts by a piece of thread, or a white mouse in a shoe box with a breathing hole.

When the giant red and white striped tent appeared as we drove south on Route 45 over the Route 57 overpass, you heard a chorus of "oohs" and "aahs" from the carryall full of brothers and sisters.

Our sense of smell is closely linked with memory. Scent-connected memories are strongest when we first experience a smell as a child. Whenever I smell sawdust or roasted peanuts, it evokes memories of opening the truck door in the circus parking lot.

The entrance to the big top tent was over-decorated with balloons, posters, streamers, and advertisements for the side shows, which required an additional ticket. For me, that opening signaled the entrance to a fantasy land. A world that included every animal who made the trip on Noah's Ark: lions and tigers, hyenas, elephants, giraffes, dogs, horses, and even a "hippo gator" (a hippo's head on one end and an alligator head on the other). The circus acts went on for what felt like the entire day. It left me with the euphoric feeling that anything was possible. Still, the real highlight was collecting my prize on the way out.

Mom welcomed all pets into our menagerie. A group of my brothers once captured a baby raccoon near the Kankakee River-banks. "Zeke" became the family pet for years. No room at the inn? Zeke made his bed in the dirty clothes basket. Later, my Zeke stories became legendary with my youngest daughter, Stella. Stella demanded a Zeke bedtime story every night from ages three to ten. Her number one stuffed animal was a raccoon named "Zeke" that one day showed up at our doorstep unannounced.

On all prior circus visits, I came home with a chameleon, a lizard-like animal that magically turned the color or colors of the material on which it was crawling. These old-world lizards camouflage themselves for hunting and protection. Chameleons had a short life expectancy at 118 South May Avenue. Someone in the family found a way to pull the lizard's tail off so we could watch the tail twitch and curl for minutes following the amputation. We justified the cruelty by telling ourselves and others it was okay; the chameleon would grow another tail. We weren't sure about that. The lizard never lived long enough to prove or disprove the theory. It turns out that chameleons cannot regrow body parts.

We had lots of pets we didn't want. At May Avenue, we had a continual mouse infestation. They were everywhere. You saw them throughout the tiny house. We heard them scratching in the walls at night, almost as prevalent as the crickets and cicadas in the summer, just part of life. There were traces of mouse droppings in every cabinet. Fortunately, the mice never spoiled any food because the food was never around long enough to give them a chance.

Polly, my sister, was one year younger than me. She was always excited to discover another nest of baby mice, whose litter size ranged from six to twelve. They were cute, hairless, and bright pink with closed eyes. Mom taught us not to disturb or touch these pups; it would cause the mother mouse to abandon the babies and deprive them of her milk. In a house infested with mice, our mother wanted to protect the lives of more mice.

Late at night, Polly and I would wait and watch the mice drop out from the kitchen cabinet kick panel and from the upper cabinets, like soldiers paratrooping behind enemy lines. For most children, this would be traumatizing. For us, it was a sport.

I have since questioned how many mice could have resided at May Avenue, so I did a quick web search to learn more. Theoretically, two mice can give birth to as many as sixty pups per year. Conservatively, let's assume only twenty-one of the sixty pups are female. With the females of each litter giving birth six weeks after their arrival, you could see as many as 5,082 mice in one year. Do the math: if you start with ten mice, five couples, the nest could produce over 25,000 mice annually!

As I exited the big top, the band was playing fast and loud, almost deafening, and that meant it was time to pick the final prize of the day, a mouse or chameleon. I always liked the chameleon because May Avenue did not need another mouse. But this year, I chose the white mouse in a box with a hole. I named him Henry after my dad's father. Henry was a beautiful, snow-white mouse with coordinating pink eyes, nose, feet, and tail. So different from the May Avenue field mice of dirty gray and brown.

Back then, the Kankakee winters were much harsher than the present day. In 1963, I was twelve years old, and I remember the temperature never rose above zero degrees that January. Always looking for ways to make a buck, I had a paper route covering Bird Park to the "Easy Way Bumps" in West Kankakee; I dreaded winter.

Forty newspapers were dropped off by the *Daily Journal* truck at 5 a.m. each weekday. I un-banded and folded each newspaper into a spiral and placed it in my special newspaper bag, one with a wide shoulder strap to lug around my route. I had to deliver the papers by 7 a.m. and be at school by 8:30 a.m. I would make ten cents per paper, four dollars per week, plus tips earned when I collected the payment on Friday from the subscribers.

With never-warm-enough clothing, I froze while making the hour-long trek. Shoes were always in bad repair and short supply. My shoes always had large holes in the soles, making for wet, nearly frost-bitten feet. When the cold, damp weather hit, my dad made inner souls out of cardboard and wrapped the inserts with wax paper to keep our feet dry. As I recall this memory, I feel we should have experienced heavy doses of self-pity for our circumstances, but we did not. During the shoe insert ritual, my dad told us a secret; how these inserts gave us boys special powers so we could run faster and jump higher than all the other kids. I didn't believe him, but I wanted to.

Walking through Bird Park was a shortcut, but still the longest, coldest part of the route. There was a giant concrete table and benches on the way that we claimed was the dinner table for Alley Oop, a famous cartoon caveman from the dinosaur era. This was the halfway point so I stopped there, removed my socks used as gloves, took off my actual socks and shoes, and massaged my feet to bring the feeling back. Some kids on the playground at recess had leather gloves with rabbit fur lining. I don't recall having envy for the things we went without, but I dreamed about the day I could afford those fur-lined gloves.

Henry lasted less than twenty-four hours after we got home. He didn't die, and no one pulled his tail off; he escaped. Like most carnies at the circus, Henry just ran away from home.

Six months after Henry's escape, the herd at May Avenue began changing. We started seeing "palomino" mice. Brown and white coats with black patches on some. They were beautiful and captivating, and they were everywhere. It was a first, almost fantasy-like. Maybe they had special powers like the wax-covered inserts.

As Polly and I sat and counted the number of palomino mice dropping from the cabinets, Polly yelled, "Mouse skin gloves!" *What?* Polly quickly explained her flash of genius: catch all the palomino mice possible, skin them, save their pelts until we had enough, and make two pairs of mouse skin gloves. We both longed for leather gloves with fur lining. If Polly said she could do it, she would do it.

All the Menard children were problem solvers, but Polly had

unique gifts and endless energy. She made do with almost nothing. All the girls in Polly's class wore sneakers, usually Keds. Most girls in town had a pair in each color to coordinate with their outfits. Polly had one pair she would color with different shades of shoe polish. She would die that one pair of Keds two to three times a week. They began looking different from the other girl's Keds, thicker, almost leather-like. Polly would occasionally scrape off all the polish and start over with the quick-change act. Polly had wavy hair as a youngster, and she regularly ironed her hair with Mom's iron to straighten it. She was poor, but she always looked great.

So, how did we harvest the herd of speckled mice? Mouse traps could damage the pelts with blood. I tried setting out lassos to snare the mice as they dropped from the cabinets, but there was no chance in hell. Then, I had my flash of genius: shoot them with Jamie's BB gun as they dropped onto the floor. *Brilliant!*

The next night, Polly and I waited until everyone in the house was sleeping, and I set up camp under the kitchen table like a military sniper. Polly would hold a flashlight at the high-traffic locations. We had immediate success. When the BB hit the mouse, it jumped high into the air as if it wore springs. Usually, the mouse was dead when it hit the floor. With others, the mouse flipped like a bluegill pulled out of Bird Park quarry and slapped on the sidewalk. To finish those mice off, Polly scampered over and whacked the mouse on the head, dealing a death blow with her spoon.

The hunting season continued for a few weeks, with no reduction in mice showing up nightly, even after eliminating 100 or more. My dad once told me that if we ever went to war with China, the Chinese military would have enough fighters to keep sending them to our shores until we ran out of bullets. *Were these mice Chinese?*

After a night's hunt, Polly wrapped each mouse in wax paper

and put them in the freezer. You wouldn't think there would be room in our tiny freezer, but think about it. There was nothing else to put in our freezer besides a few ice cube trays. Nothing to freeze. Nothing from the store required freezing, and there were never leftovers.

What kind of mother would allow this brutal, hopeless activity in her home? Our mom. She didn't care; she encouraged us and was proud of us.

Once we hit our goal of 300 mice, Polly began the skinning and tanning process. She would thaw ten mice a day, skin them with the precision of a thoracic surgeon, and soak the pelts in rubbing alcohol. After all hides were tanned and dried, Polly went to work sewing the paper-thin skins to each other to make one large pelt. She then covered and attached the skin side of the pelt to a sheet of pillow ticking reclaimed from a fallen pillow.

Though the gloves were thin and fragile, she did it. They fit exactly like a glove, with vents and darts between the fingers so we could squeeze a fist with the glove on. Never mind that the gloves didn't offer the functionality of keeping our hands warm —we had fur-lined gloves.

Polly was ten years old when she made that first pair of gloves. She became an accomplished seamstress, making clothes for herself and her brothers and sisters. At age thirteen, Polly made me a pair of bell-bottom pants and a pirate-type shirt as the required uniform for my first performance with my garage band, "Those Guys."

## REFLECTIONS

I recently googled "Mouse Skinning." Maybe I was looking for something to convince myself that Polly and I weren't a little off in the head. I found an article and a YouTube video about this guy who was an expert in skinning mice. He did it just like Polly and me. The guy did have a strange, glassy-eyed look as he demonstrated how the skin slipped off the tiny mouse legs. I'm sure most of you are asking the same question I had when watching the video: why? This guy skinned mice to make a coat for his cat!

It's said that true innovation and big original ideas come from "aha" moments, a flash of genius. The phrase "flash of genius" describes that moment of epiphany when an inventor makes a connection between a problem or need. This is like the English proverb: "necessity is the mother of invention."

This is the May Avenue story people find to be most unbelievable. I don't blame them.

It was an exciting experience that Polly and I remain proud of. It was an opportunity to be creative and productive. As we made the gloves, we considered making a business out of them and discussed our marketing pitch.

Whenever I put on a pair of fur-lined gloves, I smile and remember how proud and excited Polly and I were while making those gloves. I reflect on how unique and extraordinary our mom was for supporting such an extreme craft.

We were poor but had more freedom than any child I knew. When my daughters were young, I did my best to encourage their far-out ideas.

What did we learn? Creativity, resourcefulness, and we could do anything if we put our minds to it.

I still shake my head at this story. It feels like it took place in a dream. When I ask Polly for reassurance, she always says, "Yep, that was us."

# HUMPSKY-GUMPSKI!

## CHAPTER 2

---

"Children see magic because they look for it."

– Christopher Moore

---

IN THE EARLY DAYS at May Avenue, life was normal. There was no doing without; everybody had a pillow, and Jamie, myself, Polly, and David had lots of Mom and Dad time. I fondly remember Mom and Dad taking Jamie and me out to dinner, usually to Blue's Cafe on Station Street. Jamie was six and I was four. We would dress up and have a date night. The food at Blue's wasn't as good as Mom's, but they did have special small bottles of orange drink shaped like miniature old-fashioned milk bottles.

Dad was always happy and fun. He played hide-and-seek with us in the dark basement. I never liked the dark, but I couldn't resist playing the game with Dad. He would start the game in the evening by looking out the backyard window, then look back at us with wide eyes. He was scared. He was looking to see if it was a full moon because that's the only time the werewolf would come out. He would look back a second time, then turn back to us with even bigger eyes and nod his head in a slow yes. *He saw the werewolf.* We would scream and run down to the basement and hide. We heard the basement door open, and the lights would go out.

"Don't scream, the werewolf will know where you are,"

THE KITE THAT COULDN'T FLY

Jamie would whisper. The werewolf stood still for a few minutes to let the suspense build, waiting for one of us to screech. Then we heard the wolf's feet start to move. Sometimes, he threw something out into the darkness to get movement or a reaction from us. He began to breathe heavily just before he grabbed one of us. When he did grab someone, he let out this hideous laugh, then a howl. That laugh, the howl, and the captured child's scream made me wet my pants every time.

Dad also created "Yahowdie and Yahoodie Itchkomatobitch," the Balto-Slavic twins. They were tiny boys, the size of a pea, and they were everywhere. Dad explained that when someone opened the fridge door, a little needle stuck one of the twins in the butt and that twin ran over and pulled the light switch on the inside of the fridge. When someone rang the doorbell, a pin stuck Yahowdie or Yahoodie in the butt, and one of them hit a bell with a little hammer. When Dad turned the radio on, a pin poked both the twins, and they would begin broadcasting or singing.

The game I remember most vividly was "Humpsky-Gumpski." Dad would lie on the living room floor and pretend he was sleeping. We knew the game began when Dad snored like a big bear. That was his signal for us to pile on top of him. Our job was to keep the bear from getting on all four legs. If Dad did get up on all fours, which he always would, he was allowed to shake us children off his back and eat us. We were safe when he shook us off his back and we made it to the sofa. Once Dad started snoring, he would attempt to get on all fours, but the bear was weak; he couldn't get off the floor with all those children on his back. But then the bear opened his eyes and peered at the children, smacking his lips. The bear was hungry. This is when the screaming started. But the bear still couldn't get up until he called the magic words and swallowed the Humpsky-Gumpski.

"Humpsky-Gumpski, come to me!" the bear yelled. Then suddenly, the bear gulped and swallowed the imaginary Humpsky-Gumpski. With the screaming at a fever pitch, the bear muscles grew, and he began swinging us off his back but allowed us just enough time to get onto the sofa. The bear went back to sleep, and the fun started all over.

REFLECTIONS

Dad was fun and playful until he changed jobs from furniture building to the stove-making factory. At about the same time, the house was filling up with a new child each year. Life got very busy. He changed. Maybe he needed to make more money to feed more mouths. Maybe the stove factory was too strenuous for a man with a weak heart. Perhaps it was the pressure of his need to provide for his family. I wish I could go back and ask him. The young dad with just a handful of children was a different dad than you will read about in the following May Avenue Stories.

Once Dad started working second shift at the factory, I rarely saw him. He was gone from 2 p.m. to 1 a.m. He slept a few hours and began his second job, making cabinets with his brother, my uncle Bob. On the weekends, Dad worked odd jobs, "Mr. Fixit" jobs. I wasn't able to spend time with my dad until he had his first heart attack when I was eighteen.

Dad's games brought us joy, and I played them with my five daughters. I hope they reflect on those days as favorably as I still do about my dad.

To young fathers: play with your children, be the bear, and tell them about Yahowdie and Yahoodie Itchkomatobitch.

# WE HAVE A LIGHTBULB!

## CHAPTER 3

> "Gratitude is one of the strongest and most transformative states of being. It shifts your perspective from lack to abundance and allows you to focus on the good in your life, which in turn pulls more goodness into your reality."

> – Jen Sincero

IT WAS 1956. THE latest technology was a transistor radio with an earphone. Elvis had just released "Blue Suede Shoes." Eisenhower was president. It was such a different, simple time.

We knew we were poor, certainly at the poverty level, but we were never destitute of dignity.

I grew up with a hierarchy of fears: no food, electricity, heat, water, and lowest on the ladder, no phone. Doing without was a way of life. It was inconvenient when services were turned off because the bill wasn't paid, but we always got by. In addition to the inconvenience and discomfort of going without, we also suffered embarrassment when others outside our home knew just how poor we were. The neighborhood kids could be cruel, so we did our best to fake it.

Across the river at Alpine Park was a clubhouse. The park district sponsored arts and crafts five days a week in the summer. It was free, so all the Menard kids took full advantage. We made things from popsicle sticks, like log cabins and birdhouses. A woman at the Alpine Park clubhouse helped me stain the projects with redwood stain; I can still smell the color. Another of my favorite crafts was painting salad dressing jars. Kraft Wish-Bone Italian Dressing was the go-to dressing in the fifties, and it came in a glass bottle with raised vegetables on the glass. The craft leader collected these empty bottles, and we would paint and decorate them as flower vases. I painted the entire bottle white and the embossed figures in natural vegetable colors. I gave my bottle to my mom, and she cherished and displayed it for years. It looked best with Mom's favorite flower, the lilac.

The club always put on a talent show at the end of the summer. The performance was given for all the parents and relatives at the Kankakee Civic Auditorium, and it was always a great show. In second grade, I was paired up with Donna Brown from a park on the east side of Kankakee. We performed a tap dance and song. We practiced once a week for all of August. Donna was my first true love. Donna's mom was a beautiful, kind woman who knew I was smitten with Donna. After one practice, Mrs. Brown invited me for dinner. "I'm sure it will be okay with your mom, but we will call her when we get to my house to make sure," said Mrs. Brown. I was all in!

They lived on the east side, down the street from the Kankakee Country Club. Their home was spectacular, with fancy everything; I had never seen a house like this. I met Mr. Brown and Donna's sister, Nancy, who were both so kind.

"Better call your mom, Mike," Mrs. Brown said.

But there was a problem: our phone was disconnected because we needed to catch up on payments. I could not tell them this—I would risk going home without dinner and time with Donna, and the embarrassment would have been unbearable.

"Okay," I said to Mrs. Brown.

I picked up the phone and dialed 933-8100. After the message played, saying the phone number was out of service, I said, "Hi, Mom, Mrs. Brown invited me over for dinner. She said she would drive me home when we finished." After a credible pause, "Yes, Mom, I'll wash my hands." Another pause. "Yes, Mom, I'll say grace. Okay, bye, Mom." The Browns never caught on. Mrs. Brown drove me home after dinner.

Now back at my May Avenue home, the lighting was provided by single pale light bulbs hanging from the ceiling by a corded wire and an open socket with a pull chain. We couldn't purchase replacement lightbulbs back then; the electric company provided them at no cost. You got an electric bill in the mail and paid it at designated hardware stores around town or the electric company. You received your lightbulbs when you paid your bill, and the size of your bill determined the number of bulbs. The system worked. That is, if you had the money to pay your bill.

It was hard for Mom to make ends meet with Dad's small paychecks and so many mouths to feed. She was a master at juggling the bills, but most of the time, Mom was late paying the electric bill, and as a result, we were always short on lightbulbs. Most of the time, we were down to one working lightbulb at a time. I remember being without electricity, but I never remember a time when we didn't have at least one light bulb, which is impressive given the low life expectancy of light bulbs in the 1950s.

On this evening, like most evenings, we were all in the kitchen, with our one pale lightbulb burning in the center of the room. The house was heated by coal when we had it. When we didn't, Mom opened the lit oven, warming the downstairs nicely until it was time to bake the daily sheet cake.

Bedtime was the ritual that signaled the end of the day. During the school year, the ceremony started with Mom baking the daily sheet cake, which was dessert for the next day's school lunches. It was made in a 9 inch by 13 inch pan, always from scratch. Just before we went to bed, she made the cake as the last act of the day. She tried to make it earlier in the day and hide it a

THE KITE THAT COULDN'T FLY

few times, but somehow, she always made a second cake before bedtime. It is hard hiding a sweet-smelling cake from a bunch of children in a 900-square-foot home.

Mom's hands were always adorned with medical tape and, at times, even electrical tape, to cover the cracks in her hands from eczema. Mom was plagued with this skin disease from childhood until she was around fifty years old, when she outgrew it. She told us that we all had a cross to bear and that her cross was eczema.

Once the cake went into the oven, Mom made the frosting from milk, powdered sugar, butter, and vanilla extract.

Mom played a game with us while mixing the frosting by asking, "What flavor icing would you like for tomorrow's lunch?"

We knew the options were chocolate, vanilla, cherry, strawberry, mint, or lemon. After everyone shouted out a different flavor, Mom took the vote. This evening, it was cherry. As we watched Mom take out her box of McCormick's food coloring, she stirred a few drops of red in the white icing. Magic—cherry icing! The power of imagination is incredible. It tasted like cherry. I still love cherry cake. This ritual brought us joy and hope because we would have cake for dessert the next day.

With the cake frosted and placed high on the refrigerator, Mom turned off the oven and shut the door. Silently, we drifted to the center of the room, under the lightbulb, waiting for Mom. She moved to the center of us, grasped the bottom of her threadbare apron, and pulled it up to grab and unscrew the hot lightbulb. Now, in the dark, with each of us gripping that apron, we shuffled over to the narrow stairs and ascended.

As we moved in the dark, Mom found different ways to say the same thing. "We have a lightbulb!" "Do you know how lucky we are to have a lightbulb?" "How many families don't have a light bulb?" "Thank you, Jesus, for our light bulb!" She continued until we reached the center of the attic floor, where she screwed our treasured pale light bulb into the socket, and once again, we had light.

Think how that situation could have played out. Maybe pity, anger, resentment, or depression for her and our circumstances. Not our mom; she was thankful for everything. She repeatedly taught this to her children. To this day, my siblings and I have an uncommon joy and thankfulness for everything.

REFLECTIONS

This has always been my favorite May Avenue story to tell. If I'm going to tell a few stories to an audience, I begin with this story. It shines a light on some of my best memories as a child. The central message teaches a priceless lesson: gratitude and thankfulness are indispensable parts of happiness and well-being. The light bulb story is just one example of the hundred lessons Mom intuitively taught her children.

As it turns out, gratitude was our superpower, our Humpsky-Gumpski.

Mom taught us gratitude by example and reinforced it with scripture: "Rejoice always, pray continually, give thanks in all circumstances; for this is God's will for you in Christ Jesus." 1 Thessalonians 5:16-18

Mom's favorite quote was "Our Lord loves a thankful heart."

In a book of Jewish ethical teachings, *Pirkei Avot*, there is a saying that translates to: "Who is the rich one? He who rejoices in his portions. Who rejoices in their portions? Those who are happy with what they have." Mom taught us to have a deep appreciation for everything we had and for life itself.

Some magic took place growing up in the house on May Avenue. The magic potion was created by the combination of gratitude and scarcity. Not having what we wanted was a way of life, a fact of life. This reality greatly reduced our wanting. Knowing most all "wants" were out of our reach trained our minds to want less; just as Henry David Thoreau wrote, "I make myself rich by making my wants few." As it turned out, this wasn't a bad thing.

My earliest memories of Christmas are bittersweet. The sweet: celebrating of the birth of Jesus was the main event. Midnight Mass, hot chocolate before bed, the excitement of Santa coming. The bitter: always getting so much less from Santa than my friends and relatives. I knew I was a better boy than Tom Boules and Mark Andrews across the street, yet they made a haul from Santa. To reduce this wanting but not getting, Mom would break the news to us at a very early age, too early, that there was no Santa—that Mom and Dad were Santa and, as we knew, they had no money for gifts, even though we deserved them. Yet, even in delivering devastating news, Mom found a way to lessen the sting and build our self-esteem:

"Michael, I have decided that you are now mature enough to join the special club."

"What club?"

She reached down and whispered in my ear, "The Santa Secret club." She would then wait, building excitement to make me ask.

"What secret?" I whispered back.

She turned her head from side to side making sure no one else could hear her and said, "There is no Santa, I am Santa. I buy the presents for all of you. And you know, because we have such a large family, we don't have enough money to buy nice presents for Christmas. This must be our secret, don't tell anyone else. Promise?"

"I promise. Who else knows?"

"Only Jamie and your dad. That's why this year your younger brothers and sisters might get more gifts than you and Jamie, they don't know the secret yet. And when you are in the special club, you get special privileges; like sneaking away with Mom to go grocery shopping and get a secret treat. When it's time, you can let Polly into the club."

What a master of psychology she was. Delivering demoralizing news and making me feel special at the same time. The following Christmas my wish list was much shorter.

Mom worked hard at counteracting the pain of our deficiency. She acknowledged it could be good to have more, but that we already had enough. She taught us that no matter what was missing, there was always an abundance of things to be thankful for. Gratitude for what we did have became more profound when contrasted against the backdrop of unfulfilled desires.

Not getting what we wanted led to our personal growth and self-discovery. As an adult, when my desires went unfulfilled, I was prompted to reflect on my real motivations, which in turn caused me to reassess my priorities and wants.

Not getting what we wanted also gave me a knack for surrender and acceptance. It helped me recognize certain things were beyond my control and that I couldn't always bend the world to my will. I learned at an early age to navigate the complexities of life without.

Mom knew gratitude was valuable and correct, but did she know the gift she was giving her children? Did she know it would be a potent lifelong tool in our toolbox for happiness and fulfillment? Having this gift of gratitude, and after coming out the other side of the trauma, most of my siblings and I saw everything clearer, brighter, and more appealing. Coming into adult life with gratitude has given most Menards a heightened sense of joy, play, and a continual commitment to making the most of their lives. I can confidently say that I have squeezed every bit of joy I could out of my life.

Scientific evidence shows that gratitude can change brain function when practiced consistently and correctly, making us feel more content and joyful. In his groundbreaking book *The Neuroscience of Gratitude: Why Self-Help Has It All Wrong,*

Andrew Humington compiled scientific data compelling that gratitude changes the brain's structure.

"The benefits span across all areas of your life—from the physical to the professional and even the spiritual—that are touched by the stress and anxiety of modern life. On a physiological level, gratitude can bolster your immune system, enhance your sleep quality, and reduce your pain and sensitivity. Professionally, a consistent practice of gratitude will leave you brimming with motivation, while your productivity soars and decision-making processes occur with ease and clarity. Spiritually, gratitude deepens your sense of purpose and meaning and can finally uncover that piece of your life that has eluded you for so long. It empowers your personal compass that continually guides you toward personal growth and appreciation for your life and life in its entirety."

Sound too good to be true? It's not.

While gratitude is a superpower, it is not the end-all. Gratitude is fantastic, but it has limitations. Gratitude did help some of us power our post-traumatic growth, but it was not enough to save Patrick and Adam from post-traumatic stress.

To identify the need for and possible benefits of gratitude, consider the converses: envy, materialism, cynicism, stress, and depression.

Achieving a mindset of gratitude is possible but not easy. If you do not have an outlook of gratitude and thankfulness, I invite you to try it. There are great resources that can teach you how to have gratitude. I have listed Andrew Humington's book in the resource section of this book.

# MICKEY COOPER

## CHAPTER 4

---

"You must have chaos within you in order to give birth to a dancing star."

– Friedrich Nietzsche

---

DAD WAS A PEOPLE, pigeons, and fighting specialist.

Don't confuse fighting with boxing. While the goal (knock your opponent unconscious) is the same, there is a difference between the two.

Boxing is a sport where two people face off and strike each other only with their hands. A set of rules governs boxing and includes protective gear like padded gloves, mouth guards, and at times, head protection. Boxing has rules and typically takes place in a public forum.

Street fighting is when two or more people engage in combat without rules and protective equipment. No rules in a fight means it's almost always unfair for one of the fighters.

Street fighting ran through Dad's entire being. The best way to settle anything man-to-man was with your fists. Dad would raise his right fist and say, "This one will put you in the hospital," then he would raise his left fist, "This one will put you six feet under." With the amount of fighting in our youth, one might think we went looking for fights. We didn't have to. Fights found us.

Until the Mickey Cooper fight with Jamie, there wasn't much

talk around the house about fighting. We knew our dad was a boxer in the Navy, and Jamie and I would go with Dad to his father's house and use the makeshift boxing ring. Dad boxed with his brothers, friends, and sometimes strangers. Dad always won and regularly knocked out his opponents, including his brothers. Once Dad struck Uncle Jimmy so hard, I thought Dad had killed him.

Mom disapproved of Dad talking about fighting with us. We talked about it at Grandpa's house and during "Saturday Night Fights."

Before we had a television, the center of entertainment at May Avenue was our old chipped and nicked-up RCA Victor tube radio—the big wooden box with speakers wrapped around the sides. The radio was fussy and always needed tubes we couldn't afford. It was also used almost exclusively to listen to boxing matches.

The fight of the week was broadcasted by NBC on Saturday late at night. It was the highlight of the week for Jamie and me. The ritual began with Dad taking us to the West Kankakee Liquor Store. Mrs. Ravens put our usual on the counter: one quart of Papst Blue Ribbon beer, two tall bottles of RC Cola pulled right out of the ice water-filled machine, and a package of TV Popping Corn. The package had two sides attached and was perforated down the middle. On the left were fat yellow corn kernels. On the right was the "finest nut oil" sleeve. This semi-solid gunk would go in Mom's soup pan, and once melted and boiling, the kernels would go in.

Dad had a process for everything; "If you're gonna do anything more than twice, you best figure out how to do it right."

With the fire on high, the nut oil spit and two kernels were put in the pan and quickly covered with the lid. When the first kernel popped, in went a half cup of corn. With the lid back on, we waited for the popping to begin. Once it started, Dad waited until the kernels stopped hitting the inside of the lid. He turned the fire to medium and slid the lid off center just enough to let the steam out. Dad explained each time that the steam and built-up heat made the popped corn tough. Once confident no corn would fly out of the pan, Dad removed the lid until the popping slowed and took it off the fire. He poured the popped corn into our largest bowl. Dad sat between Jamie and me, holding the big bowl.

I always wanted the fights to go the complete fifteen rounds and go to the cards. This allowed me to finish the popcorn and spend more time with Dad—Mom's rule was straight to bed after the fight.

We got our TV in 1955, much later than the rest of the families on May Avenue. I had seen *The Mickey Mouse Club* on my friend Mark Andrews' TV before and could not wait to see Annette Funicello again. Dad couldn't wait to see boxing.

Boxing came alive on our black-and-white screen as Dad became our blow-by-blow announcer. The room was dark except for the glow from the TV screen, and the fog of Dad's cigarette smoke. He explained every punch, stance, and counter punch. Jamie listened to every word; I had no interest at all. I was there for the buttered popcorn, RC Cola, and most importantly, time with my dad.

The May Avenue neighborhood was full of boys around the same ages as Jamie and me. Mark Andrews, Tom Bowles, Tom Dupree, Rick Reardend, and Mike and Kim James from Kentucky, who spent summers with their grandma two doors down. Like most teenage boys in the '60s, we grew up fighting amongst ourselves. Nothing vicious or hurtful. When it came to fighting, the rest of the boys stayed clear of Jamie, who had developed into a much stronger boy than the rest of us.

It was 1962. I was eleven, Jamie thirteen. We spent most early evenings playing Kick the Can in the middle of May Avenue. As dusk turned to dark, Jamie and I sat on the concrete stoop, waiting for the night to cool off so we could sleep in our attic dorm.

Mickey Cooper was older than the rest of us and lived down the street close to the Illinois Central Railroad tracks. While we spent lots of time around the tracks, we stayed clear of Mickey Cooper, who had the reputation of being a bully and a fighter. Cooper scared me; his neck was bigger than his head, and he had an evil face. His face was poxy, and he had a buzz cut. He looked like a Doberman Pinscher.

On this evening, I saw Cooper peddling toward us. He curved to our curb and spat on our yard as he approached our house. I felt safe. Jamie was with me, and he could take anyone.

I ran to the curb and yelled, "Hey Cooper, don't spit in our yard!" Cooper did a figure-eight U-turn while leaning deeply on his bike and pulled up onto our yard, about three feet away from us. Off his bike, Cooper walked up, grabbed my head between his thick hands, and spit right in my face.

"Don't do that, Cooper," Jamie said, almost apologetically.

Cooper turned, grabbed Jamie's head, worked to summon more saliva, and spit with force into Jamie's face.

Jamie stood up and wiped his face all in one movement. In street fights, the one swinging always goes for the head: head-hunting. Cooper hit Jamie with a flurry of strikes to the head, taking Jamie immediately out of the fight. It looked and sounded ugly. Street fights are like bad car crashes, instantaneous and destructive, more like an explosion. Jamie was beaten badly. I helped him into the house.

Dad sat Jamie on a kitchen chair. He rinsed a dirty dish towel from the kitchen sink and wiped Jamie's face, slowly going from forehead to chin. Mom had lost it, crying and trying to get around Dad to get to her son. Jamie sat motionless and calm. No tears, no whimpering. Once Dad had the chance to survey the damage, he led Jamie down the basement stairs. I followed.

Out of nowhere, Dad produced a dented metal box, opened

it, and started on Jamie's face. Dad pulled out these large Q-tip type sticks, applied a salve, and pressed the cotton tips into the two largest gashes on Jamie's brow. He held the two sticks on Jamie's face with one hand while he cracked open a mesh-covered cylinder with his other hand and stuck it under Jamie's nose. Jamie jerked his head backward and snapped out of it. I'd seen many Saturday Night Fights. *Dad was a cut man?*

The cut man was an essential guy on the boxer's team who worked between rounds to stop the bleeding and reduce the swelling on the boxer's face. A cut man was either trained by a professional or came up the ranks by being a boxer.

"He'll be okay," Dad said, giving me a rare smile.

"I'll be okay, Mike," Jamie said, giving me that same smile.

In addition to the physical damage from losing a fight, losing your first fight was humiliating. It could crush a boy. It was worse than being dumped by the prettiest girl in school or losing your best friend. You might as well take your self-worth and throw it in the trash.

By the next evening, our old, damp basement was transformed into a war room. Dad must have borrowed it all from his friends: jumping ropes, weights, a heavy bag hanging from the ceiling for bodywork and uppercuts, and a punching bag for endurance and speed which looked like football leather. Sunday night was the first fighting lesson—the first of many to follow over the next two years.

Dad only talked for most of the first lesson. He explained that we were going to be trained to fight. The sole purpose was to make sure what happened to Jamie never happened again. He was going to teach us self-defense. Two things stuck in my mind from that first lesson. First, never provoke or start a fight. If we were ever caught starting a fight, we would have to fight Dad. And second, if you think you might lose the fight, don't fight. But if you must, ensure your opponent will never want to fight you again.

Dad learned his fighting skills defending himself from his drunk father. After that, from being taken to bars by his dad and forced fight other men's sons, which was a blood sport like cock-fighting. Because of his proven fighting skills as a teen, Dad was taken under the wing of a local boxing gym owner. The combination of natural strength, street fighting experience, boxing, endurance, speed, and agility training prepared Dad to become the US Navy boxing champion—coupled with the chip (tree) he carried on his shoulder, Dad was a dangerous man.

It was unspoken, but Dad was preparing us for something. He taught and trained us with purpose. The training was holistic and far-reaching. We were trained to build strength, endurance, and agility by weightlifting, running, and jumping rope. Using the punching bag to increase hand and eye coordination, speed, power, accuracy, shoulder and arm strength, and mental focus, he taught us boxing and street fighting tactics. Both were needed.

Dad said the speed bag would be the training tool we would use the most. When introducing the speed bag training, Dad gave us a demonstration of his skill with the bag. It was beautiful to see. I couldn't believe this was my dad. He started with a left-left, right-right pattern. Slow, then faster. He used a rolling design with his fists that created such speed that the bag and his hands became a blur. He employed a rolling figure eight pattern as he walked around and under the bag, bobbing and weaving, incorporating forward and upper-cut movements. Dad was coming alive.

During the physical training, Dad wove in the physiological aspects of the fight. He was a real Sun Tzu when teaching us the art of the wars to come. A typical training session in the basement would start with warm-ups, jumping jacks, and jumping rope.

While jumping rope, Dad taught, "The more you know about fighting, the less you will fear the fight."

Then onto the speed bag, more teaching, "Street fights last only a few seconds. Adrenaline spikes in the body and drains all your energy in the first burst of action. Adrenaline is your enemy. Stay calm." We moved on to feet shuffling, "Don't stop fighting when you think you have won; stop only after you have disabled your opponent." While sparring, he continued to teach, "If you do not believe you will win, don't fight. Use surprise to your advantage. If a fight is going to happen, hit first, and hit hard."

We sat at the end of each training session, and Dad finished his lesson, "Fighting is brutal. You will hear bones break and teeth snap off. It's ugly to feel and hear. But it's a lot worse if it's your bones and teeth."

"Anger is your enemy. Let your opponent rage angrily and begin swinging like a windmill while you calmly sidestep and deliver your combinations."

"The best fighters will break their opponent's will before the fight begins."

Dad was a man of few words; he often said, "People are going to assume you are stupid; why open your mouth and prove them right?" Now, I understand this was his take on Mark Twain's "It is better to keep your mouth closed and let people think you are a fool than to open it and remove all doubt." But in the basement, he sounded like a professor teaching his students how to fight. I remember one lesson precisely:

"Work to create fear in your opponent. When you see that fear in their eyes, don't rush into the fight; give that fear more rope. Give the fear time to work on them. Let the fear become terror; the terrified fighter fights himself. Let the opponent attack desperately because the panicked man can always be trusted to make a fatal mistake. I will show you how to detect and use these mistakes to win."

"Voir deux fois" is the French term for seeing twice.

Two years later, I'm thirteen, and Jamie is fifteen. I shaped up a bit, but Jamie grew six inches, added thirty pounds of muscle, and burned away all unwanted fat. His knuckles were covered with callouses.

Another summer night, brother David joined Jamie and me on the stoop.

Like a slow-motion movie, Cooper came out of his yard. Although he was driving age, he was still riding a bike. As Cooper got closer, I wondered, *Will this be the day?* Jamie gave me a knowing glance. David was too young to remember the first fight.

Cooper swooped over to the curb and spat far into our yard. David daringly shouts, "Don't spit in our yard, Cooper!" Cooper smiled at that.

"I can't believe this is going to happen again," he smirked as he rode up and spat in David's face.

Jamie turned to Dad, who was standing at the screen door, in slow motion. Dad gave Jamie an almost undetectable nod of approval.

Jamie stood up. Cooper got off his bike and approached Jamie. Jamie jabbed Cooper in the face, then another, followed by a left hook. Jamie wouldn't let Cooper fall to the ground; he was kept erect by Jamie's continual, perfectly timed uppercuts. Then Jamie let Cooper fall. He was down, and he was hurt. We watched as Cooper stood clumsily, stumbled to his bike, and rode off.

It wasn't long before Cooper returned, walking behind his father. Dad was outside the screen door. Cooper's dad looked hot and ready to fight.

Our Dad said, "You better turn and go home unless you want your face to look like your son's." That's all he had to say.

As a show for Mom, Dad dragged Jamie to the basement steps to teach him never to fight again. Once David, Jamie, Dad, and I were downstairs with the door closed, Dad did an uncharacteristic victory jig. I'd never seen our dad this happy. After the quiet cheering, we went back to business. We all sat as Dad explained and demonstrated what Jamie could have done better.

## REFLECTIONS

I heard from Jamie much later in life that he didn't like to fight, didn't want to fight, but fighting was a way Jamie got to spend time with Dad. With Dad working two jobs and a side job painting houses, time with Dad was precious. Doesn't every child crave time with their father?

All my brothers went through Dad's fight club training; he should have written a book. A few of my brothers and I had no interest in fighting and avoided it at all costs, but what we learned about fighting served us well later. To this day, I fear no man. In a stress-filled situation, I know how to keep my cool. I know how to be patient and quiet as fear builds in my challenger. Knowing how to win a fight has helped us avoid the fight.

This was Jamie's maiden win, setting off five years of fights of ever-increasing intensity. Each fight by Jamie was prompted by either protecting himself or one of his siblings.

# BREAKING BOUNDARIES: AN UNEXPECTED WARDROBE CHANGE

## CHAPTER 5

---

"I think that there is a problem with rewards and consequences because in the long run, they rarely work in the
ways we hope. In fact, they are likely to backfire."

– Marshall B. Rosenberg

---

WHEN TELLING MAY AVENUE Stories to family, friends, and
strangers, I'd always weave in stories of my grade school years
and the nuns. While I still twitch recalling my elementary school
years at Saint Rose Catholic School, it makes for great storytelling.

The May Avenue Stories included comedy, drama, suspense,
action, love, and tragedy. The nun stories were initially intended
to be comedies; they got some laughs, but I also saw frowns,
head shaking, and pity. Given that they were true, the stories are
sad and disturbing.

Attending Catholic grade school midcentury meant every
teacher, clerk, leader, and even the cooks were nuns. The nuns at
Saint Rose were from the order of Notre Dame. Their habits
(uniforms) had a white starched thin helmet with a point on the
top like a steeple, a white collar, and a full black gown with a
veil-cape. Just walking into the room with their faces squeezed
and crunched up made them look pissed, and for some reason,
Jamie and I believed it was our place in life to make them even
more pissed.

The nuns had complete authority—a nun could never be wrong. It wasn't possible to say anything negative about a nun without severe repercussions from my mother.

Suzy Andrews from across the street held preaching services on the curb at May Avenue. From a family of devoted Baptists, Suzy told all who listened about being saved. She was genuinely concerned that all Catholics were going to hell because we were not saved. Straight to hell, no stopping over at purgatory. Imagine the scene when I told a 300-pound, already pissed-off nun that she was going straight to hell because she was Catholic. Sister Margarete Joan descended upon me with a flurry of shots to the head. She must have been a prizefighter in a previous life. I think she could have taken Dad. When I got punished by a nun, it would be best not to share that with my parents, or I would get punished a second time.

Entering grade school, the deck was stacked against me; the nuns already had two years of Jamie and painted me with that same brush. But I was different. Not better. *Different.* Jamie revealed his combination of charm and malice at an early age. The nuns had this love-hate relationship with Jamie. He wouldn't do his work and was a runner, causing constant stress on the system. I did my work and got straight A's. Jamie taught me to have no fear of the nuns.

Catholic grade school was all about memorization and repetition, just like Catholic prayers and repetitive and rote recitals. In second grade, I misspelled my name. My punishment was to write my name 500 times before school the next day. This was a positive punishment. Its purpose was to ensure I never misspelled my name again. It worked. I learned to read, write, and do arithmetic. Even today, as I write, I am edited by my inner nun.

The Catholic schooling system is based on structure and discipline. That didn't work for me or Jamie. I revolted against it quite early and regularly. The reaction was always corporal punishment. The stories you hear about the brutality delivered by the nuns are true. Corporal punishment began in kindergarten.

I'm guessing my arrival as a happy and productive adult is a testament to being a survivor, but I still wonder if I've paid an unknown price. The nun stories here are written from direct, personal experience. The stories are true, not taken from old jokes, other accounts, or lines from the novel-turned-Broadway-musical *Do Black Patent Leather Shoes Really Reflect Up?*

Saint Rose Catholic School nuns delivered physical and psychological punishment for a number of offenses: not listening, poor performance, wrong answers, and a litany of rule-breaking. At times, there was punishment for no known reason. Maybe it was the unclean thoughts I was having. The type and intensity of the punishment was unpredictable, having to do with a combination of the severity of the offense, the level of rage built up in the nun on that day, and the number of repeated crimes from the felon. The punishments were intended to inflict pain, shame, isolation, and even torture.

Jamie recalled one specific type of psychological punishment he found most disturbing: "Sister Saint Regina would habitually, for no known reason, make all the boys in her class stay after school, seated at their desks, and she would just sit and stare at the boys. She would go into a trance, her eyes glazed over. One time, Denny Hosier stood up and said, 'Hi, Sister,' hoping it would break her trance. She just kept staring, no response; it was freaky. Eventually, we would just all get up and walk out. The next day, it was like nothing happened."

Other punishments were physical. Holding my arms extended out for an hour. Kneeling in the corner on the hardwood floor, with my open hands on the floor, palms up, while kneeling on my knuckles. Raps on the back of my hands with a wooden ruler and across my back with a three-feet-long pointer. We are talking about real pain here. The most disturbing punishment I received was being put in a dark, locked closet for hours. If I made a sound, the time in the box was extended. I regularly wet my pants while in solitary confinement and was not allowed to go home to change.

The most interesting punishment was making me hit myself on the hand with a ruler. If I didn't beat myself hard enough, Sister Saint Emma would hit me three times harder. So, I developed skills in acting, cringing, and wincing at the right time. How twisted is that? It wasn't that I was singled out—many children, primarily boys, received the same abuse.

## WHEN PUNISHMENT REWARDS

We entered the school from the playground door at the back of the building. Inside was a long, narrow hallway with three stairs going up, halfway down the hall. The hallway was lined with classrooms on both sides. The cafeteria was at the end of the hallway.

Nuns prepared lunch, and the smell of the food filled the hallway. Meal tokens were round and blue with the school's name embossed on one side and twenty-five-cent marks on the other. Tokens were sold on the first of each month. It was a rare occasion when my siblings or I had the privilege to eat the day's hot meal, but I remember every meal as excellent. Great food and lots of it.

We brought our lunch, which included a sandwich made with bologna, ham salad (made with bologna), or cheese, and a two-inch square of Mom's cake of the day. You can imagine the amount of bread we consumed. Jamie and I walked once or twice weekly to the Wonder Bread Bakery's day-old bread store. There, the bread not sold in the stores around town the day prior was collected and brought to the day-old store. Our sandwich and cake were wrapped in wax paper that we returned to Mom every day. Lunch bags were as scarce as light bulbs, and Mom cut plastic bread sleeves in half and repurposed them as lunch bags.

Kids with meal tokens sat in the front half of the cafeteria, closest to the food line. Those who brought their lunch sat in the back.

I loved cake then and still do. After picking up a carton of chocolate milk (provided by the school district free of charge), I sat and ate my cake first, then my sandwich. I always ate my entire lunch. My lunch ritual went on for three years under the radar, and then one day, the nun in charge of lunch duty noticed I ate my dessert first. She gently told me that was not allowed, that from now on, I must eat my sandwich before I ate my cake.

I mistakenly asked her why, and she not-so-gently told me, "Because I said so."

I told my mom what had happened at lunch, and she dismissively said, "Well, that's silly," which I translated to, "Of course, you can eat your dessert first, don't listen to that cranky old biddy."

Of course, the next day, Sister I've-Got-My-Eye-On-You caught me unwrapping my cake first and instantly floated to me (I'm still unsure if nuns have feet) and told me to collect my lunch. She brought me to a classroom and made me eat my lunch there, alone. Being a social creature, this punishment hurt. I was sentenced to five days of eating alone.

Some children don't learn. Once allowed back in the cafeteria to eat with my friends, I did it again. After consultation with Sister Superior, I was officially excommunicated from lunchtime for the rest of the school year. At age eight, the nuns expected me to go home (which was a mile away) or eat outside somewhere. They pressured my mom to ensure she enforced their rules. I told my mom about the punishment and could tell she was on my side, but there was no way she would take on the nuns. But Mom had a brilliant solution; I would go to my grandma Myrtle's house two blocks from the school for lunch.

I loved my grandma, my mom's mother. She was short, always wore a dress, and had an ass so big she waddled when she walked. Grandma Myrtle was a comedian. Jamie and my brother, Warren, must have inherited that gene from her. When she farted, which she seemed to enjoy doing often, she picked up the edge of her dress, waved it, and said the same thing each time, "Catch it and paint it green!" She told us regularly that she was going down to city hall to change her name because it sounded like a fart in a bottle, as she blew air into her palm to make the most astounding fart sound. Funny and kind, Grandma Myrtle was the only family member who came regularly to help my mom with the children.

When I'd walk in to have lunch with Grandma, I'd be greeted with a vanilla ice cream cone. I'd eat my cone, then my cake, and then my sandwich. The punishment that rewards.

Recess on the playground is where it all went down. It was like a circus sideshow. Beth Dupree hung upside down by her knees on the monkey bars with her jumper draped over her face. Ken Richards sold black market pretzels, competing with the nun who walked around with her tray selling snacks. Lee LaMontagne was over in the far corner masturbating a stray dog and giving the boys sex education talks at the same time. That dog stealthily showed up in that corner every day at recess time.

While the classrooms were coed, the playground was not. The school building was across the alley from Saint Rose Church. The playground was an ample asphalt space doubling as the church parking lot on Sundays. Starting at the school's back door, a broad white stripe ran the length of the playground— boys on the right, girls on the left. Do not cross that line.

I've always found girls more interesting than boys. Beyond simply being better to look at, they don't fight, don't sweat, and never gave me wedgies. At recess, I was allowed to stand at the edge of the line and talk with Connie, Claudia, and Beth. Some-times, you must cross the line, and I did. *How bad could the punishment be? Let's see.* So, I joined the girls in Double Dutch, as a crowd of boys grew at the line, waiting for Sister Sergeant to see me. It took about thirty seconds. Sister Regina was a lovely nun. She never yelled, never hit me, and always gave me a light sentence. Grabbing me gently by the elbow, she walked me back to the manly side of the playground. First offense, sentence suspended for good behavior.

The next day at recess, the girls encouraged me to cross the line. The second offense got a bit more attention. That time, I was pulled by my ear to the other side of the line by that 300-pound Sister Joan Margarete. I was given a fair warning, "Do that again, and you will see Sister Superior." Something no boy wanted to experience.

The next day at morning recess, offense three. Straight to the third floor with my escort, Sister Joan Margarete. Saint Rose School was on the ground floor. The other two floors were what we called the nun factory, where they made nuns—a Convent. And the third floor was where all the nuns lived. In a strange way, I was looking forward to visiting the never-seen third floor.

Once up the two flights of stairs with beautiful carved railings and balusters, I walked down the long hallway with doors closely placed on both sides. I felt like Dorothy on her way to see the all-knowing wizard. Sneaking a peek into one open door, I saw what must have been a bedroom for a nun. Small, with one twin bed and a tiny wooden night table. No pity from me; I slept on a mattress on the floor with eight other stinky boys.

I must admit, walking into the Holy Mother's office did give me a little shiver, but the wonder of being behind the curtain with the wizard who pulls the strings intrigued me. Whatever my punishment was going to be, it was worth it.

"So, you want to play with the girls? I'm going to help you. Put this on and wear it the rest of the day." Sister Superior handed me a girls jumper uniform of plaid green and blue. It slipped over my light blue shirt and dark blue pants uniform.

For almost any other eight-year-old boy, this punishment would have been devastating. The teasing by the other boys in the classroom would have been brutal, and the boy wearing the girl's jumper would have spent the rest of the day with head down and tear-filled eyes. But in this case, Sister Superior picked the wrong boy, and the wrong punishment. This time, she gave the jumper to the class clown, lover boy, and the one no boy would dare tease. At afternoon recess, with envy from every other boy on the playground, I went right over to the girl's side and loved all fifteen minutes. With the girls' admiration and envy of the boys, this was yet another punishment that instead rewarded.

The next day, just before recess, I raised my hand and told my teacher nun I needed to see Sister Superior. Thinking I must have had an appointment, my teacher sent me up... I knew the way.

I walked into Sister Superior's office as she greeted me with an unexpected smile: "How can I help you, Michael?"

"Sister, may I have the jumper? I want to play with the girls."

REFLECTIONS

While it certainly makes for good storytelling, we must call this one by its name. Abuse. I still consider the punishment of wearing a girl's uniform as pure comedy. No harm, no foul. It just played into my hands. But as I reflect, what damage could have been done to a child suffering from insecurity or shyness? What if I wasn't the class clown who loved attention?

The jumper aside, the totality of my punishment and abuse has had a long-term negative impact on me. I began bed-wetting days after being locked in a crowded, dark closet by a nun for eight hours. I am incredibly claustrophobic. *Could this also be a result of the punishment in the closet?*

My siblings and I have a strange trauma bond, having experienced abuse from the nuns. I find it interesting and somewhat comforting when I connect with others outside my family who were also taught by the nuns in the '50s and '60s. We quickly get to comparing notes on the specific abuse levied on us. It's always the same experience. *Did they teach abuse at the nun factory?*

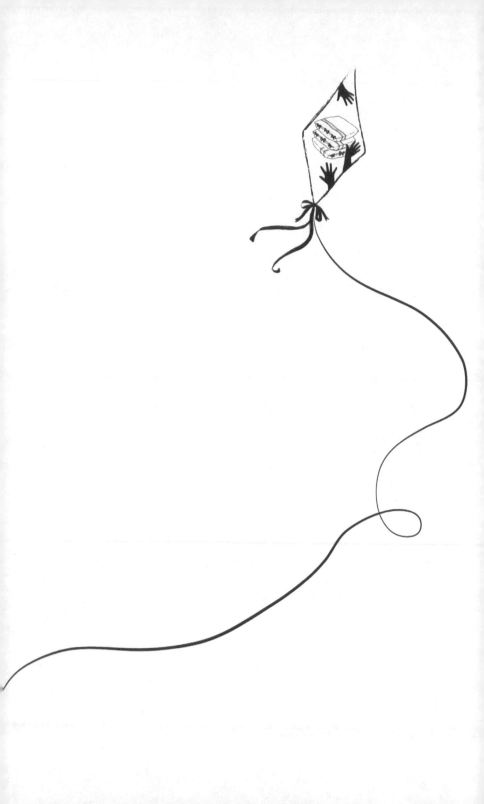

# PILLOWLESS DREAMS

## CHAPTER 6

"Your struggle is your strength. If you can resist becoming negative, bitter, or hopeless, in time, your struggles will give your everything."

– Bryant Gill

THE MENARD FAMILY ALWAYS welcomed bedtime.

Dad had converted the attic into two small rooms, one for the boys and the other for the girls. The girls' room had two double beds; the boys' side started with two bunk beds but evolved to mattresses on the floor to accommodate ten boys.

Once we made the trip upstairs with Mom and our one dim light bulb was screwed in place, we took turns peeling off the soles of our feet. We sat on the side of the mattress, took the butter knife that stayed in the bedroom, and took turns scraping off the crust of dirt from the bottoms of our feet—sixteen people in and out of the house all day long. With barefoot children tracking dirt onto the well-worn linoleum floors, Mom couldn't keep the floors clean. It was a game; try and get the dirt crust off our feet in one piece. It was a mix of earth, human hair, dog hair, cockroach wings, and dust bunnies. I'm sure it had some undiscovered commercial use. The dirt soles were deposited in a cardboard box.

For the most part, we had assigned beds, where we piled our few belongings, mostly clothes. I always ended up next to Jamie.

Even in a sardine can of a room, I never wanted to be the last one to sleep. I was afraid the Holy Host Burglar was going to get me on the way up the attic stairs.

In the Catholic church, communion was served at every Mass. The priest prepared to administer Holy Communion to the congregation during the Mass ceremony. It was my favorite part of Mass. I understood that it was the foundation of our beliefs. The priest, who we were taught to believe had divine powers, consecrated the thin round pieces of bread: the Host. The consecration was transforming the Host from bread to the Body of Christ. There was Latin chanting and a giant pipe organ blasting. When you took the bread into your mouth, you were receiving Christ and reenacting the Last Supper, where Jesus held up bread and said, "Do this in memory of me." The leftover consecrated hosts were stored in the church tabernacle, locked in a box made of gold. When a Catholic walked past the altar at any time, you were expected to genuflect (take a knee) and bow your head. It made sense; God was in the tabernacle.

We learned all about the Catholic doctrine at Saint Rose School. The rules, guilt, punishment, and penance. When it came time, we learned about the consecration. It was dramatic. As part of the lessons, we were warned that bad people wanted to steal consecrated hosts and use them in satanic rituals. The people who stole the Holy Hosts were devil worshippers, and they were tricky. They would offer a Catholic altar boy treasure to steal and hand over one consecrated Host. Maybe a new bike or a BB gun.

The nuns were skilled at implanting fear into the souls of their young students. They often lectured that a child who stole a consecrated Host went straight to hell—no stop off at purgatory. I was obsessed with the Holy Host Burglars and believed they were everywhere. I had an image of them, tall with wire-like hair coming out the sides of a dunce's hat. Thin-faced, large nose, like a giant troll; ancient. They wore thick wool clothing, and I assumed they lived in the woods.

I was confident a Holy Host Burglar was watching my every move—and I didn't even have any hosts to barter with. When walking up the stairs to our attic dormitory, I closed my eyes as I walked past the window at the top right. I was sure the Holy Host Burglar's face would be peeping through the window. Once, in bed next to Jamie, I mustered the courage to look out the window quickly, and there he was.

I told Jamie about the Holy Host Burglar, but he was never there when Jamie looked. If Jamie fell asleep before me, the burglar's face instantly appeared in the window, and the burglar was looking right at me out of all the children in that dorm. *Why?* Jamie had to stay awake until I fell asleep. Jamie was a great big brother; he still is. He never criticized or teased me about the burglar and always did his best to stay awake until I was sleeping. And poor Jamie, I wet the bed most nights. I should say I wet the Jamie.

If Jamie nodded off, I'd nudge him to wake up. I devised the plan for Jamie to jiggle his leg next to mine to let me know he was still awake. Jamie complied, and it worked. To this day, some sixty years later, just as I begin to fall deep into the arms of Morpheus, I jiggle my leg to let a not-there Jamie know I'm not yet asleep.

There was a time when there was a set of bunk beds in the dorm. Billy always got the bottom bunk; Allen got the top. After lights out, Billy raised his left hand, squeezed it between the wall and the upper mattress, and tapped Allen's arm. Allen instinctively took Billy's hand and played "Thumbs" until either would doze off. Recently, Billy's wife, Karen, told me that some nights, when Billy is in the twilight between awake and asleep, he raises his left hand into the air, reaching for Allen's hand.

We always needed more at 118 South May Avenue: food, toilet paper, clean towels, hot water, heat, light bulbs, and pillows. I wanted more pillows. On the boy's side of the dorm, there were three pillows: no pillow covers, and the ticking was made of traditional cotton material with thin blue lines. The material was thick and a little rough. When I was lucky enough to get one of three pillows, I would run my hand slowly over the ticking, searching for little pokey things sticking through. I'd tweeze the points with my fingers and would pull out feathers. I would look closely at each feather and wonder where this feather came from on the goose or duck.

Living in such tight quarters, you can imagine how vital it was to have order and peace. We were taught to be quiet, respectful, and kind from an early age. A disagreement or argument disrupted the entire 900 square feet. We had rules we lived by. Some spoken, some not. Suppose you ended up with a pillow; good for you. Those without a pillow used their small pile of clothes as a pillow. You might think deciding which ten boys got the three pillows was a constant source of fighting. Nope. Jamie created and taught us all the rules of pillow getting:

1. The first three to go to bed get the pillows.
2. If you get up after securing a pillow, you must leave the pillow on the mattress. Do not take your pillow with you.
3. You cannot reserve a pillow.
4. A brother may not reserve a pillow for another brother.
5. Once a brother is asleep on a pillow, another brother may steal the pillow; however, if the brother stealing the pillow wakes the pillow holder, the robbery is over, and the original holder is now entitled to keep the pillow uninterrupted for the remainder of the night.

Jamie was the master thief. He could slide the pillow out

from under a brother's head while effortlessly sliding their pile of clothes in as the replacement. They would never wake.

## REFLECTIONS

Years after we moved out, our 118 South May Avenue home was purchased and relocated to a lot about four miles west of Kankakee in the small village of Limestone. On a trip home for a reunion, while I was writing this book, I took a ride and found our old home. It had been renovated, with new siding, windows, and roof, but it was still a tiny home. It was about the size of a two-car garage.

I felt a rush of memories and emotions, but they were all positive. I reflected on how difficult it must have been for my mom to raise so many in such a small space. I sat on the front porch and relived the famous Jamie vs. Mickey Cooper fights. I looked around the right side at the single window on the second floor and smiled—there was no way the Holy Host Burglar could have peeked at me through that window. Maybe he had a ladder.

On my bed nowadays, there is a pile of decorative pillows at the head of the bed. Without fail, I smile every night as I take those pillows and pile them in the corner.

# FEATHERS & FATE: THE BOY AND THE PIGEON'S DESTINY

## CHAPTER 7

---

"In a deeper sense, a great deal of human suffering exists because of the denial of the past and an inability to acknowledge and integrate it. But when the decision is made to finally look at and feel the past, everything shifts."

– Thomas Hübl

---

PIGEON RACING IS A sport where a particular breed of pigeon, called Homers, are taken 100 to 500 miles from their nest and released. The pigeon registering the fastest speed wins. While the first recorded history of using Homer pigeons goes back to 3,000 BC, the first long-distance race occurred in Belgium in 1818.

Dad raised pigeons for two reasons. He was a pigeon fancier and loved the sport of racing pigeons. He also raised pigeons for food. Pigeon races took place in the summer, and race day was always on Sundays. All the fancier club members from Kankakee County brought their pigeons to Jebb Turner's garage; he was the president of the pigeon club. The setting of the clocks and banding of the birds for the race happened on Saturday at 6 p.m., the night before the race. It was an all-evening event and included much beer drinking. Dad always took Jamie and me to the Saturday night meetings. We loved being there. Rare times with Dad, we visited with two of my dad's brothers, Uncle Bob and Uncle Bud. My uncles were impressive men. My dad and two uncles were WWII veterans. Uncle Bob lost both legs in the war and struggled to walk on his two wooden legs. Jamie and I noticed that Dad looked up to his two older brothers. Bud and Bob treated Dad with respect and admiration.

I think Dad wanted Jamie and me to witness him as something more and better than the guy who worked so hard yet still couldn't provide for his family. Among his thirty fellow fanciers, our dad stood tall. At the pigeon meetings, he was proud; his posture was different, with his shoulders back and chin up. Looking back, we understood why Dad was treated as the king. First was his reputation of being tough as nails and undefeated in fistfights; he was badass. Second, he represented the Navy in the Army-Navy boxing championship in 1945. Dad lost; Mom had told us that his arms were sore and swollen from receiving five shots in prep for his deployment to the Philippines. Third, Dad was the undisputed all-time winner of the pigeon races. Dad treated racing as a science. He was an expert in breeding, nutrition, and training, and never passed up an opportunity to win ugly. Finally, Dad, hands down, used the most beautiful pigeon crates to transport his birds to the Saturday night meetings.

A clear status was assigned to the members based on the type of pigeon crates they owned. The crates had to be a specific size for shipping the birds: twelve inches tall, sixteen inches wide, and thirty-two inches long. Most fanciers bought crates with canvas sides and bottoms, and a bird cage-type top. One side had small toggles to quickly drop the canvas side so the birds were released quickly. The top was made of various types of screening or mesh with a door at the top to take the birds in and out.

After losing his legs, the VA offered to train my uncle Bob in a trade, and he chose woodworking. Using that training, Uncle Bob built a successful cabinetmaking business. Uncle Bob hired Dad to work on weekends to make some extra money. I have fond memories of being with Dad and Uncle Bob in the cabinet shop. The smell of freshly sawed wood, the opportunity to view and feel beautiful pieces of wood with their intricate patterns of grain. Maybe this is where I developed my love for acoustic guitars made from walnut, Brazilian rosewood, and mahogany. The most popular type of countertops was Formica. In his shop, Uncle Bob had hundreds of sample pieces the customers would use to select the tops for their new cabinets. When new samples arrived, Uncle Bob always gave me the old ones to take home. Aunt Edna would serve lunch for Dad, Uncle Bob, and me. It was such a special time. Dad became a master cabinet builder working under Uncle Bob and passed his woodworking skills on to some of his sons.

Dad built beautiful custom crates for himself and his two brothers using wood scraps from the cabinet shop in his minimal spare time. They were like pieces of fine furniture.

On Saturday night, the birds were banded and placed back in the crates for the trip to the release points. The distance for the races gradually increased, starting at 100 miles and ending the season with the 500-mile race. The routes to drop off the pigeons were always due south. The birds were released at sunrise. The club used one of Sonny Meyer's bread trucks from the bakery to transport the birds, and they always used the same driver, Russ, who sounded as rough as he looked.

As we got older, maybe ten or twelve, Dad arranged for Jamie and me to ride along with the pigeons and Russ. I believe Dad's intention was to have eyes on his pigeons to ensure there was no funny business with the timing of the release. God forbid some other fancier would scheme to win ugly.

Jamie and I treasured these Saturday night expeditions. The adventure of staying up all night, and Dad always gave us each a bottle of RC Cola and a large bag of Frito Lay corn chips. Jamie and I sat on the metal floor of the truck just behind Russ. For me, the longer the trip, the better.

Russ arrived at the release point about an hour before sunrise. We unloaded the cages and stacked them three or four high with the escape sides facing north. We would loosen one of the two toggles on each cage, and upon Russ's count, we released all the birds. It was a beautiful sight and sound. The timing of the release of each crate wasn't necessary; the birds grouped and circled the bread truck for a few minutes. It was like they were all resetting their inner compass. And then suddenly, the flock headed north, and the race was on. Jamie and I slept all the way home.

Russ was a smoker; in the '60s, everyone smoked. If it were a hot summer night, Russ left the bread truck's back door open so we wouldn't cook. It was windy and loud, but Jamie and I enjoyed the cool air. On one memorable race night, we were near the release point; the back door was open and Russ tossed his lit cigarette butt out the driver's door window. The draft sucked the lit cigarette back into the back door of the bread truck and into one of the crates. The crates had sawdust floors to make cleaning the pigeon poop easier.

Jamie saw the smoke filling the back of the truck and yelled at Russ. When Russ could pull over and stop, open flames were coming out of the crates. We pulled the burning crates off the truck and onto the side of the deserted road. We watched in horror as several crates and pigeons burned to a char. Russ was in a trance, and then he panicked. He released the rest of the birds right then and there. Dad's pigeons survived the catastrophe. After the release, we sat and listened as Russ frantically developed the plan to save his ass.

We could never tell anyone what happened. Russ implied that if the truth came out, Jamie and I would somehow be in big trouble. There was no fire, and the release went off as planned. And on the trip home, with the back door open, somehow, several crates broke loose, flew out the back, and were smashed by the traffic behind us. Jamie and I were sure Russ would tell the story in a way suggesting that Jamie and I must not have properly secured the crates for the trip home.

As soon as Russ dropped us off at home, we took Dad into

the basement (this is where all solemn men's things were discussed), and Jamie told him precisely what happened.

Dad had one question. "Are you sure none of my birds burned?"

We were 100 percent sure Dad's three crates were back at Jebb's house. Without Dad saying anything, Jamie and I immediately understood Dad's position. This was a good thing for him. The odds of Dad taking first, second, and third just increased—a blessing in disguise. Dad decided that we would never speak of the tragedy again.

When the race results were read, Dad took all three places and won the twenty-five-dollar pot. Mysteriously only fifty percent of the birds made it home that race. Some of the members lost their entire racing flock; it would take them years to rebuild.

Race days had two benefits. We watched Dad win, as he almost always did, and we had Sunday dinner. Race day Sundays were enchanting. After breakfast, Jamie, David, and I took our place in the middle of our tiny May Avenue yard. We lay flat on our backs and waited for the pigeons to arrive from their race. We started early to watch the clouds morph into exotic shapes. We spied dinosaurs, elephants, and Mickey Mouse. Once, we even saw Santa... and his reindeer. Our mom taught us this skill; she was a master at nurturing our imagination.

Dad always saw the birds first; he knew where to look. We knew it was showtime when Dad sounded his well-known whistle, the birdcall his pigeons grew up with. His whistle told the birds that it was time to come into the coop after exercising or "winging."

As soon as Dad whistled to welcome his birds home, he rattled seed corn in a tin can. The pigeons would not stop for the entire race; they came home hungry. Getting the birds into the coop and clocked in was the most critical step in the race. Getting his birds in five seconds faster than his competition could make the difference between winning and losing. The birds entered through the trap door; they could go in, but not out. Dad removed the rubber band placed on the bird the night before. The band was placed in a brass capsule and dropped in a hole atop the pigeon clock. When Dad cranked the handle, the capsule disappeared into the clock's turnstile and was stamped on the side of the capsule with the date and time. When the pigeon clocks were calibrated on Saturday nights, a lead seal was placed as a lock on the clock. At the Sunday night meeting at Jebb's house following the race, Jebb would cut the lead seals, and the club secretary would unload all the capsules and list the arrival times. At the beginning of the season, the distance was calculated from the release point to each member's coop. The average speed for each pigeon in the race was calculated, and the fastest average speed determined the winners.

Those pigeons returning late from the race were dinner—survival of the fittest. We quickly killed and cleaned the birds, and into the pressure cooker they went. We only cooked the breasts; it took many pigeons to feed the Menard clan. Pigeon pot pie, pigeon stew, and my favorite, creamed pigeon on toast. It was delicious. It's not that tough meat you'd get from bridge or common pigeons. Dad reminded us that we were eating grain-fed squab, a delicacy in France. (Yeah, but I was in Kankakee, and none of my friends ate pigeons.) Dad clocked in the first six birds to arrive at his coop. Every bird coming in after that went into the crate for Sunday dinner.

At a young age, I learned that Native American cultures revered the buffalo as a sacred and vital animal. Native Americans relied on the buffalo for food, clothing, shelter, and other necessities. In Western movies, the Native Americans touched a freshly slain buffalo they had just killed with kindness and respect. In some ways, pigeons were our buffalo. We valued Dad's pigeons. They were essential to him and a source of food for us. As children, we knew nothing about the importance of protein to the human diet, but Mom and Dad knew. The process of killing and dressing the pigeons was a solemn event, a ritual. Jamie, David, Tim, and I followed Dad as he carried the crate of soon-to-be dinner pigeons into the basement. I dreaded being part of the assembly line, but I knew there was no way to get out of it.

On the assembly line, everyone had a role to play. No one spoke on the assembly line. No laughing, smiling, or joking. At the head of the line, Dad reached into the crate and took out a pigeon. He soothed the bird before placing it into a five-gallon bucket. Dad twisted and pulled the head off in one smooth motion and let the bird bleed out into the bucket. Jamie plucked the big feathers then I removed the smaller ones. David and Tim finished the job by removing all the tiny pinfeathers. The pigeons' bodies were placed in an old rusty Radio Flyer wagon that Dad lifted up the stairs to Mom. If we found any pin feathers on our cooked pigeon, David and Tim heard about it.

When I was ten, Jamie would have been twelve, David eight, and Tim six. Dad announced that it was time Jamie began pulling the heads off. I was paralyzed with fear. I knew this meant, at some point, I would have to pull off a pigeon's head. *No way!* Jamie was the fighter; I was the lover. Jamie was all in. He couldn't wait to get that poor pigeon in his hands. Just being one position closer to the killing made me sick. I was hoping this would be a permanent position for Jamie.

Dad spoke slowly as he instructed Jamie. "When taking the bird out of the crate, get control before you lift the pigeon out of the crate. Hold the bird with two hands with the feet between the fingers of your left hand. Hold the bird's right wing to your ribs as you free your right hand. Grab the bird's head between your pointer and middle fingers. Point the head toward the bucket, twist and pull the head off in one fast movement. Hold the bird there until the bleeding stops."

Jamie followed instructions well, but at the last moment, as

Jamie pulled the head off, he forgot to hold that right wing to his ribs, and that wing started slapping Jamie in the face. Bang! Bang! Bang! In Jamie's attempt to secure that wing, blood sprayed all over Dad and Jamie. It was all very disturbing. Jamie got a second chance. This time, he did it perfectly. Dad and Jamie were proud.

A few weeks later, Dad decided it was time for my rite of passage into manhood. Dad repeated the instructions. I wouldn't make the same mistake Jamie made. I had both wings secured. I remember so vividly the beautiful, almost iridescent, multi-colored neck feathers. I commented on their beauty to Dad; I was stalling. Dad told me that it was a "splash" pigeon. My heart just wasn't in it. I didn't get the snapping the head off part right; I slowly and chicken-heartedly stretched that poor pigeon's neck about three inches long. When I let go, the head dropped and dangled. Dad grabbed the bird, snapped the head off, and without looking at me said, "Go to the back of the line."

I had made one of my dad's birds suffer; no second chance for me. I was demoted to pin feathers for the rest of my child-hood. *Fine with me.*

Some thirty years later, I attended a business dinner at the Le Hare restaurant in Princeton, New Jersey. Squab was on the menu, creamed on toast points. Mom's was better.

## REFLECTIONS

The transition from boyhood to manhood doesn't happen automatically or overnight. Experiences, relationships, and chal-lenges faced along the way shape us into unique individuals. All these factors help a boy turn into a man. While most males learn and grow on this journey, others do not.

There is something to this rite of becoming a man. While I believe the Menard boys were over-initiated, I know many unini-tiated men. Our dad certainly gave us multiple opportunities to "be a man." I do think the initiations came too early and were too harsh for most of my siblings.

At the cemetery, just before lowering Dad into the ground, my brother Tim released a crate full of Dad's pigeons. At the same time, Tim turned on a recording of Dad's pigeon whistle. The flock circled Dad's grave site until Tim turned off the recording, and the birds headed home.

Dad wasn't a General, no twenty-one-gun salute at his funeral. But there were many who loved Dad, the man who did the best he could with what he had. His twenty-one-bird flyover was a beautiful finale.

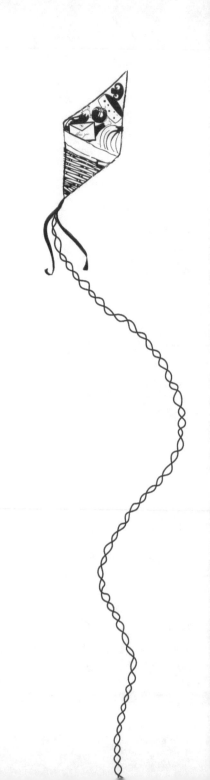

# GOD'S LOVE COMES FROM EVERYWHERE

## CHAPTER 8

"When you view your world with an attitude of gratitude, you are training yourself to focus on the good in life."

– Paul J. Meyer

I ASKED MY SIBLINGS what they remembered most about our mother. They said her love, faith, teachings, selflessness, capacity to do anything, and joy. Further down the list of praises, I heard about her cooking: the potato dumpling soup, her Thanksgiving Day stuffing, or the cake we had in our lunch bag each day. When we talk about our childhood, we have some of the best food stories. When we dig deeper into the subject of food and eating at 118 South May Avenue, we unearth a richness, revealing more about Mom and Dad and why we are the way we are.

One day, I was hungry and knew there was no food or money to buy dinner. Dad had the bottom of a bunch of celery, just the bottom, no celery. We sat around the table as if we were playing a game, not eating. Dad sliced across the celery root, producing ten little crescents of celery. Each pass delivered about ten pieces, three passes in total. The game divided the number of little celery pieces evenly for the people at the table, and then we could eat the pieces. Before the division started, Dad salted all the pieces. Jamie did the math, and we all ate our shares. That was dinner. I was sad for Dad, not myself.

While we all truly honor our mother, we took all she did and accomplished for granted. To this day, I have never known or heard of a mother who did more or better for her children and did it with so little.

It would be inaccurate and unfair to say we went without food, but sometimes we did go hungry. I didn't starve, but most of the time, I suffered from not knowing when my next meal would come.

We often reflect on the weight on Dad's shoulders to make enough money, and on Mom to shop, buy, and prepare the food to feed so many. Whether we had money or not, it was completely on Mom to provide the food.

When I was a young father, I would, from time to time, take Laura and Jenna to Dunkin Donuts for breakfast before dropping them off at grade school. These were always fun mornings, such great memories. On one particular morning, I forgot my wallet at home. I had enough change in my pocket for a donut each for Laura and Jenna, but they had to share a carton of milk. Knowing I didn't have enough money for a donut for myself, Laura and Jenna broke their donuts in half and offered me half of theirs. Such a tender memory. I thought of my Mom and about the hypothetical pain I would experience if I were ever in a situation where I didn't have enough food to feed my daughters. *How did she do it?*

Sister Saint Regina told Mom I had difficulty staying on task and paying attention. "Michael must learn to mind his own business. If there was a child across the classroom whose pencil needed sharpening, Michael will be there to sharpen it." (I'd prefer to view this quality as my desire to serve others.) So, when I was worried about where my next meal was coming from, I also worried for all my siblings. The FDA says that when a child is uncertain as to when their next meal comes, they suffer from food insecurity.

When I was uncertain, I would ask Mom what we were going

to eat for our next dinner. She would tell me, "God will provide." Mom would then recite Matthew 6:26 from her King James Bible: "Behold the fowls of the air: for they sow not, neither do they reap, nor gather into barns; yet your heavenly Father feedeth them. Are ye not much better than they?" My mom believed God would provide; she *knew* God would provide. I became a believer after witnessing repeated miracles at 118 South May Avenue. But why did God always keep me on the edge of my seat about getting my next meal?

From the time Mom had her first child until the last child left home, she shopped for, cooked, and served somewhere around 315,360 meals. This staggering number doesn't include meals provided for others. No one within a two-mile radius would go hungry if Mom knew about it. The parish priest would, like clockwork, stop over uninvited for dinner. *NO!* My mind would scream every time a priest walked into the house. *They had plenty of food. Why eat ours?* Dad disliked it but never said anything to discourage the freeloaders from returning. He had his own little ways to get back at them.

Dad was a master at evening the score, so you never wanted Dad as your enemy. Once, Dad placed a pair of my sister's dirty panties in Father White's black suit jacket pocket. Dad knew the rectory had a woman who came in to care for the priests and that woman would likely find those incriminating panties in Father's pocket. Busted!

When Mom cooked, the miracle of the fishes and the loaves was recreated. Most meals were stews, soups, and things in her big pot. She served her family. The pot should have been empty, but there was always plenty for seconds. Visitors intentionally stopped by at mealtime: Aunt Bee, the widow from down the street, Beaupre, the bum from the shack in the alley, and Father White. There was always enough to feed them.

Most meals consisted of potatoes, milk, Bisquick, and bacon fat or Crisco lard. We couldn't afford milk, so Mom made three gallons of powdered milk each morning and put it in the recycled wax-covered cartons.

Dad had a few bad habits that drove Mom up the wall. One habit was drinking out of the milk carton. We were not allowed to do it, so why was it okay for Dad? Mom often preached, "Ask, and thou shalt receive." Mom misused her power of prayer when she thought it was needed. I believe Mom asked God for Dad to stop drinking out of the carton.

118 South May Avenue had only one bathroom. Even in the middle of the night, the bathroom was occupied. When little boys have to go, they have to go. Next to the bathroom door, there was always a half-gallon empty milk carton to pee in if the toilet was occupied. We were supposed to wait till the door opened and pour the pee into the toilet. One night, someone peed in the carton and mistakenly put it in the fridge.

Dad was always the first one up in the morning. He opened the fridge, grabbed that milk carton, and took three swallows before he realized it wasn't milk. In a home with only 900 square feet, you hear everything. Dad was hurling in the toilet. He gagged when he tried telling us what happened and could not get the words out. We believe that was the last time Dad drank out of the carton. Prayers answered?

There were times when there wasn't enough food to make the next meal. There were a few fallback maneuvers I turned to. I went down to Chouinard's food store and asked the butcher, Bill Chouinard, if I could have the ham bone to make soup. Regardless of how much ham remained on the bone, Bill wrapped it in that white butcher paper, taped it with masking tape, and handed it to me over the tall glass meat counter. He tossed me two bags of dry Northern Navy beans on my way out. Thank you, Lord; bless Bill Chouinard.

The West Kankakee Liquor Store had a small deli that sold cold cuts, cheese, and other food items. Mom would send me to the liquor store to buy one dollar's worth of bologna. The first thing Mrs. Ravens did when I placed my order was give me a bottle of RC Cola and two pretzel sticks from the big plastic container with a metal screw lid. As I savored my snack, Mrs. Ravens packed two large paper grocery bags chock full of milk, lunch meat, cheese, bread, smoked oysters, and sardines. The bags were so heavy that I'd have to stop every block or so, put the bags on the sidewalk, and stretch my arms. Bless Mrs. Ravens.

Mom only let me make these trips when it was a true emergency. Other angels helped Mom feed her family. The stories about the nuns from grade school were true and deservingly revealed the nuns in a bad light. However, the Saint Rose Convert nuns often answered Mom's prayers. During times of no money and no food, two or three nuns delivered trays of hot food to us. "Sister Francis cooked too much food again," they explained. On those delivery days, the nuns ate well, and so did the Menards. Chicken baked in butter and parsley. Pork chops in cream sauce. Full sheet cakes. Bless the sisters of Saint Rose.

Myer's was the go-to bakery in Kankakee, mostly known for donuts and pastries. Sonny Myer, the owner and baker, was Dad's good friend; they were both pigeon fanciers and met every Saturday night at the Kankakee Pigeon Club. Sonny regularly showed up with a tray of day-old glazed donuts, enough for us to eat our fill. Mom popped them in the oven. Once warmed up, they tasted fresh enough for us. Bless you, Sonny.

Summertime was easy pickings, literally. Jamie and I walked over to the Small Woods two blocks west of May Avenue, each with a pocket full of sugar. Illinois Governor Small was born in a house on this land that was later named Governor Small Memorial Park after his death. It was a wonderland for young boys to explore and play. The woods were loaded with wild rhubarb. Break off a stalk, dip it in the sugar, and you almost have rhubarb pie. With a saltshaker in our pocket, we openly hunted for ripe tomatoes in many of the May Avenue alley gardens. Pick the tomato and lick it so the salt sticks to the skin for that first bite. *Mmmm.* I'm sure the neighbors knew what we were doing, but we never heard a complaint.

We called it "dimple corn." More widely referred to as dent or field corn, it's grown mainly for feeding cows or for corn byproducts like high fructose corn syrup. It received its namesake because each kernel has a slight indent at the top, unlike sweet corn. This corn wasn't intended for people; it was not sweet nor corn-on-the-cob-like. But Dad knew there was a week-long stage where the dimple corn was edible. Dad drove to the country near smaller towns like Herscher and Irwin and parked on a dusty gravel roadside. We scurried out like stormtroopers and disappeared about four rows deep. We filled the containers Dad provided in less than a minute, climbed back in the truck, the Chevy Carryall, and went home for dinner.

Dinner was dimple corn. Mom boiled two pots of corn for precisely six minutes, or the sugar turned to starch, and all the taste evaporated. One of us slathered butter on a heel of bread. With the steaming plate of corn in the middle of the table, we each grabbed an ear and waited our turn. In birth order, each sibling ran the corn over the buttered bread, like sliding a hot dog through a bun. The last person won the prize and got to eat the bread still soaked with melted butter. Three rounds were enough for most.

In addition to pigeons, our protein came from hunting. Dad, Jamie, and I hunted for rabbit, pheasant, and squirrel all winter. Mom made fried rabbit, making her famous gravy with the drippings. Dad stacked four slices of bread, each with its layer of gravy; it always reminded me of pancakes and syrup.

Dessert was ice cream. Down the railroad tracks, about two miles from May Avenue, there was a large grain elevator and an ice cream factory that also manufactured ice. On one of our expeditions, we struck gold. We discovered trucks loading ice cream from the factory in the daylight. We reckoned it was possible to crawl up the chute where the ice cream came down and out to find ice cream to steal.

We hopped on a freight train the next night and took a short ride to the ice cream factory. It was Jamie, our friend Tom Dupree, and me. We planned a sleepover in Tom's backyard so we could stay up and eat ice cream all night long. The plan worked! In the freezer room, pallets of every type of ice cream imaginable. The choice was easy for me: ice cream sandwiches. We loaded up, each boy carrying the maximum possible. I had four cases of ice cream sandwiches, two in each arm. And then, just like we bought a ticket, a return freight train approached the ice factory.

To jump a train, one must first run along the train to match its speed, grab hold of the ladder that goes up to the roof at the end of the car, and jump on, staying on the ladder until jumping off at the May Avenue intersection. Easy enough.

The first challenge was to grab the ladder, which meant I had to let go of two cases of sandwiches. On departure, Tom jumped off just a bit early and right into a cesspool, an open pool of sewage as part of the water treatment plant. Tom went under, and when he climbed out, the ice cream was gone, and Tom was covered with sewage from head to toe. We returned to the tent, and Tom crept to the bathtub to clean up—a big mistake. Tom's mom woke up and caught him. Tom sang like a canary, thinking it would deflect blame on the Menard boys. His mom called our mom, who ordered us home immediately. No ice cream, and we, like Tom, were in deep shit.

While stealing steaks, ice cream, and corn seemed acceptable and expected, Dad's pride would not allow anything in the house that he defined as "charity." Rather than accept charity, he would rather starve and let his children starve alongside him. If a handout came while Dad was home, he would say, "No thank you, give it to someone who needs it." Our hearts would sink.

Dad had an unhealthy ego that he instinctively transferred to his children. When it was noticed that the family went without, Dad said, "We may not have a car, but we are Menards. Do you know how many people want to be a Menard? All of them!" To challenge Dad's ego was the worst thing that could happen to him.

Mom raised her children to know and trust in Jesus. She taught it and lived it, and our Lord reinforced it with what we all knew and believed to be miracles. One never forgets a miracle.

Dad was in the hospital—one of his many stays caused by his heart problems. He was at the VA hospital in Dwight, Illinois, too far for us to visit him. One Sunday, there was no food and no money. Mom and I knew it.

I asked Mom, "What will we do for dinner? Chouinard's and the liquor store are closed."

"Don't worry, Michael, God will provide."

But this time, I thought I saw that she didn't believe He would. It was late afternoon, and the sunlight came through the window in thin slices through the Venetian blinds. I sat on the sofa beside Jamie and talked about the crisis. As we spoke, Jamie was slapping the velvet-type material on the arm of the couch. Billows of ultra-fine dust rose in the air, magnified due to the sunlight streaming right onto the sofa. In the warmth of the sunlight, we both fell asleep.

A rapid knock on the door woke me. Startled, I jumped up to answer it—no one was there. On the stoop was a large basket. It was full of food: canned ham, bread, orange juice, fresh fruit, cookies, and candy. I could barely lift the basket into the house. Jamie remembers this day like it was yesterday. He remembers Warren wearing only oversized tighty-whities, tossing oranges and bananas to the other children, all screeching and laughing with joy and excitement. Jamie remembers it as monkeys in a zoo sharing their food.

A white envelope was on the top of the food. Inside was $500 and a note. "God's love comes from everywhere." I took the note and cash to Mom. She looked to Heaven, made the sign of the cross, and then looked down and gave me that didn't-I-tell-you look. The value of that $500 in 1966 would be $5,900 today. That $500 was enough to buy food for six months for our entire family.

In her last months, we had the privilege to cook for Mom. She was diagnosed with stage four uterine cancer a few days after her eightieth birthday. When she heard her prognosis, she refused any treatments. She said she was already homesick for Heaven. And while Mom lived a life of poverty and going without for so many years, once her children began making money, Mom wanted for nothing. She died four months later in the new home her children bought for her years earlier.

There was no need for hospice. Two of Mom's daughters were nurses, and one of her sons was a physician assistant. We took shifts, a week at a time. Two siblings per week provided twenty-four-hour coverage. One of her children provided Mom's care, and the second on duty did cleaning, laundry, shopping, and cooking. During my weeks with Mom, I was the cook. Planning the menu and shopping for Mom's meals created some great memories. Mom had a robust appetite right up to the end, requesting and enjoying steak and lobster at least twice a week.

Mom loved food, especially when there was no shortage of money. She loved high-end foods once she reached the place where she knew we would give her anything she desired—one of the small fruits of her labors. She loved lobster. Laura, Jenna, Melissa, and Anna loved and adored their grandma. They often quote her still today. They loved it when Grandma Arletta visited us in Doylestown, Pennsylvania. I remember Jenna sobbing when it was time for her grandma to return to Kankakee. In between gasps of breath, Jenna would say, "My heart hurts."

During her visits to us, Mom counted on dinner at the Cock and Bull restaurant every Tuesday night at Peddler's Village. It was billed as King Henry's Feast: all you could eat for twenty-nine dollars and ninety-five cents. An impressive spread including prime rib, baked salmon, shrimp, and a mountain of steamed Maine lobster tails, a tank of clear melted butter alongside. On one of these Tuesdays, I noticed Mom struggling to finish her fourth lobster tail.

"Mom, don't worry; you don't have to finish that lobster."

"I will, honey," she said, "You paid $29.95 for my supper, and I want to make sure you get your money's worth."

We counted on Mom leaving the Cock and Bull with butter stains on her dress. It was her hallmark. She fussed and tried to clean it off as soon as she noticed it. It always happened; we waited for it and would have a laugh with her when it did. Even after being gone for fifteen years, my daughters still talk about it and get especially tickled when I drop food on my shirt; I explain it away as being genetic.

## REFLECTIONS

While it's in my nature to always look for the lessons, for the good that might come from my childhood experiences, I can't come up with much that was good about going hungry or experiencing food insecurity. No child should experience this.

Doing without food when you need it must be classified as neglect, which is a documented form of childhood trauma. However, going without has multiple possible root causes. Neglect can result from a parent or caregiver just not caring. Neglect can also be created by the parent using the withholding of food as punishment. But in our case, there simply wasn't money at the time to buy food.

None of us, then nor now, hold anything against our parents for when we went hungry. Of course, it was their responsibility, and I believe it was excruciatingly painful for Mom and Dad, knowing we were hungry. I *can* fault my dad's pride for sometimes keeping food from us. He wouldn't take charity. He wouldn't take advantage of food stamps or any government welfare.

Did our food insecurity cause harm and disorder? The answer must be yes. While it's often a source of jokes, I still order the large pizza when a small would be enough. I overeat; I fit the medical criteria of being obese. I still get anxious when the fridge is low on real butter.

There is a silver lining to going without. Mom used these little miracles, like the basket on the porch with the cash envelope, throughout childhood to build our faith and gratitude. Even after fifty years of enough money to buy whatever food I want, I remain genuinely thankful for every meal I have. I remember with fondness in my adult years making sure Mom had more money than she needed for food, especially at Thanksgiving when Mom put out a dinner spread that would rival a buffet at the Ritz.

# WHEN THE TRUTH REALLY HURTS

## CHAPTER 9

"I've gotten the short end of so many sticks that I could start a bonfire."

– Craig D. Lounsbrough

"Spare the rod, spoil the child" was the chant of adults of my parent's generation and every nun I encountered. And so often I heard, "This is going to hurt me more than it will hurt you." *My ass.*

Today, psychological research and general wisdom state that corporal punishment isn't good for a child; that it will build resentment and result in the child acting out later in life. Paul and Arletta sincerely believed in corporal punishment and embraced the virtuous benefits of spankings, immediate compliance, reinforcement of boundaries and rules, and teaching respect and self-control.

Imagine the level of discipline required of a mother to keep order among fourteen children, including ten boys—boys raised by Paul Menard. As an adult, I spent a considerable amount of time in Japan. One of the interesting things I learned about the Japanese while living among them was of their universal kindness and politeness. A Japanese friend offered an explanation when I complimented the country on these admirable traits. He said that while most Western civilizations originated with people and families spread out across vast land areas, Japan's early

THE KITE THAT COULDN'T FLY

development forced villagers to live in small places, given the terrain. Families lived in a single room. If they had more than one room, only rice paper separated them, so it became essential to be quiet and polite to maintain civility and peace. For thousands of years, the Japanese valued manners and etiquette.

This all connected with how I grew up. Harmony was important. Any disagreements not quickly resolved created havoc and discord within our home. There weren't many involute rules, but when Mom established a rule or a law, it was in everyone's best interest to obey. One of those rules was not to speak until spoken to when there were adult visitors. I violated that rule when I was five years old. Mom had a friend over for coffee. Her name was Evelyn, and I remember how fancy she was dressed compared to my mom. Evelyn wanted nothing to do with me, but I needed her attention, so I butted in and tried to talk with her. I got the death stare from Mom, screaming to me with her eyes, *Don't speak until spoken to!* But I didn't stop. Mom, not so gently, took me by the arm and led me to her bedroom. That usually meant a spanking was coming. But instead of a spanking, Mom squeezed my two lips together right in the middle with her fingernails. I froze.

She spoke slowly and quietly, "Don't ever speak again unless the adult speaks to you." She held my lips sealed for what seemed like an eternity. It was painful. That was the last time I violated that rule.

Being loyal to your brothers and sisters was one of Dad's hard and fast rules. It's okay to rat out others, but never your family. I received my first real spanking for violating Dad's rule—I snitched on Jamie.

The Benoit family lived to the right of 118 South May Avenue. Renee was the dad, Julie was the mom. Renee had the most enormous beer belly we had ever seen. His jeans were four sizes too small, and his belt went way down under his belly. Julie's butt was even bigger than Renee's belly. It was a real sight to see Julie walking behind Renee. They had two boys, John and Jimmy. John looked exactly like Renee, belly and all. And there was Grandma Bisolac, Julie's mother. Grandma Bisolac was a cheerful old lady who always wore what our mom called a babushka, a scarf tied across her head. I discovered years later that a babushka isn't a colorful scarf; a babushka is a Polish or Russian grandmother. Mr. Benoit was French, and Mrs. Benoit was Polish. Because we were French, this meant the Benoits were half okay.

Mr. Benoit worked on the railroad, which meant to the Menards that the Benoits were rich. Their home was beautiful but clearly out of place on South May Avenue. The house was made from cut stone on all four sides. It was new and had an oversized two-car garage on the alley that matched their home. There was an old-time picket fence between our backyards, and the Benoits always had a large garden. Mom told us Polish people liked to have gardens. The Benoits grew vegetables we had never seen before: asparagus, cauliflower, kale, and broccoli. Of course, they grew what we recognized and enjoyed, like watermelon, tomatoes, and carrots. We scavenged from all the gardens in the neighborhood except the Benoits; they were always so generous in sharing from their garden, so it was off-limits to us boys. A mature plum tree was on our property right at the fence line. The Benoit and Menard boys used that tree to get between our yards.

The Benoits did their best to be good neighbors, but we knew they weren't happy with us. We had a scraggly-ass antenna strapped with metal bands to the chimney. It got three channels, but only one was viewable. The Benoits had a giant antenna atop a post that looked like it came off some bridge. The antenna was shiny and new. One could easily climb it like a step ladder to tilt and adjust the antenna. We had strict orders to never climb on the Benoit's antenna tower.

Dad bought Jamie a real bow and arrow set with the plan for

Jamie to learn how to hunt and kill rabbits for food. Jamie became an expert archer. Jamie had two types of arrows: metal-tipped for target practice and razor-tipped for hunting. I loved to stroke the feathers on the arrows. Jamie always reminded me that the arrow would be ruined if I messed up the feathers.

Jamie seemed to be constantly doing what he knew he should not do. Late one summer afternoon, Jamie decided to see how high he could shoot his arrows in the sky. I imagined one of those arrows coming down and going through my head. I told Jamie not to do it, but he never listened. Jamie aimed his arrow toward the sky and let go. The arrow went so high that it went out of sight. When it came back into view, we watched the arrow hit Jamie's intended target: the Benoit's roof. *Bullseye!* Jamie strung the next arrow and bullseye, right in the middle of Benoit's roof. He did it a third time, bingo!

Arrows were expensive, and money was scarce, so Jamie had to retrieve those arrows and remove the damaging evidence. If Renee knew, he would flip out on Dad and us. Jamie broke another rule and climbed up the Benoit's antenna tower and tippy-toed toward his arrows. In a flash of genius, I decided it was time Jamie learned a lesson. I went over the plum tree, up to the Benoit's back door, and knocked hard.

Mr. Benoit answered the door, and I spilled the beans. "Jamie shot arrows on your roof, and now he is up there getting them."

It was an absolute shit show. Renee came to our front door, and when Mom answered, he screamed at her. He wasn't just yelling because of the arrows shot into his roof; all of Renee's unhappiness with the Menards was coming to the surface. Our front yard was dirt, and our house was old and filthy. He knew we were stealing his tomatoes, and there was noise twenty-four-seven.

Mom was apologetic and embarrassed. Dealing with this had to wait for Dad. The following Saturday, Dad went over while Renee worked in his garage. Dad apologized, promised that it would never happen again, and agreed that Dad would go up on the roof to patch the holes with tar to ensure the roof wouldn't leak.

After that, it was time to deal with Jamie. "Jamie, go down to the basement." Oh, that was it. Jamie was going to get the paddle.

Dad was a carpenter as well as a factory worker. Knowing he would use it often, Dad made a beautiful and functional paddle. It looked like a short canoe paddle and even had holes drilled into it, so there would be less wind resistance. The spankings were ritualistic. We knew exactly where to bend over with our pants down around our ankles. Dad would tell us how many swats we would receive. He would hit hard; I think he was trying to lift our feet off the ground.

"And you too, Mike, go with Jamie to the basement."

*What? Me? I didn't do anything. Maybe Dad's going to let me watch. Dad never lets us watch!*

Dad told us, "Jamie, you are getting spanked for damaging the Benoits' roof and climbing on their antenna tower. Mike, you did something worse than Jamie: you told on your brother. No matter what your brother does, never squeal on him."

As I dropped my pants, I tried to use some psychology on Dad. "You are right, Dad, I deserve the spanking. I was wrong."

"You're damn right, you deserve it. Now bend over."

I got three swats, and Jamie got only two. I remember Jamie and me going out behind Dad's pigeon coop, sitting down, and talking about how our butts felt hot. Then we began laughing— no hard feelings from Jamie for me tattling on him.

I received about a dozen spankings while growing up on May Avenue. I don't recall any spanking as traumatic (the beatings from the nuns were never deserved and were much more disturbing), and I believe I deserved each spanking from Mom and Dad. All except one, my worst and last spanking.

The truth was sacrosanct at 118 South May Avenue. For

Mom, it was one of her core beliefs that she drilled into her children. Even Dad stood firm about truth. Given Dad's pathology, I always found his sermons on truth counterfeit. Still, I guess there is some truth to the saying, "There is honor among thieves," like not stealing from each other or not squealing on or testifying against a fellow criminal.

The Kankakee swimming pool was the children's social center in town. It was a large, beautiful pool that always smelled like chlorine. When entering the front door, there was a person at the counter that you either paid or showed your metal season pass, which was pinned to your trunks. It costed thirty-five cents to swim for the day or eight dollars for a family season pass. Of the ten years I used the pool, I can only remember having a season pass one of those years, and it was heaven. I never understood how it was possible for my parents not to buy that season pass. Think of how much it would have saved Mom and Dad. But Mom couldn't come up with eight dollars at once. I rolled my trunks in a towel and walked across town to the pool. I could not leave the pool and return unless I paid another thirty-five cents. That never seemed fair.

Once admission was paid, you were given a small wire basket. The basket had a number on it with a metal pin attached, and the number that matched the basket was pinned on your trunks. After changing into your trunks, you passed the basket with your towel and clothes inside a small window. Before leaving the locker room, you had to walk through the shower room and shower unless the attendant wasn't there. You had to walk through a foot bath when leaving the shower room and just before leaving the building. The bath was always filled with a milky liquid that we believed to be concentrated chlorine. Maybe it was Pine-sol; it had the distinct odor of evergreen.

My siblings, relatives, friends, and I loved the Kankakee pool. It was a main event. On a hot summer day, the alternative was swimming in the Kankakee River, Soldier Creek, or Rock Creek.

I went to the pool as often as possible and stayed the whole day, from open to close. The pool was where I first noticed girls. The lifeguards were mostly girls, and they were the cutest girls in town. They were always nice to me because I was Jamie's little brother, and every girl in the city loved Jamie. He was handsome, charming, the toughest boy in town, and he did a perfect double off the high dive.

You needed at least thirty-five cents to go to the pool, but fifty cents was always the goal. Thirty-five cents to get in and fifteen cents for a snack at the end of the day. Swimming all day made a boy desperately hungry. A small, tidy, detached snack bar was beside the pool entrance. It was in a trailer, maybe an Airstream trailer, with a shiny aluminum exterior and rounded corners. The female servers wore white dress uniforms with cool little hats tilted to the side. The manager was Mrs. LaPorte, the wife of the superintendent of parks. Mrs. LaPorte was businesslike, while the other two women were always happy to see you.

The menu at the Airstream snack bar was limited, but all good stuff in order of popularity: popcorn, Turkish Taffy in chocolate, strawberry, vanilla, and banana flavors, oversized tubs of vanilla or chocolate ice cream, hot dogs, BBQ beef sandwiches, and Coca-Cola. Fifteen cents bought any item except the hot dog and BBQ. Add ten cents, and you could have a drink with your snack. I only headed to the pool if I had at least fifty cents.

That morning, I was hired to cut Grandma Maddingly's grass. Grandma Maddingly was the widowed mother of Mr. Maddingly, my dad's foreman at Roper Stove. My dad respected Mr. Maddingly, and we kids knew to be on our best behavior around him. This meant I had to do an exceptional grass-cutting job for Grandma Maddingly. After I finished the job, I collected my pay and went home for a towel. I would spend the rest of the day at the Kankakee pool. It would be a good day because Grandma Maddingly paid me fifty cents for cutting her grass and added a twenty-five-cent tip. After soaking myself in the sun, I would have a tub of chocolate ice cream *and* a Coke. It was going to be a great day.

Mom was washing clothes in the basement when I yelled to tell her I was going to the pool. I rolled my trunks into the first towel I found. I followed my path to the pool: down May Avenue Alley to Chouinard's grocery store, take a right on Station Street, over the Kankakee River bridge, take a right, and there was the pool.

After being at the pool for only an hour, Jamie came to the cyclone fence and yelled my name. "You have to come home right now! You are in big trouble! Mom sent me to get you!"

*No! Coming out means I won't be able to come back to the pool today.* Thirty-five cents wasted. But Jamie said, "Mom said," so I had to go home.

Jamie was gone when I left the pool changing room. I walked home alone. I was the good one, never in trouble. Jamie was the problem, not me. There must have been a misunderstanding, but I also knew Mom didn't make mistakes.

I sensed trouble when I walked in. Mom wasn't smiling. "Go into my bedroom, remove your pants, and get under the covers. I'll be there in a few minutes." This was serious. I was going to get a spanking and didn't know why. But I knew better than to say anything; I did as Mom said.

"I put thirty-five cents on the corner of the second shelf in the kitchen. When I came upstairs, the thirty-five cents was gone, and you were at the pool, which costs thirty-five cents. Did you take the thirty-five cents?"

"No," I said emphatically. "I got seventy-five cents from Grandma Maddingly for cutting her grass."

"The grass mower has been in the middle of the yard all morning; you could not have cut her grass," Mom said.

"Grandma Maddingly had me use her push mower."

Mom didn't buy it. "I'm going to give you five minutes, and if you don't tell me the truth, you will get a whipping with your father's belt."

This was not a problem because I didn't steal Mom's money. After the five minutes, I stuck to the truth and got five lashes on my bare butt. I got the usual "This hurts me more than it hurts you, Michael, but you must tell me the truth."

Confused and pissed, I yelled at her, "I didn't take your money! I'm telling you the truth."

"I will give you another five minutes; you'll get more if you don't tell me the truth. Please tell me the truth, and I'll stop the spanking. If you keep lying, I'll keep spanking you until you tell me the truth." And then I got another five lashes.

Something was very wrong. Mom was possessed and obsessed; it was like she didn't know me. She should know that I would never steal from her, and if I did, I wouldn't lie about it. *Has Mom finally lost it?*

She came in a third time, and this time, she was crying. "You have to tell me the truth, Michael, even if I have to beat the truth out of you."

I considered lying and telling her I stole the money to stop the beating. I was confident that she would not stop until she heard me confess. But I had the toughness of my father, and I was not going to buckle. "I did not take the money. I'll never admit that I took it because I didn't. Go talk to Grandma Maddingly."

Just as Mom pulled the covers off me to start the third round, Jamie burst into the bedroom yelling while out of breath, "Mikey didn't take the money! Dad gave me that thirty-five cents to buy him a pack of cigarettes; Dad took the money."

Jamie hadn't known why Mom sent him to summon me. Dad followed Jamie into the bedroom and confirmed Jamie's story. It was only the second time I witnessed Mom falling apart, weeping with her head in her hands. It looked like Mom was having something like a nervous breakdown. She had made a terrible mistake. Maybe she was exhausted, hungry, and perhaps worried about no food for supper. Mom grabbed me while she sobbed and kept saying how sorry she was. It was a bad scene, even by Menard family standards.

After Mom settled down, she asked me to forgive her and told me she would never doubt me again. She gave me one dollar as restitution, and with that and my twenty-five cents left over from the pool, Jamie and I went down to the Dairy Queen, where the dollar-twenty-five bought us both a large chocolate milkshake. It was my worst and last spanking. Truth can hurt.

REFLECTIONS

With only two exceptions that I remember, Mom didn't resort to physical punishment. Mom used patience and applied teachings when most other children in the 1950s would have received spankings.

Mom taught us that there is always a silver lining. My silver lining? Mom believed me indisputably for the rest of my life. On the other hand, Jamie was constantly in a dilemma when he had to lie to Mom. Jamie worked every angle. When required, Jamie put me up to lie to Mom to validate Jamie's untruths. Mom believed me, and Jamie always went scot-free.

Throughout my adulthood, and always with an audience, I would retell the unfair beating I received at Mom's hand. Mom would put her hands in her face and then burst out in a deep, infectious laugh as I would lie to her again, saying, "Mom, I'll never tell that story again."

# YOU GONNA EAT THAT?

## CHAPTER 10

"Bullies don't like to fight, son. They like to win. Being afraid is normal. The only fight you really have to win is the one against the fear."

– Kwame Alexander

IN THE 1960S, I went from a nine-year-old to an eighteen-year-old; it was a unique decade. Growing up in a sixteen-person family in the '60s created a background that bred interesting experiences, stories, and trying times. I couldn't make up things this crazy.

It was a time of polarization, skepticism, and youth rebellion. The decade saw the end of innocence and the rise of cynicism. It was a decade of extremes in transformational change and bizarre contrasts: flower children and assassins, idealism and alienation, Beatles and Jimmy Hendrix, rebellion and backlash.

Racism and the Civil Rights Movement were at a fever pitch throughout the '60s. Kankakee was split evenly between blacks and whites and was still heavily segregated. Riots were a common occurrence in our town and our schools.

118 South May Avenue was also a home of polarization and extremes. The Menard children grew up with a devil on one shoulder and an angel on the other. Our parents represented the age-old battle between good and bad, right and wrong. It was

THE KITE THAT COULDN'T FLY

East of Eden. Nothing highlighted this more than our parents' vastly differing viewpoints on how to love thy neighbor or not.

Mom taught us about Jesus and the Bible. Not only did she teach it, she also lived it. "Love thy neighbor, forgive, and turn the other cheek." She taught us about the injustices and sinfulness of racism. Mom was shopping at the Wonder Bread day-old bakery when she reached for some individual fried cherry pies.

"Oh, Arletta, don't buy those. They are spoiled," said the lady behind the counter.

"Why are they still for sale?" Mom asked.

"We sell those to the black kids," she replied.

With disapproval, Mom asked, "Are the black children's stomachs any different from ours?"

Racism is a complex knot to untie.

Dad openly professed and practiced racism. Mom forbade the N word in her home, and Dad wouldn't let us use other descriptors for a black person. For Dad, it was more than prejudice; it was hatred. We knew Mom was right; she was always right, but she never debated the point with Dad. She caringly made excuses, suggesting we forgive and pray for him. *Love thy neighbor.*

Driving downtown as a youngster, Dad had me roll down my window whenever there was a black person on my side of the street. "Wave and yell 'Midnight' to that guy. He's my friend." I did as coached but was puzzled when they never waved back. And wasn't it strange that Dad had so many friends with the same name?

Integration was front and center in Kankakee in the '60s. A new junior high school was built three blocks from 118 South May Avenue in a white part of town. Black students were bused in, creating a new dynamic. There was ever-present tension. The whites didn't like it; the blacks didn't like it. My dad hated it.

I moved from Catholic to public school in eighth grade where I began to played football on a team made up of blacks and whites. We quickly bonded and were a team. Coach Owens made it clear that no racial bullshit would be tolerated. He was much like the coach played by Denzel Washington in the movie *Remember the Titans.*

Charlie Tuna, or "Tuna" as we called him, was a black guy who played right guard; I played right tackle. Tuna was the largest person I had ever seen. He was fat but fast. He often grabbed me in the locker room, telling me he wanted to be my girlfriend. I think he meant it. If I told my dad about that, I would have been ordered to take Tuna's head off. I would have had to do it but would have been crushed. The next fight would be with Jamie and Tuna, and Tuna would have been destroyed. So, I kept it to myself.

Kankakee Junior High served excellent lunches—a full buffet with hot food and homemade desserts. A stack of bread and a giant bowl of butter were at the end of the tray line. Take as much as you want. This must be what Heaven will be like. I continued eating my dessert first.

Tuna had a nasty habit. He never paid for lunch. He walked around, sucked on his finger, and searched for what he wanted to eat next off any white guy's tray. Tuna stuck his wet finger into the food and asked, "You gonna eat that?"

"No, Tuna, you take it."

Most whites were intimidated by blacks. Whites thought blacks were stronger and meaner; most black guys wanted us to believe it. When fights were in the hall, the white guys almost always lost to black guys.

When Tuna realized I had eaten my dessert first, he made me his favorite target. He waited for me to put my tray down and then stuck his cigar-sized pointer finger in the middle of my spice cake; "You gonna eat that, Benard?"

"Here you go, Tuna."

This was a tough one. "If you are positive that you will not win, don't fight," my dad said.

Tuna was twice my size and, I'm sure, a few years older. To top it off, I wasn't Jamie. There is no question I would be the one on my back with Tuna on top rearranging my face. Even if I could win, I would have been jumped by Tuna's friends as soon as I got the upper hand. But I had something Tuna didn't have: Paul Menard. After losing my dessert multiple times in a row, I had to take some action. I talked it over with Dad and Jamie. Then Dad gave me an order.

"Before you put your tray down, grab your fork with your right hand with the prongs away from your thumb, like this. Put your tray down and hide your right hand under the table. Put your tray toward the middle of the table and put your dessert at the top to make him reach for it. When Tuna extends his hand, raise your fork as high as you can, stand and drive it with all your might through his hand, make sure it goes all the way through."

Dad demonstrated the movement for me three times. "The school will call home. I'll be ready and will be there in five minutes. Tell the principal and the police I told you to do it."

It happened that following Monday. I did not want to do it, but I had to or face the repercussions from Dad. *No, thank you.* The fork went easily through Tuna's right hand. They took him by ambulance to the emergency room to remove the fork. I was in the principal's office with a policeman and Tuna's father when Dad entered the room. Behind Dad came Tuna, his hand bandaged the size of a boxing glove. I had lost my fear of him.

Unexpectedly, my dad immediately took over the room. *Hit first and hit hard.*

"This boy has been spitting on and putting his finger in my boy's food, making sure he won't eat it, and then your fat ass son eats it. He's been doing it to all the white boys, and only the white boys, thinking nobody can stop him. The cafeteria teachers knew this was happening, but they were too chicken shit to do anything about it. I ordered my son to put that fork into your son's hand; he deserved it. And if Mike would not have done it, he would have gotten a beating from me at home. So, if you are going to charge someone, charge me." Tuna's dad started yelling at my dad in a threatening voice. My dad cut him off. "Say another word, and I'll drag your black ass outside and give you the beating of your life." It was exactly what Dad wanted to do.

There was an agreement reached between the white men in the room that I was justified to do what I did; no charges would be filed. I was elevated as a hero and badass among the whites in school. The blacks thought I was crazy and never bothered me again. Tuna began buying his lunch.

REFLECTIONS

I wasn't fighting Tuna that day; I was fighting my fear of him.

There are two possible reasons why the victims of bullying don't put a stop to it. The first is that they don't know how to stop it. The second reason is fear. If the bully isn't stopped, they will continue doing more and worse.

There is now massive research on the disastrous outcomes of bullying. Being bullied can affect everything about a child: how they see themselves, their friends, school, and their future. Students who are bullied often experience depression, low self-esteem that may last a lifetime, shyness, loneliness, physical illnesses, and threatened or attempted self-harm. Some students miss school, see their grades drop, or even leave school altogether because they have been bullied. Verbal and social/relational bullying can be just as harmful as physical bullying. Bullying is a complex subject. Why does a person become a bully? How should a child (and an adult) stop the bully?

While my actions with Tuna stopped him from bullying me, I believe "Stand up for yourself, hit back" is terrible advice. Hitting back usually makes the bullying worse and increases the risk of serious harm. The person doing the bullying is often bigger, so the target could get seriously hurt by hitting back. Fighting with the other child can escalate the situation, and your child may be reprimanded for their part in a fight. There are other options; any resolution involving a child being bullied requires a caring adult's intervention. There are things we know: bullying is terrible and should not be tolerated.

My dad's solution to put a fork through Tuna's hand was wrong and risky, but it worked. Not only did it stop Tuna, but it also stopped any future bullies from messing with me or with any of my younger siblings. That day, my actions established me as a badass and possibly a madman.

I'll repeat myself: the violent action I used to stop Tuna was dead wrong. Don't try this at home. It changed me immediately and forever. I won the fight against fear. From that moment onward, I feared no man. When I did experience a bully or anyone who intended to harm me or anyone within my sight, I would immediately send a message by words or action: *You aren't tough enough.*

My siblings all carry this confidence and badassery.

# THE HALF-GIANT
## CHAPTER 11

"The worst poverty isn't about not having enough money to survive. Real poverty is when there is no one in the world who loves you. When there is no other human to make you feel like you matter. As if you aren't worth the air you breathe. Poverty of love is the worst thing you can be deprived of."

– Paige Dearth

THE ALLEY BETWEEN MAY and Alma Avenues was the center of my universe. Most homes in Kankakee had alleys, which you rarely see in newer developments. Alleys are for parking your car, depositing your trash, playing kick the can, and dumping your ashes from the coal furnace (dumping the clinkers).

Many homes in the 1950s burned coal for heat. A chute would go down through a window into the basement, where the coal was deposited. The home on 118 South May Avenue was built with a cistern, a swimming pool-type room in the basement where rainwater collected from the home's gutters. The water from the cistern was pumped through the house for drinking, washing, and cooking. When city water was piped into the homes around the '40s, many cisterns, like ours, were converted to the coal room. With coal heat, once a day, someone had to shovel the small pieces of coal into a hopper that fed the furnace. Once a week, someone had to shovel the coal ashes out, also called "cinders" and "clinkers," into the cinder bucket, a metal bucket with a strong handle. The bucket was then taken and dumped in the middle of the alley. Most good neighbors evenly spread the clinkers in the alley, and the not-so-good neighbors left them in a heap for cars to eventually even out. Clinkers served a purpose; they helped pave the alleys and kept the grass and weeds to a minimum. The alley behind our home looked paved with asphalt, black and smooth. It was not smooth enough to roller skate or write on with railroad chalk, but smooth enough for playing kick the can and walking from the tracks to Chouinard's.

The alley was well-traveled. Take a left at the alley, and it was the preferred route to get to the Illinois Central railway tracks. Up and over the Kankakee River, trestle over to White City where all the cute schoolgirls lived: Beth Dupuis, Susan Ciocio, Vicki Parker, Sharon Habercorn, and Kathy Johnson, to name a few. The tracks were only one short block from 118 South May and were a hot spot of activity for the boys. When a freight train came down the tracks, we got as close to the tracks as possible and yelled, "Chalk, Chalk, Chalk!" at the engine and the caboose cars. Most of the time, someone on the train threw us long fat sticks of chalk, ten times the size of the chalk the nuns used on the blackboard. The railroad people used chalk to write stuff on the box cars. We used the giant pieces of chalk to draw hopscotch diagrams and all types of sidewalk art.

Take a right at the alley, and you soon come to Station Street, where the Chouinard grocery store was on the left, and Mrs. Wertz's basement store was on the right. Behind Mrs. Wertz's store was Walker's shoe repair business. Across Station Street was Home Appliance and Lola's penny candy store. Take a left on Station Street, and down two blocks, there was the Dairy Queen and the Bird Park Quarry.

The Menards were frequent travelers up and down May Avenue Alley. It's where we met our friends and where I garbage-picked for treasures. What you could find when diving into a fifty-five-gallon drum of someone's trash was amazing. There was no garbage collection in those days, so the homeowner stuffed the drum to the brim and lit it on fire. The bottoms of the garbage cans were soot and char, but anything glass or metal survived. I went from garbage can to garbage can and collected anything I could resell: glasses, plates, clothes hangers, anything. I polished it up and then walked door-to-door, selling my treasures. More than once, a homeowner told me they threw one of my items for sale away a few days ago. Most people bought something for pennies.

But I had competition. Old Man Beaupre traveled the May Avenue alley more than anyone. He tried to beat me to the trash. His target was empty pop bottles. When he returned the bottles to the Kankakee Westside Liquor store, he got two cents per bottle, the deposit paid by the person who bought the pop.

Some in the neighborhood called Old Man Beaupre a bum. Others called him a hobo, tramp, or vagabond. Mom called him Hector, and my siblings and I called him Beaupre.

Mom told us that Beaupre was a half-giant and possibly a descendant of Goliath (as in David and Goliath). Beaupre was at least seven feet tall and looked to be 500 pounds. It was hard to tell his actual size. We always saw him with his calf-length thick fur overcoat. I only saw him with one pair of shoes: old-time galoshes, waterproof overshoes made from black rubber with adjustable metal clasps. Beaupre never used the clasps; his boots were always unbuckled and loose. His hair was thick, long, and snarly, always dirty. His beard matched his unruly hair, and he was toothless.

When a person has no teeth for a long time, their entire face changes, making them almost cartoon-like. The shrinking jawbones made Beaupre's face look shorter than it should be. His shrinking lower jawbone also caused it to rotate forward. Because his lips no longer had support, the muscles around his lips changed, creating more wrinkles that made Beaupre look much older than his age. In addition, his upper lip became much more pronounced and looked long, making his nose more prominent. But Beaupre had a welcoming, toothless smile even with all the distortion.

Mom had a warm spot in her heart for Beaupre; she understood and trusted him. It was as if she knew more about him than she told us. Even though she didn't have enough food for her family, Mom ensured no one within her influence went hungry. Mom often sent me down with food. When delivering food to Beaupre, she reminded me, "Stay with Beaupre while he eats; he doesn't like to eat alone."

I once brought Beaupre a platter full of Thanksgiving Day food and watched him eat the entire spread in one sitting. Watching him eat with no teeth was fascinating.

Beaupre's house, or shack, was sad. It was a garage on the alley's edge converted into a living space. The outside of the building was covered with what looked like asphalt roof shingles. He had electricity but no heat, toilet, or water; instead, a hand water pump in the backyard and an outhouse that stunk of sewage. When invited inside, I was always amazed and a little scared. The house was full of junk and clutter, with little room to move. Things, mostly treasures from his garbage picking, were stacked from floor to ceiling, and they looked as if they were about to topple on me. Chickens moved freely in and out of his shack but stayed in the yard between Beaupre's garage and the main house. His home had a horrible smell.

I never understood the relationship or connection between Beaupre and the people who lived in the main house. Teresa Hebert lived in the house with her parents. Teresa was older than Jamie, and she was a badass. More brutal than any of the boys except Jamie. But Jamie never fought Teresa. I saw a resemblance between Teresa Hebert and Beaupre, but we never discussed it.

Making so many trips to Beaupre's place, we became friends. Contrary to his ogre-like appearance and rumors that he ate children, Beaupre was a gentleman and a man of faith. I spent three or four long summers with Beaupre, swinging on his yard swing and talking about everything.

Beaupre's main staple was chicken. He had a whole flock in his yard. When it was time to kill a chicken, Beaupre advertised a few days in advance to draw an audience and hear the neighborhood girls scream. The executions occurred on a big old tree stump in the middle of Beaupre's yard. In the center of the tree stump were two large rusty nails pounded halfway in, each bent with the head of the nail facing down at the tree. Beaupre snatched a chicken, brought it to the chopping block, stretched its neck, and placed it between the two nails. He twisted the head of the nails to form a kind of strap over the poor chicken's neck. Next, Beaupre released the chicken as we watched it hopelessly flap its wings. Beaupre grabbed his hatchet, pulled the head out until it was about six inches long, and raised it as the girl spectators' screams reached a crescendo. Down came the hatchet. With blood squirting like a water gun, the headless chicken ran around the yard as Beaupre roared with laughter.

When the chicken expired, everyone got quiet, and Beaupre would say, "You know what happened?"

"He died," some child answered.

"Nope," said Beaupre, "He ran out of gas."

Beaupre had some kind of hot plate he cooked on. On days when he planned to kill a chicken, Beaupre had a five-gallon metal bucket heating water to scald the chicken, which made plucking the feathers easier. With the pot of hot water in the yard, Beaupre collected the dead chicken and quickly submerged it in the hot water. He counted to ten, pulled the chicken out of the bucket, and plucked its feathers. He told us he had to pull gently to ensure he didn't rip the skin. After the bird was bald, Beaupre shooed us away and cooked his dinner.

Beaupre had many chickens, producing more eggs than Beaupre could eat. He regularly brought eggs over to Mom; he knew we needed them. But we never got to eat Beaupre's eggs. They were caked with chicken poop, and Mom never knew how old the eggs were or what the chickens ate, so she always threw them out. It was always difficult for her, but Mom knew best.

Beaupre also made a mean apple pie. He made them in a deep cast iron skillet. He had no oven, so he must have cooked the pies on the stovetop. Occasionally, Beaupre took one of his pies to Mom as a gift, maybe to repay her for all the food she gave him. We loved those pies; there was always enough for seconds. Then, one day, Mom found a used band-aid in one of Hector's pies; that was the last time we ate his apple pie.

Mom told us that Beaupre was in the circus after he left the Navy. He was strong until he injured his back and was forced to retire. We knew Beaupre was strong. One day, when Warren was a young boy, he climbed up Mom and Dad's bedroom dresser, using the handles as steps. It was a tall dresser with doors on the top and drawers on the bottom. Warren somehow pulled the dresser down, pinning himself to the ground. Mom panicked because she couldn't get Warren free. Out of nowhere, Beaupre entered Mom's bedroom through the back door and lifted the dresser in the air with one arm.

We lived in peace with Beaupre. He chased the other neighborhood kids away and made them scream. With us, he just winked and smiled.

One summer, as a neighborhood project, all the boys on May Avenue got together to build a go-cart. Jamie, David, Mark Andrews, John and Jimmy Benoit, Tommy Boules, and I made up the team. Mr. Benoit and Mr. Philips agreed to help. Mr. Philips donated his lawn mower motor, and Mr. Benoit welded the frame. The men did all the work while we watched and waited. The go-cart was a real success; it was fast and fun. But we had a problem: the wheels. We burned through a set of tires in minutes. So, we all went on the hunt for wheels. We stole wheels from wheelbarrows, lawnmowers, and even baby strollers, yet we never had enough wheels.

One day, David made a big mistake; he stole the wheels from Beaupre's rusty old Radio Flyer wagon. The wagon Beaupre depended on to gather his pop bottles and transport them to the West Kankakee Liquor Store to collect his two cents per bottle deposit. David had just removed the fourth wheel when Beaupre saw him. David ran much faster than Beaupre, but Beaupre knew where David lived. David flew through our backyard gate, threw the wheels in the yard, and ran into the house. Beaupre arrived at the back door minutes later, knocked, and waited for Mom to answer. Beaupre was mad and hurt. How could a Menard do that to him? While trying not to yell, Beaupre explained what had just happened. Mom summoned David to the door and asked if what Beaupre said was true. David knew he was busted and confessed. Mom made David return and put the wheels back on Beaupre's wagon—all ended well.

## REFLECTIONS

I learned so much from our half-giant. Time with Old Man Beaupre was the birth of empathy for me. He was different and scary, but Mom taught me that he was a person, that everyone has feelings, and that we are all God's children. I remember feeling good about sitting with him while he ate.

I also learned the gift of giving—another paradoxical example of the many in this book. Mom had so little to give, and conventional wisdom said she was taking food from her children's mouths. Common belief says that the less you give, the more you have. But our mom taught us that the converse is true —the more you give, the more you will have. Abundance creates the ability to give; giving creates more abundance. Brother Mark shared this reflection which strengthened Mom's teaching.

Thanksgiving was always a special holiday for Mom; it was the one day when she filled the table with traditional foods. Turkey, prime rib, ham, all the sides, pies, cakes, and Mogen David wine. Mom would beg, steal, and borrow to have a memorable Thanksgiving dinner for her family. On this Thanksgiving, Mom shared with Adam that she only had one hundred dollars saved of the two hundred dollars she needed for her holiday meal.

"I'm going to put my hundred dollars in the offering basket at Mass this Sunday; you must give in order to receive."

"Do not do that, Mom," Adam replied. "A hundred dollars is better than nothing; we can make do with a hundred dollars." Attempting to change Mom's mind on anything was futile. That Sunday, she confidently put the hundred dollars in the basket.

Mark, living in Michigan and working at his first job out of college, had decided to come home for the Thanksgiving holiday. The prior month, Mark had excellent sales and received a two-hundred-dollar bonus. When Mark walked in to see Mom the Monday before Thanksgiving, in front of Adam, Mark handed Mom two hundred dollars.

"Hey, Mom, I know how important Thanksgiving dinner is to you; here is two hundred dollars to help with shopping."

Mom calmly thanked Mark, turned to Adam, and gave him that famous over-her-glasses look that said, "Oh ye of such little faith."

Adam falsely accused Mom of putting Mark up to giving her the two-hundred dollars.

One of the reasons Mom was so willing to have us spend time at Beaupre's was because he was a Christian. One day, when Beaupre told me again how he had lost his family and house, I asked him how he could still be so happy. He told me he would see his wife and children again in Heaven. He also said that he read Jesus' words, the ones in red in his Bible, and prayed every night.

After I moved from May Avenue, Mom called me to tell me Old Man Beaupre had died. It was a sad ending. Mom heard that Beaupre was found a few days after his death and that the chickens had eaten away most of his face. Reflecting on my time with Beaupre, I didn't know whether to laugh or cry. I took comfort in knowing he was back with his wife and children.

After writing about Beaupre, I researched to see what I could find; there wasn't much. I discovered in Beaupre's 1940 census data, he had five children; in 1940, he lived at 137 North Alma Avenue. When I knew Beaupre, he lived in the garage at that address. Beaupre had told me multiple times that he lost his house and family, but how did Beaupre end up desolate and living in that shack that used to be his garage? I tried, unsuccessfully, to locate several of Beaupre's descendants. I guess we will never know the whole story. Still, to this day, we Menard siblings reflect joyfully on those long-lost May Avenue summers spent in Beaupre's yard.

# THE KITE THAT COULDN'T FLY

## CHAPTER 12

"Hope lies in dreams, in imagination, and in the courage of those who dare to make dreams into reality."

– Dr. Jonas Salk

OUR MOTHER WAS A blessing who made every day joyous. She rarely ran out of energy. She was our teacher, protector, guide, and friend.

All of Mom's children took turns staying with her for a week at a time when she was dying of uterine cancer at age eighty. Through it all, she was her cheerful self. She told us she was already homesick for Heaven. During one of my stays with Mom, I asked if she had any regrets, anything she would do differently. There was a thoughtful pause, and then she said, "If I could do it over, I would change one thing. I wouldn't worry about my children not having enough. I was worried that growing up without would negatively affect you. But look at all of you; you are wonderful, happy, and successful. Going without didn't hurt you at all. Maybe it helped you. Look at the mothers and fathers you have become. No, I wouldn't worry at all."

As a dad to five daughters, I could not imagine life knowing my children had to do without. Not without a second Cabbage Patch doll necessarily, but without a pair of shoes, the money to participate in a field trip, or a baseball glove.

Our playground, Bird Park, was a five-minute walk from 118

South May Avenue. The swings, slides, teeter-totter, and picnic tables spread out over a stretch of wooded land with the Kankakee River on one side and the quarry on the other. There was a stone-paved walkway along the north side of the quarry for walking and feeding the fish: bluegills, sunfish, and the occasional smallmouth bass. And there were sea monsters in there. The water was a beautiful dark blue, and you could see deep down. When someone fed the fish, it created a frenzy at the water's surface. If observed closely, a monster fish or two would show their glittering scales. The goliath fish were either bass or northern pike. There was no fishing allowed in the Bird Park quarry.

It was created from a stone quarry that some say went down a thousand feet. Once the miners had struck the water, they escaped immediately and left machinery and vehicles at the bottom to never be recovered. At the top of the hole, up behind the walkway, was the home of the current park district supervisor—a cozy Hansel and Gretel-type stone cottage. Ed LaPorte was the supervisor, and he took his job seriously.

Every kid in Kankakee wanted to fish the quarry, and we did. We mostly fished at night when Ed LaPorte was sleeping. The cyclone fence along the walkway had "No Fishing Allowed" signs every thirty feet. One lazy summer day, Jamie and I decided to go quarry fishing. We wound up a handful of fishing line with a hook and a sinker and put them in our pockets. Pieces of bread in the other pocket—quarry fish bit on anything, even an empty shiny hook. Always catch and release. It was about sunset when Jamie and I reached the quarry. It was a quiet day, with no one at the park; Ed LaPorte's car was gone. *All clear.*

Jamie and I had fished the quarry a hundred times or more. On this day, we had our lines in the water, waiting for one of the monsters, when Ed LaPorte grabbed us firmly by the back of the neck. "I finally caught you!" he exclaimed. *You little shits*, I'm sure he thought. We were busted. Ed turned us around and said, "You are both in big trouble; you've broken the law."

Jamie was so quick on his feet. "What do you mean?"

Ed LaPorte turned Jamie's head to the nearest "No Fishing Allowed" sign.

Jamie, almost offended, cried, "We ain't smoking!"

*Brilliant!* Jamie knew most townspeople thought the Menards were poor and ignorant, so why not try this? *Maybe they can't read*, Ed LaPorte must have wondered. Ed didn't know what to say.

"That sign says 'No Fishing Allowed'. You are not allowed to fish in the quarry, go fish in the river," Ed ordered.

But Jamie wasn't finished. "Why can't we fish here?"

"Because the sign says no fishing."

"Yeah, but *why* can't we fish here?" Jamie was not going to go easily.

Ed LaPorte did not have an answer and told us to go away.

Years later, the town leaders opened the quarry to fishing; it was a wonderful day. Brother David has dedicated his life to fishing; he is a master. Soon after the ban on fishing the quarry was lifted, David landed one of the quarry monsters, a nineteen-pound twelve-ounce northern pike—an Illinois state record and the second largest pike ever caught in the United States. The article and picture in the Kankakee *Daily Journal* title read, "Bird Park Behemoth."

Bird Park also had football and Little League fields on the other side of Court Street. There were baseball games almost every night in the summer. Little League was a big deal in Kankakee, like most cities across America. The Menard boys went to most games. There was a concession stand, and we smelled the popcorn all the way to May Avenue. While there was never money for popcorn, we always had our fill at the games. If you caught a foul ball or a home run and brought the ball back to the concession stand, you had a choice of a free drink or a bag of popcorn.

Dad taught us the strategy that guaranteed success. Three brothers placed strategically behind the concession stand and home plate, and two brothers at the fence, one in right field, the other in left. The other kids competing for the foul balls all had baseball gloves. Menards had no gloves and caught home runs with our bare hands. We were all fast runners and collectively snatched ninety percent of all balls. When we each had a bag of corn and a drink, we stopped retrieving, gave the other kids a chance, watched the game, and enjoyed the spoils of our work.

I loved watching baseball: the uniforms, the hats, the home runs. I planned to try out as soon as I was old enough. When tryouts for Little League finally came one spring day for me, it was humiliating. I did well in hitting tryouts. We played half-ball in the streets. Half-ball was the same as stickball, but you used half of a ball. Hitting a half-ball with a broomstick was difficult. Hitting a whole hardball with a fat bat was easy.

Next was fielding tryouts. This was a problem; I didn't have a baseball glove. The coaches provided the bats and balls, so I counted on them providing the gloves. I was wrong. I still have bad feelings about the men who watched me struggle to field a baseball with my bare hands. They thought it was funny. I missed every ground ball they hit to me but caught every pop-up. No surprise, I didn't make the team.

Bird Park was also the site of all kinds of cool activities: Fourth of July festivities, Punt/Pass/Kick competitions, dog shows, and the annual Grand Kite Contests. The kite contest was a big deal and filled the park each year.

All children have needs and wants. Needs are few: love, safety, food, and clothing. Needs are things every child should have. Without these, the child will experience neglect. Unmet needs create Adverse Childhood Experiences (ACEs), which is classified as neglect, ultimately creating trauma and stress.

Wants are desires. Getting wants satisfied will make a child happy; wants are birthday gifts and Christmas lists. Growing up in poverty teaches a child that there is little hope that they will ever get those wants. But even the smallest hope is enough to keep that longing alive.

I always seemed to need more food, heat, and a pillow. But I have memories of wanting only three things. A shiny, sleek, porcelain black panther TV lamp with green eyes that I was sure were jade gems. It was in the window at Woolworth's store on Schuyler Avenue. The second want was a baseball glove. The third was a trophy, any trophy. I wanted these three things desperately. I dreamt about them, daydreamed about them, and made my mom crazy by asking for them, relentlessly.

The Grand Kite Contest was grand indeed. Hundreds of children and adults would bring their kites to compete. The sky looked like a postcard, all sizes and colors. Trophies would be awarded. There was free popcorn and lemonade for all, and the contest always fell on a day with great wind. I'd attend the event each year and looked forward to the awards ceremony. *Someday,* I would tell myself as the giant trophies were handed out.

In 1961, when I was ten, I began begging Mom for a kite weeks before the Grand Kite Contest. Then, on one magical day, I couldn't believe my ears. "You want a kite? Do you want a trophy? Then let's build a kite!" There is no way she would tease about such a serious subject. I heard, "You, Michael, will win a trophy!"

That night, Mom kept me up after the other children were put to bed; we would make a plan. Mom already had the idea to make a large kite with a drawing of Jacob's Ladder, just like in our Bible. She showed me the picture, and I was all in. The painting by William Blake was breathtaking: gold, silver, sky blue. I could already see it flying in the sky. I actually visualized myself flying on top of my kite, with me holding my trophy.

Every little boy wanted to fly, and I would get my chance. I was euphoric. We made the plan.

Mom gave me two jobs to get the project going. Go to the meat market on Station Street and get the butcher to give me three sheets of white meat paper; each piece had to be four feet long. *Check.* I had to find a way to buy a box of crayons with all the colors we needed. I knew exactly what box I needed. They were advertised on my favorite TV show, Captain Kangaroo—sixty-four brilliant colors with a built-in sharpener for one dollar.

I got paid twenty-five cents to cut a lawn on May Avenue. I worked like a crazy boy, mowing four lawns in two days. I went to Woolworth's, bought the crayons, and then onto the meat market to get the paper, and we were ready to go. I couldn't believe my eyes when I got home and opened the crayons. I didn't know that many colors existed in the world. I hid the crayons and the paper in Dad's pigeon coop.

We had two weeks before the Grand Kite Contest. Each night after my brothers and sisters slept, I snuck downstairs, got the paper and crayons, and Mom worked on the drawing. I had to clean the kitchen floor before putting the paper down. We sat on the kitchen floor, and I'd watch her draw and color. Mom was tired, I was tired, but there was always excitement as we began the work. Occasionally, she let me fill in some areas; it was very serious work. While we colored, Mom told me the whole story about Jacob's Ladder.

Jacob was not a good man initially; his name meant "cheater." He didn't believe in God, but God fixed that. He gave Jacob a dream about a beautiful white spiral staircase that went from Earth to Heaven, with angels along the sides to guide Jacob to Heaven. After that, Jacob became a believer and a good man. Mom told me that Jacob's dream was God's way of teaching us that Earth and Heaven are connected and that we all have a pathway to Heaven. *Maybe I could skip those steps and fly to Heaven on my kite.*

Mom colored the kite for three nights in a row. She was just as excited as I was.

"Where will we keep the trophy?" I'd ask Mom.

"Right on top of the TV, so all the neighbors can see it out the front window."

I must have asked her that question ten times. I loved hearing her answer. She believed.

We stood when she finished the coloring; Mom held it up as I stepped back for a better look. It was beautiful; it glowed. It was as if the sun at the top illuminated the entire kite. It was huge, four feet tall and three feet wide. We went into the basement that night, and Mom built the diamond-shaped kite frame. She used Dad's wood glue to secure the paper onto the frame and cut away the excess. When we returned upstairs, she attached a long burlap tail and added four stunning silk-like streamers, two on each side. The streamers were used gift-wrapping ribbons she had saved. The next day, Mom tied about twenty feet of cloth line rope to use as a string. There was no way skimpy kite string would hold this monster.

It was time to test drive this baby.

I walked the kite to Bird Park, to the field where the contest would occur. The kite was big, and it was heavy. Thankfully, it was a windy day; maybe I wouldn't have to run too far to get my kite in the air. My excitement and anticipation were off the charts. *Perhaps I'll be able to jump on and fly with the kite today.*

Standing on the grassy hill that sloped from the field to the Kankakee River, I raised the kite above my head and ran downhill. When I let go of the kite, it didn't soar into the sky like I expected; it fluttered briefly and plunged to the ground. My heart sank. I didn't understand why my kite didn't fly.

At ten years old, I was a chubby kid. I was already gasping and sweating, but I was not going to give up, so up the hill I went for another try. This time, I ran faster and changed the tilt of the kite. No luck, the same disappointing result. I adjusted the string and the tail. No improvement. But I needed my kite to fly. To win my trophy, my kite had to fly. After many attempts, I was exhausted and carried my kite back home.

On my way home, I stopped by my Uncle Dan's house. Uncle Dan was an auto mechanic; he was the guy who kept my dad's old truck running. Uncle Dan could fix anything. I loved listening to him talk while he worked on Dad's truck or fixed our furnace. My dad was smart, but Uncle Dan was smarter. *He'll know what to do to make my kite fly.*

Uncle Dan came out on his porch and studied my kite. After long consideration, he said, "Mikey Joe, this kite is beautiful. It's a very special kite, but it isn't made to fly; it's made to look at." Maybe Uncle Dan wasn't as brilliant as I thought. It's a kite. Kites fly. I went home and put the kite back in the pigeon coop.

The next day, I tried again. I ran up and down May Avenue to get my kite to fly. I gave up and sat on the curb as the kite slowly drew a crowd of the neighborhood kids. They all loved the kite. I told them the story of Jacob's Ladder. I don't think their mothers had Bibles. I didn't try to fly my kite again until the contest.

When I arrived at the Grand Kite Contest, the sky was full of kites. I was sure they would get all tangled and come crashing down, but they didn't. Maybe my kite would fly today; the wind might be just right. As I approached the table to sign in, a kid was flying the smallest kite you could imagine. It was smaller than a penny, with sewing thread as string. It was in the air just above my head. When he brought the kite down, he placed it in a small aspirin tin, about two inches square, coiled the thread on top of it, and snapped the lid closed. Maybe my kite was too big to fly.

I tried flying mine with the other kites—no go. The kite dropped to the ground like it had weights on it. I kept trying. All those watching wanted my kite to fly. Some kids even tried to help by holding the kite and launching it as I ran, holding the rope. The kite would not fly. I was beginning to panic, but after many tries, I knew it couldn't fly. I took the kite to the judging area and leaned it against a picnic table. Like on the curb, the kite immediately drew a crowd. No one recognized the picture Mom had drawn and colored. I told everyone the story of Jacob's Ladder and how God's dream taught Jacob and all of us that there is a way to get from Earth to Heaven. Adults and children came close to see all the details. They wanted to touch it, but they didn't. I remembered Uncle Dan's words, "Some kites are made just to look at."

It was time for the awards. My kite didn't fly, so I knew I could not win a trophy. Trophies were handed out for the smallest kite that flew, the biggest kite that flew, the kite that flew the highest, and the most acrobatic kite. Then, it was time for the overall winner of the Grand Kite Contest. That trophy was the most enormous and ornate. Three feet tall with a flying kite suspended on the top, almost like it was held on by kite string. Who would be the lucky winner? The judges took too long to decide; I saw some disagreement between them, and then the head judge came to the microphone.

"The first-place trophy for this year's Grand Kite Contest goes to Michael Menard for his Jacob's Ladder kite. Michael wins for beauty and creativity."

I was lightheaded; everything got blurry. The crowd erupted in applause and cheers. Slaps on my back pushed me around. In a daze, I walked up and received my trophy.

When I turned to face the crowd, I saw my mom in the back with her arms folded and a confident smile. *How did she know my kite would win? Of course, she knew.* She didn't say, "We will build a kite and try to win." She said before we started, "I will build you a kite that will win you a trophy." *Did she know God believed it was my time to win? Did she have a direct line to God?* We all thought she did.

We walked home to May Avenue. Mom held our kite, and I carried the trophy. A group of May Avenue neighbor kids carrying their kites walked with us. Everyone was happy. It was a glorious day.

I kept the kite in Dad's pigeon coop for years. I would often bring it out into the yard to look at it. Occasionally, I'd try to get it to fly, but I knew it couldn't fly. I often took the kite to the curb, sat, and waited for someone to see it, admire it, and hopefully, they would listen to me tell the story of Jacob's Ladder.

So, the kite that couldn't fly remained grounded. I wish I had kept track of that kite and the trophy I just had to have.

REFLECTIONS

Think of the gift my mom gave when she decided to build a kite for me.

Looking back on that kite that couldn't fly, this May Avenue Story taught me so much. Kites are supposed to fly, but sometimes things and people don't have to do what we expect of them to be winners. I wasn't supposed to grow up prosperous, but I did. The kite remains a testament to the enigmatic nature of existence, a symbol of the paradoxes in life, reminding us that the pursuit of dreams, even though unattainable, can enrich our lives with purpose and meaning.

The memories of the kite that couldn't fly remain vivid some sixty-two years later. Every time I see the cover of this book, I can't help but have a sense of gratitude for the paradox that helped shape me and my perspective on life. I cherish the memories of those late nights watching my mom create that masterpiece, teaching me to believe and never to give up, to always look for the beauty in life, that true beauty lies in appreciating the artistry, even when it defies conventional expectations. I never think about my kite not flying. I think about my mom and her dedication to her children. I think about the wind blowing against my face when running with my kite, trying to get it to fly. I remember the beautiful colors of the kite. All these memories remind me that sometimes, the journey is more important than the destination.

I got the trophy that I wanted so badly.

Fifty years later, I met Emilie, who became my wife. She listened to all my May Avenue Stories and memories with interest and love. Emilie was the motivation for me to finally write this book. One Christmas, Emilie surprised me with a beautiful black leather Rawlings baseball glove and a baseball. I finally got to do something I had dreamed of since I was a little boy—oil my glove, place a ball in the pocket, wrap it up, and leave it for a week. I got to break in my new baseball glove. What a simple, beautiful, healing gift.

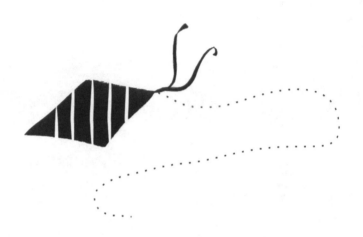

# BEHIND FALSE BARS

## CHAPTER 13

"Then, one day, it clicks.

The pain you had turns into peace as you accept that everything had to happen exactly as it did for you to be exactly who you are now. You hold no blame, bitterness, or resentment toward the experience, person, or yourself. Instead, you see it as the catalyst that led to your change and development. The very storm that shook so much in you also worked to clear your path."

– Morgan Richard Olivier

TWO DIFFERENT STANDARDS FOR boys and girls applied at 118 South May Avenue. My dad had a shameful saying that spoke volumes, "If you have a son, you must worry about one penis. If you have a daughter, you must worry about them all."

Dad had a puzzling moral code. We were not allowed to tell any jokes that reflected poorly on women. While we never received any fact-of-life talks from him, the message to his sons was clear regarding sex: "screw them all." Once, when the brothers were teasing Jamie about his latest girlfriend being homely, Dad said, "It doesn't matter. Stand them all on their heads; they look the same."

We received corporal punishment if we did or said anything to disrespect our mother or sisters. However, Dad lacked respect for women other than his wife and daughters. One talk with his

THE KITE THAT COULDN'T FLY

adult sons revealed Dad's twisted and awful view of rape, "It's not possible because a woman can run faster with her skirt up than a man can with his pants down." I was never quite sure if he was making a bad joke or sharing his authentic self.

We were all blessed to have a mother who made sure we knew about relationships and sex. She taught her sons to respect and honor all women. She taught us the fine print when it came to sexuality. She taught us about the hearts of women and that our wives would be the mothers of our children and the givers of life. She untied the knots created by our dad. In our later years, my brothers' wives publicly thanked our mother for raising such great husbands.

While he offered no advice to my sisters, he watched them like a bodyguard. My four sisters were all beautiful girls, now very beautiful women. They attracted boys like bees to honey: the good, the bad, and the ugly. For a boy to get close to one of my sisters, they had to get past her father and brothers, an almost impossible mission.

When Mary was fourteen years old, she looked much older. There was an eighteen-year-old young man named Westeroff who developed an interest in Mary. Not sure how he met her, maybe at the city swimming pool, but she made it clear she wasn't interested in him. He continued to hound Mary. He declared his love for her, which only confused her. He wrote Mary a love note, saying that he would put his head in an oven and kill himself if she didn't see him. You can imagine how anxious and nervous this made Mary, and she shared it with Mom and Dad. A day after Mary shared the note and her fears, Dad caught Westeroff trying to shimmy up the gutter to get to Mary's bedroom—big mistake. Westeroff escaped.

This happened around 8 p.m. Dad summoned Jamie and me and told us what had happened. Enough was enough. Dad told Jamie to find Westeroff and bring him to Dad. "Let's talk with this guy." Jamie took off in search of Westeroff. He knew his car model and color. Kankakee is a small town, and he would be easy to find. I stayed home and helped Dad finish painting the kitchen. Around 10 p.m., Jamie spotted Westeroff's car at the local Steak and Shake and waited for him to leave the restaurant. Jamie stepped out as Westeroff approached his vehicle and said, "Hey, Westeroff, I need to talk with you."

Knowing what was about to happen, Westeroff ran to his car and opened the door just as Jamie grabbed Westeroff's arm. Westeroff pushed the door and Jamie away from the vehicle—a bigger mistake.

Jamie stepped back toward the car. Westeroff was in the driver's seat when Jamie pulled him onto the pavement through the door window. By then, Jamie was a seasoned fighter. He unleashed his dangerous combination of strength, skill, and rage on Westeroff. Westeroff didn't land one punch. Jamie beat Westeroff within an inch of his life, literally. The beating ended with Jamie repeatedly smashing Westeroff's face into the windshield of his own car, turning Westeroff's face into mush. Lifeless, Westeroff fell to the ground.

Around 11 p.m., the police arrived at our door. With me close behind, Dad answered. They were looking for Mike Menard. I was arrested for attempted murder. Dad turned to me and placed his finger over his lips, telling me to say nothing. Dad knew what had happened and was already planning his next steps. I was cuffed and taken to the police station, processed, and placed in a jail cell with three other men, all who looked like Falcon Eddie, the most evil bad guy television ever created. I was only sixteen.

Westeroff was taken to the emergency room and was in critical condition. When asked by the police who did this, Westeroff mistakenly said, "Mike Menard." Around 2 a.m., Jamie burst into the police station yelling, "I did it!"

After his victory, Jamie had gone out drinking with his buddies to celebrate. On the local radio station, he had heard that Mike Menard was arrested for attempted murder. Jamie couldn't stand the thought of his little brother doing time for something he did. Jamie was staggering drunk, his shirt covered with blood that wasn't his. "I did it! Mikey didn't do it. Arrest me!"

The police were dumbfounded. I had already been booked, and they couldn't arrest two people for the same crime. Dad arrived minutes later at the police station and brought Jamie home.

My dad's friend and lawyer got me released the following day. A few days later, Jamie, Dad, and I met at the lawyer's office to agree on a plan—Dad engineered the whole thing. It was a clear, proven case of false arrest and imprisonment of a minor. The lawyer would file charges against the police department for false arrest and jailing a child. There would be defamation charges. When I went to court, Westeroff would say it was Jamie who beat him up. The lawyer could prove it was Jamie, but then Jamie would eventually be charged, convicted, and sent to prison. My dad and my lawyer met with the mayor, the police chief, and the judge who would preside over my trial. They struck a deal. The charges of false arrest and defamation would be dropped. I would be cleared based on wrongful identification. When Jamie was arrested and at trial, the judge would dismiss the case based on lack of evidence.

The evidence presented at Jamie's trial was macabre. Westerhoff's face was disfigured, his nose broken, crushed right eye orbit, fractured skull, and sixty stitches. After one day, the case was dismissed based on lack of evidence. Gavel down!

Westeroff's family was enraged, and rightly so. Westeroff's father didn't have the balls to approach my dad or Jamie. Dad never reprimanded Jamie for going too far. Jamie did precisely what he had been taught to do. He elevated his position even higher as the county's dominant male and the social privileges that came with that title.

## REFLECTIONS

I remember all this as pure drama. I felt terrible for Westeroff and his family; the punishment he received didn't fit the crime. Dad must remain responsible for whatever his winged monkeys did. I viewed the whole jail thing as exciting, and I was proud of my dad's connections and ability to orchestrate Jamie's freedom. Had I not been falsely arrested, Jamie would have most likely served time for attempted murder. I have always felt grateful for, in a small way, paying Jamie back for all the times he protected me.

# MEAT FOR THE HEART: A SON'S DESPERATE ACT OF LOVE

## CHAPTER 14

"How starved you must have been that my heart became a meal for your ego."

– Amanda Torroni

NO PERSON OR PLACE wants to be known as the worst of anything, but sadly, sometimes that label gets assigned. In 1999, Kankakee, Illinois was mocked on *The Late Show With David Letterman* by being named America's worst place to live. As a stunt, Letterman donated two gazebos to the city, which were placed on the town hall grounds. In 2015, the gazebos were taken down, and a rocking chair was constructed from the wood and sent to Letterman for his retirement.

Kankakee is sixty miles due south of Chicago on Route 57. 118 South May Avenue is the birthplace of all fourteen Menard children and the Kankakee area remains home to four of my siblings. While it's certainly not the worst city in America, being my hometown is probably the best thing I can say about Kankakee.

The city's name is derived from the American Indian word teeyaahkiki, meaning "open country exposed to view." It is tabletop flat for a 100-mile radius. The only elevation change is the Route 57 overpass that crosses Court Street—nothing remarkable in the town except the Kankakee River. Snaking through town, the Kankakee River is 133 miles long and serves as a central landmark of Kankakee. The river water is refined and filtered for drinking, and electricity is generated from the Kankakee River Dam. The winding path includes eddies, inlets, and creeks, creating desirable fishing conditions. Fish caught in Kankakee waterways remain some of the state's record holders.

The Kankakee River was a beautiful, clean river with dots of recreational areas for Kankakeeans: Rock Creek Falls, Sand Bar Island, Beckman Park for ice-skating, and the Yesteryear Restaurant.

Frank Lloyd Wright was one of America's best-known architects and designers. Wright designed more than 1,000 structures over a creative period of seventy years. He played a pivotal role in the architectural movements of the twentieth century. Wright believed in designing his buildings in harmony with the environment. The mention of Frank Lloyd Wright still evokes a slide show of memories from my experiences at the Yesteryear Restaurant.

In 1901, Frank Lloyd Wright built his first home on the banks of the Kankakee River, a fifteen-minute walk from downtown. The house was built on an outside curve of the river, providing an almost panoramic view of the river. Two former Navy cooks, Marvin Hammach and Ray Schimel, purchased the Frank Lloyd Wright home at 701 South Harrison Avenue and opened the doors of the Yesteryear Restaurant on February 1, 1953.

A work permit was required to get a job if you were fourteen or older. In 1963, at twelve, I was hired as a busboy by Hammach and Schimel. At six feet and 200 lbs., my age was not of concern to my employers. To work at the Yesteryear was a privilege, and once in, you were part of a club. I still don't know how I got the job. I vividly recall walking into the building on my first day.

The building's entrance was tucked away under a porte cochere. Several pinkish polished steps ascended into a small reception area where exotic food was for sale, including caviar, pâté, and chocolate-covered grasshoppers. A long hallway led to a cocktail lounge overlooking the river. The lounge had once been part of the home's master suite. Other than church, it was the first time I'd seen stained glass windows. Custom designed stained glass windows were a hallmark of Frank Lloyd Wright designs.

To the left of the reception area was the sprawling dining room (the former living room of the house), with a band of cut-glass windows outlining a deep bay facing Harrison Avenue. On the room's west wall was a large fireplace faced with Roman brick. The former dining room of the house served as an extension to the main meal service area. At the back of the house was a large kitchen with two pantries and stairs leading to basement storage areas, including glass door freezers for the two-inch-thick steaks.

Advertising proclaimed the restaurant offered "Gracious dining at the sign of Yesteryear, Harrison at the River, Kankakee, Illinois." A typical luncheon menu offered fifteen entrées, including a New York strip streak, a broiled lamb chop, boneless breast of chicken cordon bleu, pan-fried brook trout, aristocrat crabmeat thermidor, and a sautéed baby veal patty.

The food and the historic Wright-designed setting generated newspaper reviews and magazine articles that drew a steady stream of well-to-do diners. While there was a loyal local following, numerous patrons—couples, small groups, even busloads—also came from Chicago and surrounding suburban areas. The owners built upon their success by opening a gift shop, a travel agency, and six inn rooms for overnight guests in the stable, and a connected two-story structure.

When I entered each day, it was like walking through a portal to a new world—a world I loved. Hammach and Schimel were more than business partners. They were a couple. Kind, polite, and dressed like Liberace. My mother explained their relationship matter-of-factly. No judgment, no warnings. Those two men taught me how to walk, dress, and talk. They overpaid me so I could afford presentable clothes. They made sure I was welcome to eat the food at any time. I was never hungry again. At Yesteryear, I acquired a taste and appreciation for fine food; South African lobster, escargot d 'Alsace, and Idaho brook trout.

Over the four years I worked there, I advanced from busing and dishwashing to training in food prep cooking of some of the finest dishes on any menu, which jump-started my love of cooking that continues today. After leaving Yesteryear at sixteen, I had a standing invitation for dinners with my dates, with exceptional service and always on the house. Hammack and Schimel taught me more than culinary arts; they taught me the difference between right and wrong, something my father had failed to teach.

I couldn't explain to my family what I experienced at the Yesteryear. I felt guilty for all I received at work and even felt a widening separation between them and me. This made me aware for the first time just how poor we were.

Dad worked the second shift at the factory, from three to midnight. He got thirty minutes to eat lunch, which was always a bologna sandwich and a thermos of black coffee. Except for paydays, Friday.

On Fridays, we had a well-oiled ritual. Jamie started walking to the factory at three in the afternoon and met Dad at a wire-covered window at four, where he passed his check to Jamie. Jamie walked back home and passed the check to Mom. Mom walked to the bank, cashed the check, and then onto the grocery store to shop for our dinner and Dad's lunch. Mom returned home and made Dad's "special lunch"—a fat olive loaf sandwich with mayo and lettuce, and a Hostess cherry-filled pie. The pie was an individual pastry filled with juicy cherries wrapped in a flaky crust with a sugar glaze. Jamie and I returned to the factory, where Dad waited by the window. Jamie handed Dad his lunch, and we talked while he ate. Dad was usually sad, mad, or distant, except on Fridays at lunch. Then, he was happy and talkative. Jamie and I cherished these times with Dad. Even though the process took over four hours to complete, it was worth it for two reasons: we had time with our dad and we each got a third of Dad's cherry pie.

My job at Yesteryear included closing the restaurant at 10 p.m. From ages twelve to sixteen, I arrived home from my job at 12:30 a.m., the same time Dad came home from his second shift. We were the only two awake at that time. I hated how Dad looked when he got off work. Regardless of the season, his work pants were soaked from sweat down to his knees. He was dirty and looked exhausted. He sat at the kitchen table with his head down, elbows on his knees, and head in his hands. I knew then that I would never work in a factory. Mom left a little something for Dad to eat. I cherished the time alone with Dad, but he never had the strength or energy to talk. Once he entered the bedroom, I went to my dormitory mattress. *Maybe we would talk the next night.*

One night, Dad was talkative. "How's the job at the restaurant?" "What did you eat tonight?" "Hey, where do they keep the steaks at night?" "How many do they have?" I explained in detail how the steaks were kept in the glass door freezer in the basement. Porterhouse, filets, and New York strip steaks. Stacks and stacks of steaks.

"Hey, I have an idea! Slip two strip steaks down your pants, and we will cook them up tomorrow night. They won't even miss them."

*Great idea. Why hadn't I thought of that?*

The next night, I grabbed two steaks from the freezer, slipped them into the back of my pants, and headed home. Dad had the broiler on. He added salt and pepper and cooked the two steaks. There we were, two big shots eating steak and talking like old friends. He was happy; I was happier. We had steak dinner two to three times a week. These were golden moments. Possibly the best times I can recall as a youngster. Spending time with my dad, talking to him, and, more importantly, making him happy. This continued for a few months, and then Dad had another idea.

While enjoying his strip steak one night, he suggested, "Hey, I was thinking your mom needs some silverware. Why don't you take a spoon, fork, and knife and put it down your pants each night? When we (*we*?) get enough for sixteen people, you can wrap it up and give it to her as a present."

*Another great idea! Why hadn't I thought of that?*

It became part of the nightly closing up of the restaurant. Clean out the grease trap, sweep and wash all floors, and put all the clean dishes and silverware away. I selected the newest-looking spoon, knife, and fork and placed them in my back pocket. I went down the old basement stairs and chose two strip steaks from the glass door freezer. It was all part of my job. Up and out the back door. No fear of getting caught. After all, I was working for my dad.

The walk from Yesteryear to home took thirty minutes. My butt was freezing from the steaks, and my pants slipped down from the weight of the place setting. I got excited when I saw my dad's car home from his shift at the factory.

Dad only liked to talk about fighting and pigeons. He was an expert on both. We enjoyed our steak one night as Dad rehashed the Liston-Patterson boxing rematch. Dad predicted Liston would knock Patterson out in the first round; he was right.

Fear is a central part of the human experience. Fear, coupled with surprise, startles the brain and sets in place several possible responses. The response to fear and surprise begins in the amygdala, the part of the brain that processes many of our emotions. The amygdala is activated due to possible danger and triggers the fear response. The first brain response to the combination of fear and surprise is to reroute energy to the amygdala, slowing down processing in other areas. That's why speaking or making rational decisions becomes problematic when we are afraid.

Once the amygdala is activated, our brain makes quick decisions about what to do next. Our brain's goal at this point is to decide to keep us safe, which will get us away from the perceived danger with minimal harm. The brain's choices fall into four categories: fight, flight, freeze, and fawn.

It was 1 a.m., and we were finishing our steaks when the unthinkable happened. Mom came out of the bedroom to use the bathroom and passed the kitchen table. She couldn't see well without her glasses and mumbled something about us being up too late. Then she stopped dead in her tracks as she caught the smell of the steak. She turned around and shuffled toward us to get a closer view. "Where did you get that meat?"

Emotions raced through me: sadness for not sharing the steaks with Mom and my siblings, regret knowing how disappointed she would be with me once the truth came out—finally, I feared the harm that would come to me in the form of punishment. My amygdala took over.

*Fight.* When the brain perceives danger, it may fight off the threat. With the fight response, our brain tries to ward off danger by defeating it. There was no way I could win this fight.

*Flight.* If our brain does not believe it can successfully fight off danger, it may try to escape, getting as far away from the dangerous situation as quickly as possible. There was no way to outrun this.

*Freeze.* This response tells the brain you must be silent and still until the danger passes. Some people with extreme social anxiety might experience selective mutism—their vocal cords become paralyzed due to fear, and they cannot speak until the fear lessens. That was my first involuntary response. Play possum, be quiet, head down, and maybe she won't know I'm here.

Some twenty-five years later, as a young dad, I witnessed a perfect example of the freeze response. My seven-year-old daughter Jenna hurled a metal toy truck at her older sister

Laura, missing her head by inches. Jenna's eyes locked on mine from across the room, and she froze—she knew she was in big trouble.

Trying not to overact, I said, "Jenna, come here."

"I can't," she said.

"Why not?"

"My legs won't work."

***Fawn.*** Fawning is a fear response where the brain decides to try and please whoever is triggering the fear response to prevent them from causing harm.

"Silverware!" I shouted as I jumped out the back door, running to the pigeon coop.

I was convinced that presenting Mom with the shoe box of matching silverware I was accumulating would get Dad and me out of this mess. As I placed the box on the kitchen table, I could tell Mom had already connected the dots.

"Michael, go upstairs."

I wanted to tell her I couldn't because my legs wouldn't work. I went up the stairs, searched for an opening between my brothers, and wedged in. I had never heard Mom raise her voice at Dad until that night. I couldn't hear what was said, but it was a one-way conversation.

Halfway down the stairs the following day, Mom ordered me to return upstairs until she called me. I was sure she would get my brothers and sisters off to school and then beat me into the middle of the next week. Once the house was quiet, she yelled for me to dress and come downstairs. Peacefully, she took my arm and led me to the Carryall Chevy truck. We drove in silence to Yesteryear, where Mr. Schimel met us. Once in Mr. Schimel's office, Mom set the silverware box on his desk.

"Your mother has told me you have been stealing from me. Is that true?"

"Yes, sir."

"What have you stolen?"

"Steaks and silverware."

Mr. Schimel handed me a pencil and pad of paper and instructed me to take my time and determine the number of steaks I had stolen. He said he needed the information to give the police when they arrived. I can't remember the formula for the total, but I wrote down 100 steaks.

Mr. Schimel took out a Yesteryear's menu and went down the side with his finger until he found the steak on the menu. "five-ninety-five a steak times 100 steaks. How much is that, Michael?"

"Five-hundred and ninety-five dollars."

There was silence for an eternity, and then Mr. Schimel spoke.

"I am very, very disappointed in you, Michael. I will let you decide what we do next; you have two choices. I can fire you, call the police, and have you sent away to the juvenile detention center for a year. Or you can write a letter of apology to me and continue to work here at the Yesteryear until you have earned five-hundred and ninety-five dollars as repayment for what you stole. What would you like to do, Michael?"

At seventy-five cents per hour and twenty hours a week, it took me ten months of working with no pay as an indentured busboy. Mr. Schimel sat me down a few weeks after the meeting to tell me a few things. He wasn't mad at me, and that I had a very good mother for teaching me the difference between right and wrong. After settling my debt, I worked at Yesteryear for three more years.

## REFLECTIONS

At what age is a child morally responsible for their actions? Biblical passages like Isaiah 7:15 indicate that there is such a thing as an "age of accountability" but doesn't provide an age.

The legal system in the US makes it more precise; it says between the ages of seven and fifteen.

I knew that stealing was wrong at an early age, probably around six or seven. Mom made sure of that. Did stealing tomatoes from the Benoit's garden count as being wrong? Well, okay, there were some grey areas. But I knew stealing steaks from the Yesteryear Restaurant was dead wrong. So why would an intelligent boy who knew it was wrong steal? Upon reflection as an adult, it all made sense. The risk was worth the reward.

I had the opportunity to make my dad happy and proud of me. I knew my dad went without. I saw his happiness when he got a box of chocolate-covered cherries at Christmas and how he treasured that small bag of peanut brittle on his birthday. I remember how he never took a second piece of chicken. I was continually hungry as a child, and so was my dad.

There is no way I can make excuses for what he did and taught. It was so very wrong. But I can easily make excuses for that twelve-year-old boy who craved time with his dad.

Dad continued to teach the wrong lessons and encouraged his children to steal, lie, and cheat. Thankfully, I had a mom who ensured her children knew the difference between right and wrong and did her best to be an antidote to Dad.

The steaks were never talked about again in our home. Dad never apologized, and Mom and Mr. Schimel continued to treat me with love and dignity.

I remain amazed and puzzled about how all his adult children treated Dad with honor and respect. Were we brainwashed to "honor thy father"? Did we pity our father, or did we continue to be his winged monkeys?

# THE PUPPETEER'S SON

## CHAPTER 15

"A narcissist paints a picture of themselves as being the victim or innocent in all aspects. They will be offended by the truth. But what is done in the dark will come to light. Time has a way of showing people's true colors."

– Karla Grimes

DAD SAW HIMSELF AS a loser. A factory laborer who worked two to three jobs at a time and still never had enough money to cover the basics of food, clothing, and medical bills. He was habitually tired. He acted like a victim, with these fourteen children somehow showing up one at a time. He wanted us to believe that he came home from his shift spent, and Mom took advantage of him. So, he had nothing to do with it all. He would let us know the kind of car he would be driving if it wasn't for all his children draining him dry. And while I'm sure he would describe himself as a failure, there were a few things that he rarely lost at: fist fights, football games, and pigeon races.

In opposition to his plight, Dad was a brilliant man. He was born with a beautiful mind that he somehow couldn't take full advantage of. With fights, football, and pigeons, Dad poured vast amounts of energy into winning, even if he had to win ugly.

Dad developed his love of breeding and racing pigeons from his father and grandfather. My grandfather, Henry Menard, was a legend in pigeon racing circles in and around Kankakee. He was a champion with tricks and secrets he passed down to my dad and his other sons, Bob and Bud.

When Mom and Dad bought their first home, 118 South May Avenue, Dad's first renovation was to convert the one-car garage on the alley to a proper pigeon coop. It was Dad's church. When he wasn't working, he was in his coop. We were welcomed there, but if you entered the coop, you had better be ready to listen, learn, and pitch in with the chores. Even though the place smelled dreadful, I loved being there. One-on-one time with Dad was priceless.

Through the front door was a small storage area with large bags of feed grain, grit required for the bird's digestion, and a bag of a white powder Dad spread on the floor after cleaning the coop, a disinfectant to keep the birds from getting sick. The floor of the coop was up three steps through a screen door. To the right and up about three feet was a platform to facilitate the bird's exit from the coop to exercise (wing), and return to the coop. The trap door was the door to let them in and out of the coop. Pigeons easily returned to the coop by going through and lifting the series of eight-inch steel rods that swung into the coop but did not swing out unless my dad dropped the bar across the bottom.

The rich experiences generated by Dad's years of racing pigeons created many May Avenue Stories. My children, siblings, and their children still associate pigeons with our dad and grandpa.

Like horses, pigeons are bred for racing. It takes years, even decades, to elevate an owner's flock to win races and championships. Any money earned by my dad from racing his birds funded the coop. I don't know how much money my dad made off pigeon racing, but I believe it was substantial. Dad paid to have a stud male mate with his pigeons. Once, Dad had six pigeons on loan from a breeder. The breeders were on loan for two to three weeks.

We had all kinds of pets—dogs, raccoons, mice, snakes, but never cats. Cats were the enemy. Cats worked hard to get into a pigeon coop. Cats loved to eat pigeons, and they loved the sport of catch and kill. When a cat got into a pigeon coop, it would kill one or two and eat them, and once they had their fill, they would catch and kill every bird in the coop for sport. If it were during the daytime, someone would hear the commotion in the coop, and there would be minimal damage to the flock. But if the attack came at night, the flock would be annihilated. Cats got into Dad's coop a handful of times, and one of those times, the cat killed every bird in the coop. As bad luck would have it, that was when Dad had the six pigeons on loan. This was an emotional and financial disaster for our family. I vividly remember the anguish on Mom and Dad's faces. The pigeon club came to Dad's rescue. They collected enough money to pay for the birds Dad had on loan, and they all donated birds from their coops to rebuild Dad's flock. After that, Dad won a race here and there but never again dominated the club.

My brother David has a whole library of his own May Avenue Stories. I especially like David's story about hunting a killer cat with my dad and his brother, Bob. A cat got into the coop and killed two of Dad's birds before Dad came in; the cat escaped. My dad and Uncle Bob agreed that the cat would be back to kill more birds. So, the next day, Uncle Bob brought over his twenty-two-caliber rifle, and they sat in the yard quietly and waited for the cat to return to the scene—and it did.

Brother David begged Dad to let him stay with them and watch. David has ever since regretted having that privilege. After a short period, the cat appeared in the two-foot open space under the coop. The cat was sitting in the middle of the coop when Uncle Bob shot him once in the head. David was instructed to retrieve the cat. He crawled under the coop twice and returned without the cat; he was scared. Dad sternly ordered him to get the cat. On the third try, David dragged the cat out, crying hysterically. He ran over and chucked the cat into the garbage can. To hear the story today, some sixty years later, the cat was the size of a bobcat, and David was covered head to toe in blood. Dad told us it was a small alley cat and that David got a few drops of blood on his hand. But it's clear that David believes everything he tells you when you listen to that story.

It was essential to keep the coop clean; a never-ending chore. The floor was covered in pigeon poop, and this white dust-like powder generated from the pigeons constantly shedding their skin. Jamie and I scraped the coop floor once a week. It was a nasty job, but doing it gave us special status with Dad, including the right to attend the Saturday night pigeon club meetings.

Fanciers who bred and raced pigeons took the sport seriously. In the '50s and '60s, almost every town of any size had a pigeon club that participated as part of a national organization. The Kankakee chapter had about twenty members, each having their own coop. The members were my dad's friends, and two of the members were my uncles, Bob and Bud. I enjoyed visiting the other coops with my dad, where the members' wives greeted me with Kool-Aid and cookies.

Even though race season was only ten weeks in the summer, Saturday night member meetings were held year-round; an excellent reason to have a few beers with your friends. Jebb Turner, who was the club's president, hosted these meetings at his house. The off-season meetings were short and dull whereas the in-season were all business, banding, bluffing, and betting.

Jamie and I loved attending Saturday night meetings during the racing season. All the root beer and chips we could consume and the opportunity to see our dad in action, in his element. In that clubhouse, Dad was happy, proud—alive. We got regular winks from Dad, signaling he was about to misbehave. The other members liked and looked up to our dad.

The main events at Saturday night meetings were to band the birds, make bets, and set the clocks. After the banding, the birds were placed in the pigeon crates and stacked in the back of a member's bread truck. The birds were driven to the destination, where they were released at the same time by dropping the side of the crates. The destination distance increased each week, beginning at twenty-five miles and ending at 500 miles at the end of the season. When we got older, Jamie and I rode along with the driver. We especially liked long-distance races because sometimes we went away for two days. The racing process and bird's skill were amazing.

On Saturday night before the race, the pigeons joining the race were brought to the meeting in their custom-built cages. Each cage held about ten pigeons. A numbered, wide rubber band was placed on one of the pigeon's legs. The number on the band coordinated with that bird's identification, the owner's name, and the bird's description. The birds were then taken to the race destination and released at sunrise. Homing pigeons have an internal mechanism guiding them to return to their home coop. The bird owners know the approximate time the birds will arrive. When the birds reach the coop, they fly in a tight circle over the coop and wait for the owner's whistle.

Jamie and I were given jobs at the club meetings, and President Jebb paid us well for what we thought was playtime. The other members were kind to Jamie and me. One of our jobs was placing the bands on each pigeon's foot. We sat on old rusty folding tables with the banding machine between us. Jamie reached into the small, hinged door and removed one bird at a time. He was trained to grab the birds without the slightest chance of injuring or agitating the bird. Jamie held the bird with its two feet between his ring and middle fingers. I loaded the rubber band onto the machine's fingers. I turned a crank to expand the fingers and stretched the band into a two-inch opening. Jamie placed the pigeon's foot into the opening, and I reversed the crank. Next, Jamie withdrew the bird's foot with the rubber band snuggly around the bird's leg. Jamie placed the banded bird into a second cage. Jamie and I banded 200-300 pigeons a night.

Early in our tenure of pigeon banding, Dad had an idea to increase his odds of winning. Dad told Jamie to discreetly squeeze the opponent's pigeons during the banding. He taught Jamie how to squeeze the bird just hard enough to injure the bird's internal organs, reducing the bird's ability to fly long distances. A percentage of birds never finished the race; expected casualties. Flying into electrical and phone wires, being eaten by predators while stopping for a drink, or... organ failure.

## REFLECTIONS

When Jamie and I get together and reminisce about our childhood, some stories make us laugh, cry, and shrink with guilt and regret.

During my first sessions with Kristin, I would bristle when she would point out what was clear childhood abuse and neglect. She would shake her head in disapproval. At some point in my relationship with Kristin, I waved the white flag in my mind. *Yes*, it happened, and *yes*, it was a complex childhood trauma.

Upon reflection as an adult, I wonder how Dad, who lived for and loved pigeons, consented to, and even orchestrated abuse to those beautiful and harmless animals. What horrific lessons to teach his children and even to be amused by the torture. He didn't love pigeons; he loved winning, even winning ugly. Given this atrocious behavior, I challenge whether he even loved me.

We were puppets and winged monkeys as children. I can make no case for this trauma contributing to our collective post-traumatic growth. Nothing good came from this. However, I am proud to say that none of Dad's children followed in his footsteps of lying, stealing, winning ugly, and getting even.

I have forgiven my dad for all the wrongs and all the hurt. That forgiveness has released me from all bitterness, regret, and pain. I only have sadness for the life Dad lived.

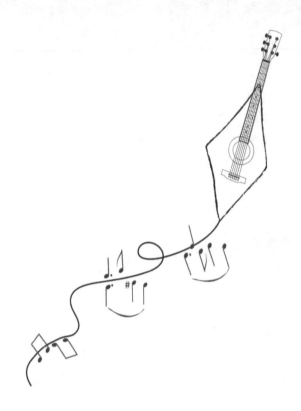

# CLAIR DE LUNE

## CHAPTER 16

"Our job is not to deny the story, but to defy the ending—to rise strong, recognize our story, and rumble with the truth until we get to a place where we think, yes. This is what happened. This is my truth. And I will choose how the story ends."

– Brené Brown

IN THE 1950S, CELEBRATING a child's First Holy Communion was a big deal. This is where a Catholic child received communion for the first time at a special High Mass. This typically happened in second grade. Before your first Communion, you received one of the other seven sacraments of the Catholic Church; penance, or more commonly referred to as confession.

At the center of the Catholic Mass was the Holy Communion ritual. The presiding priest consecrated (blessed and sanctified) small disks of bread called the Host intended to represent Christ's body and replicate Christ's giving of bread to his apostles at the Last Supper. The priest placed the bread Host on the tongue of the recipient as we single-filed toward the altar. Catholic children were taught that the consecrated bread was God, and to receive God in this form, you had to be free of sin. So, before receiving communion, one went into a tiny wooden box, knelt, and told all their sins to a priest sitting in another wooden box with a screen separating the priest. Confession was held on Friday nights; communion was taken at Mass on Sunday mornings. You better not do any sinning on Saturday, or you could not receive communion on Sunday. If you didn't take communion on Sunday, every person at Mass knew you had sinned on Saturday, including my mother and Mrs. Rabideau—which meant by lunchtime on Sunday, everyone in town knew you were a no-good sinner. Every Catholic, Protestant, French, Polish, German, and Jew knew. Oh, the shame of it all.

When a child celebrated their First Communion, it was tradition to hold a party in honor of the child. It was like a bar mitzvah for a poor child. Relatives and friends gave the child a gift, most of which was cash. I can't remember how much cash I received, but it was enough to buy the possession I had my eye on for a year—a Magnavox transistor radio with an earphone for one ear.

I was at the drugstore door when they opened at 8 a.m. Monday and I bought that radio. It was a transformational moment in my life. Music in my ear whenever I wanted. One of the first songs I heard on my new radio was "Blue Suede Shoes" by Elvis Presley. At eight years old, I became obsessed with music. It was 1959, and the music world was exploding.

I was fixated on any song or genre that featured a guitar. I wanted a guitar in the worst way. I tried constructing a guitar out of a shoe box and rubber bands. I learned that rubber bands made different sounds the tighter they were stretched. I found a Gene Autry guitar for sale for twenty-nine dollars and ninety-five cents in the Sears "Wish Book" catalog. I begged and pestered my mom for two years, and Christmas of 1960, my dream came true—I got the Gene Autry guitar. I still remember the rush as I unboxed that guitar.

It was hard to put that first guitar down. I had no training, but somehow, I was making music. To find peace, I played my guitar in my dad's pigeon coop, keeping the guitar away from my brothers and sisters. It was a cheap beginner guitar, meaning the strings were high off the frets, making it difficult and painful to play for more than a few minutes. I played for hours, until my fingertips bled. I didn't know what a pick was, so I played with my fingers on my right hand—becoming a prolific fingerstyle player at a young age.

Both Mom and Dad were proud of my ability to play an instrument. If I was awake when Dad came home from the factory at midnight, he would ask me to play while he fell asleep on the sofa. He told me it calmed his mind. Playing had the same effect on me.

Mom and Dad decided to get me lessons. Given financial constraints, lessons were not an option. It was Mom's idea that they both give up cigarettes to pay for my guitar lessons. Once a week, two dollars a lesson. I began lessons in 1963 when I was twelve.

My teacher was Mr. Stone, and he played beautifully on a white Gretsch Falcon with gold trim. Lessons were on Tuesdays at 4 p.m. I walked to my lessons carrying my Gene Autry guitar without a case. I was always proud to show it off as I walked about thirty minutes through the town center to Mr. Stone's house. I loved the lessons and was always prepared. I so enjoyed playing for Mr. Stone and getting his approving grunt. I made it to most lessons unless there was a financial emergency that required that two dollars. To put it in perspective, two dollars in 1963 was the equivalent of twenty-two dollars in 2024, the publishing year of this book.

My lessons progressed nicely, and in six months, Mr. Stone began teaching me the classical guitar version of "Clair De Lune." It was a complex song that challenged my ability. I fell in love with the song and practiced day and night.

While walking to my lesson one summer day, the town bully Scut Farkus stopped me. He was a giant of a boy with two years and fifty pounds on me. I have long forgotten his name, so "Scut" is what I'll call him here.

"Where you goin'?" asked Scut as he blocked my movement.

"To my guitar lesson," I replied.

"How much money you got?" Scut demanded.

"Two dollars for my lesson."

"Give it to me, or I'll smash your guitar."

He would, so I quickly handed over the two dollars and retreated home. I was no match for Scut; he would have creamed me. Jamie was the fighter; I was the lover and now, musician.

I returned home a broken boy. I had finished learning "Clair De Lune" and was ready to perform the whole song, all five minutes and twenty seconds, for Mr. Stone and his three sons, who were all guitar masters. My mom soothed and quieted me and told me I needed to stay up and wait for my dad to come home from the factory. I suggested Jamie go with me to beat the two dollars out of Scut, which Jamie would have enjoyed, but Mom had made her mind up—this was a problem (opportunity) for Dad.

Dad came in the door, soaked with sweat down to his knees. The factory was not air conditioned and would reach 110 degrees in the summer evenings. Dad arrived home on summer nights wiped out, exhausted, and almost shuffling across the kitchen floor. He carried with him his worn-out metal lunch box. It was steel grey and rounded at the top to hold his coffee thermos. But on this night, he gave me his full attention.

He listened to my story about Scut, and he understood. He showed no emotion, no anger, no clenched fist. He knew and taught us well that anger clouds judgment and response.

"Go to bed, Mike, and we will talk and make a plan on Saturday."

I knew what the plan needed to be: Jamie and I find Scut, and Jamie would beat the tar out of him, get the two dollars back, and I would never have a problem with Scut again.

"Go to bed, Mike."

First thing Saturday morning, Dad, Jamie, and I met in the basement. Dad walked Jamie and me through the plan. I didn't like it. The plan was to have me handle the retaliation without Jamie or Dad—a bad dream.

Dad explained that I couldn't rely on Jamie fighting fights for me, that it was time I manned up. "You can do it, Mike," Dad and Jamie said. (And if it doesn't work, Jamie will take care of it later.) *Hello!* It "not working" meant I'd lose another two dollars and get my face smashed. But I could tell by Dad's eyes and tone that his mind was made up. I had no choice.

That following Tuesday, I began the death march to my lesson. "Cross the same intersection at Court and Washington at 3:45 p.m., the same time and place that Scut stopped you the week before," Dad had said.

Like Pavlov's dog, Scut was on the corner, salivating as I arrived.

"When Scut asks for the money, tell him you put the two dollars in the change slot of the pay phone inside the phone booth at that corner. When he goes to get the money, as he will surely do, put your guitar down; he will have to wedge his huge body into the booth, and he will be facing away from you, so he will have trouble raising his arms," Dad explained in slow detail.

Scut did precisely what we wanted him to do: stepped into the booth and reached for the change return.

"When Scut steps into the booth with the folding door open, reach down and grab this club that I will place on the right side of the phone booth floor." Dad held out the club made from a two-by-two board with electrical tape wrapped around the rounded handle he had turned on a lathe.

"Swing as fast and as hard as possible; go for his head. If he turns around, go for his face. Don't stop until he is on the ground."

It worked just as Dad said it would. I hit his head twice

before he covered his head with both hands. Next, I hit his hands, and I'm sure I broke his fingers. Blood was everywhere. It was horrible.

"Once he's on the ground, drop the stick and walk to your lesson."

My hands were still trembling when I got to Mr. Stone's house. I waited a few minutes before I knocked on Mr. Stone's door and forced myself to stop shaking.

That was a big day, my "Clair De Lune" performance for my teacher and his sons. I never experienced performance jitters. As I played the song, my mind replayed the beating in slow motion. It was as if my music was the soundtrack to a movie.

We were taught never to start a fight, but if a Menard had been wronged, all was fair. We were taught to fight to win, eliminate, and destroy our opponents. Each time Jamie had a fighting victory, he was proud to give a blow-by-blow description for Dad, who loved it. I stayed up that night and waited for Dad to come home from the factory. I told Dad what had happened. He was pleased, but he knew I had no interest in celebrating.

A year later, Scut walked toward me in downtown Kankakee. I was unafraid. When he saw me, he immediately crossed the street to avoid me. The curtain to the movie had closed.

REFLECTIONS

This was the second time I had to stop a bully in the same year. Upon reflection, there had to be a less violent way to stop Tuna and Scut. Was there any possible good that came from these lessons? Well, I did learn to "hit first and hit hard." I learned that I didn't have to tolerate bullies. I also learned how much I detested fighting.

"Clair De Lune" remains my favorite song to play.

My fascination with music and guitars remains. I currently own and play some of the finest acoustic guitars made. I have been playing guitar for sixty-one years and still experience that same rush each time I unbox a new guitar, just as I did when opening that first Gene Autry guitar on Christmas morning. I still play almost every night and experience that same peace of mind my dad enjoyed.

# SAFE IN HIS SHADOW: MY PROTECTIVE OLDER BROTHER

## CHAPTER 17

"Brother, may it inspire you to know when I need a daily boost, I remember the days of yesterday and the laughter we had as children."

– Robert Rivers

JAMIE WAS THE BEST big brother. He was my teacher, best friend, and protector from my earliest memories.

Jamie and I went to Saint Rose Catholic School from kindergarten to eighth grade. The fourth to eighth-grade school didn't have a playground, so we had our morning and afternoon recesses at Alpiner Park. Lots of memories were made at that park. It's where Candy Peconino hung upside down on the monkey bars.

I was in fifth grade, Jamie was in seventh, and Lester Blanchette was in eighth. Lester was a tall boy with a severe crew top haircut. Lester was a specimen. He looked like a villain in a 007 movie—like he should speak Russian. Lester was a quiet boy but also a bully. At one afternoon recess, Lester targeted me. I was big for my age, and Lester thought I could fight. He pushed on my shoulders, asking if I wanted to fight. I kept walking away, hoping to avoid Lester while trying to find Jamie or hoping Jamie found me. Suddenly, Jamie stood next to me. I could stop evading Lester. I was safe, so I stood my ground. Lester came closer and shoved me harder on my shoulders, almost knocking me down. I stood tall again but feared Lester would hit me first. Jamie lowered his right fist almost to the ground and then uncoiled. He moved so fast that his fist looked like a blur. Jamie's first blow smashed Lester's right ear, and blood splattered in about a six-foot circle. Jamie hit Lester's head with a left hook as Lester staggered left and sprayed blood onto the white snow in an overlapping Venn diagram. On his way to the ground, Jamie hit Lester with a third strike, another right hook to the head. All three shots were from behind. Lester had no idea what happened.

Jamie stood over Lester, waiting for him to regain consciousness. "Next time, Blanchette, pick on somebody your age."

The amount of blood in the snow looked like it was a massacre. Sister Saint Margaret Joan, a six-foot tall, 200-pound nun from the Bronx, was the first one on the scene. She asked Jamie what happened, and Jamie explained that Lester was picking on me, three years younger than Lester, and Jamie stopped it. Sister Margaret Joan was the only nun that liked Jamie, so she told him to go back to class.

Sister told Lester to clean himself up and return to the class, saying, "I hope you learned your lesson."

Years later, Lester and his brother installed the plumbing on my first house. We all had a great laugh about that schoolyard fight.

1966 was a magical time for music. New bands and new music sprouted worldwide, and I was in the middle of it all. My revolution began with the Beatles, then the Rolling Stones. Great local bands emerged from the Chicagoland area.

Mom and Dad's investment in guitar lessons eventually paid off. By fifteen, I was an accomplished guitar player. My audience was my family and relatives. I could learn almost any song within an hour or so. Like Jamie, I had inherited my mother's gift of singing. Jamie often landed the lead role in the high school musicals, and crowds came from miles around to hear Jamie sing. I sang quietly in my backyard or on my front stoop.

But someone was listening because I was invited to join a local band, "Those Guys." The band's bass player and lead singer were moving to California, and a replacement was needed. I sang a few of my favorite songs for Kevin Laws, Dave West, and Brent Wadley. I was hired on the spot with one condition: I had to play bass. Having been trained to play classical guitar, playing bass guitar would be a snap. I saved three paychecks from working at the Yesteryear, bought myself a Fender Bassman guitar, and began performing with Those Guys.

At our peak, Those Guys became the go-to opening act for many up-and-coming bands: Three Dog Night, The Rascals, The Buckinghams, Paul Revere and the Raiders, The New Colony Six, and The Cryin' Shames. Most concerts were held at the Kankakee Civic Auditorium, a public venue that held about 600 people.

One summer night in 1966, Those Guys opened for The Cryin' Shames. It was a packed house. No chairs, standing only. Once Those Guys were finished, I went onto the floor with my girlfriend, Ellen, to watch The Cryin' Shames' performance.

Jamie was a fierce and prominent street fighter by this time. His skills were honed; he had Herculean strength, no fear, and an unhealthy confidence that he was unbeatable. Since he was my brother, I had an unhealthy belief that I was untouchable. I had Jamie, and he went to all my concerts.

While standing with Ellen on my right, a sizable Mexican man came and stood on my left side. He was too close, elbowing me in the side, telling me I needed to move. I elbowed him back harder. He came along my left side, looked at me, and smiled. One of his front teeth was covered in gold. It wasn't his size, age, or gold tooth that scared me—it was his eyes. They almost lit up. I decided not to push back again (don't start a fight that you might lose). Looking over my shoulder for my big brother, a sharp point pricked the left side of my ribs. The Mexican's shiny knife pointed at my side. He won. I slowly moved Ellen to the right and escaped back into the crowd. I found Jamie and told him what had just happened. I was thankful that Jamie was sober.

Jamie handed Ellen off to his girlfriend and stepped away so he and I could talk. "Go back, stand next to the Mexican, and elbow him—make sure it's the right guy,"

"You are crazy! This time, he will stick me." I told Jamie.

"Just do what I say, Mikey Joe, and you will be okay."

I went back and did precisely what Jamie said. The knife came back with the point barely touching my side. I looked at the knife, and I swear the blade was twice as long now. *Was it my imagination?* Too much time passed with that knife to my side. *What side will Jamie come from? I hope he doesn't push the Mexican toward me.* Fear was building. Suddenly, the Mexican dropped to the floor, and all hell broke loose.

The Mexican was with friends, and so was Jamie. Jamie had quickly summoned his posse of badass friends, just in case. Two Mexicans jumped on Jamie and pushed him to the ground, on top of the Mexican Jamie had just knocked out. With two Mexicans on Jamie and Jamie on the Mexican, the third Mexican came to and started attacking Jamie. Mexicans were flying off Jamie; Wally Rokus and Rick Rearden jumped in to help him. They were the number two and three best fighters in Kankakee. While wrestling on the floor, Jamie bit a chunk out of the original Mexican's ear. It was clear that Jamie and his friends had the upper hand when the police arrived. They pushed Jamie and his friends away and allowed them to leave.

A regular Friday night. It was a quick fight, and the band didn't even have to stop playing. Jamie and his friends went to the car for a beer while they waited for the Mexicans—the fight wasn't over until there was a winner. The Mexicans never reappeared. Maybe the police took them to the station.

I was at the kitchen table the following morning when there was a loud knock at the door. It was the Mexican. He was banged up with a large bandage over his left ear. "I'm looking for Jamie Menard. Is he here?"

"He is here, but sleeping," I told the Mexican.

"Please wake him up," said the Mexican

I ran up the stairs to where Jamie was sleeping. "Jamie, Jamie, you have to wake up. That Mexican, the one from last night, the one with the knife, he's here. He's on the front porch." Jamie never woke up easily, but Jamie got up quickly and put his pants on. As we came downstairs, Jamie asked, "Is he alone?"

"Not sure," I replied.

When Jamie opened the front door, the Mexican said, "We have a fight to finish."

Jamie scratched his head and looked confused, "Really?"

"Yes," said the Mexican. "Meet me behind the Luna Theater in an hour."

The parking lot behind the Luna movie theater was where all serious, fair fights occurred in Kankakee. Friday nights were the most active fight nights. You could count on a good crowd for Friday night fights. The police knew about them and stayed away; it was part of small-town life. Any boy who could fight had fought behind the Luna, but Jamie was the reigning champion. Jamie had never lost a fight at the Luna.

The Luna was in the middle of downtown Kankakee. By the time Jamie and I arrived, a crowd had already formed. *How did word get out so quickly?* Jamie and the Mexican walked into the center of the fight space. Jamie asked the Mexican if he had a knife, and the Mexican slowly shook his head no. Jamie yelled at the crowd, "Someone go call an ambulance and tell them a man is bleeding badly and needs a doctor!"

Jamie waited for the Mexican to throw the first punch. When he did, Jamie quickly blocked it with his left arm. Jamie then threw the combination he was famous for. A smashing right hook, a powerful left hook, and Jamie landed a right uppercut as the Mexican's head sagged, splitting the Mexican's chin wide open. As the Mexican's head tried to drop a second time, Jamie, with all his might, struck the Mexican's chin with another uppercut. Jamie shifted and twisted this time to put his entire body into that final punch. The Mexican was unconscious before he hit the ground. The whole crowd groaned with that last thump.

As Jamie looked down at his victim, a second Mexican ran at Jamie from behind. Jamie heard the steps and timing of the attacker as the second Mexican attempted to jump on Jamie's back. As if it were choreographed, Jamie flipped the Mexican high over his head. As the Mexican crashed onto his back, and just before his head hit the pavement, Jamie kicked him like he was drop-kicking a football. The second Mexican was unconscious.

"Anyone else want to try?" Jamie screamed.

A policeman pulled up with lights and sirens on.

The officer asked, "What's going on here, Jamie?"

"It was two on one, John, two on one," Jamie explained.

"Is that the way it was?" the officer yelled at the crowd, looking for confirmation.

"Two on one!" Confirmed at least ten onlookers. Jamie's legend continued.

### REFLECTIONS

Now in his 70's, Jamie hasn't fought in over fifty years, but remains strong and still appears musclebound. When I now tell stories about Jamie's fighting years while in Jamie's presence, a boyish grin comes to his face and he begins shadowboxing, warming up for his next fight.

Jamie made a true transformation, almost like flipping a switch. With Jamie's strength, toughness and fighting skills, he could have easily become Dad as an adult. Jamie's transformation was made possible by three factors: Mom's prayers, Joanie's love, and Jamie dedicating his life to Christ.

Jamie remains a fantastic big brother, teacher, best friend, and protector.

# ROBIN HOOD

## CHAPTER 18

"The thief, as will become apparent, was a special type of thief. This thief was an artist of theft. Other thieves merely stole everything that was not nailed down, but this thief stole the nails as well."

– Terry Pratchett

I LOVED PERFORMING. AT first, it was small gigs, and then Those Guys had a breakthrough. We performed every Friday night at the CYO, the Catholic Youth Organization, a YMCA-type location. Attendance grew to the point where people were turned away at the gate. The Friday night performances were hoppin'. We played dance music nonstop on a makeshift stage in the main CYO hall. We became well-known, joined the musicians' union, and Kevin Law's dad became our manager.

The band's popularity grew, and before long, we were hired as the opening act for more notable bands on tour across the Midwest. Then, we were hired to play at universities like the University of Illinois and Southern Illinois University. We added Mark Young on the keyboard, Mark Eckhart as bass singer and tambourine player, and replaced Brent with Micky Kilgos as drummer. We were pulling in big dollars then and bought the best instruments, amplifiers, and PA systems. We were in demand and could pick and choose our gigs. If we were playing in Kankakee, the band met after the performances at Sammy's

Pizza, which is still the best pizza I've ever had. We felt successful.

Mr. Laws had a great idea: why not put on our performances at the Kankakee Civic Auditorium? We could rent the auditorium, hire police for security and traffic control, and even buy a soda pop station, which would cost us five cents, and we could charge twenty-five cents per cup of pop. We gave it a go.

It was a remarkable success. We placed posters at all the businesses and bought radio commercials. The first concert was filled beyond capacity. It was two dollars to get in the door and get your hand stamped with a special symbol for that night only. Friday night dances at the CYO were replaced with Friday nights at the Civic Auditorium. On a good night, we sold over 1,000 tickets for an auditorium licensed for 300. We became local rock stars and rich by Kankakee standards.

People close to the band volunteered to help with the Friday night performances. My dad retired from the factory when Those Guys were in their prime. Dad enjoyed being around the band and was always willing to help. One of his self-appointed jobs was keeping the groupies away from the band after the performances. Dad openly called the groupies "snags."

"Okay, snags, time to go home to your parents," Dad said as he ushered the groupies away from the band as we exited the building.

Dad suggested he take over selling tickets for the Friday night performances. Dad and two of my brothers manned the entrance doors, collected the two-dollar entrance fee, and stamped the visitor's hand so they could come and go as they pleased. This was a critical job; Dad hauled in around $2,000 a night, not including concession stand proceeds. To put that in perspective, $2,000 in 1965 had the same purchasing power as $19,500 at the time of publishing this book in 2024.

At the end of the performance, we gathered around for the financial summary. After Dad paid for the police, the auditorium rental, and for the concession stand supplies, he then divided the profit into five piles and handed us our take for the night. It was usually around $400 each. Kevin suggested we each kick in twenty dollars for my Dad. Dad resisted but finally accepted the money with gratitude. $100 for three hours of work was generous, but the band knew my dad had fourteen kids and was a retired factory worker. I was thankful for the band's generosity. After we got home on those Friday nights, Dad tried to give me my twenty dollars back. I had just raked in $400, and Dad wanted to give me his twenty dollars back. This was not my dad, but oh, yes, it was.

Dad had his side gig going. Jamie and Dad let me in on their ruse late one Friday night. With Dad at the door, Jamie came to the door and paid Dad with a one-dollar bill. Dad said, "Change for twenty dollars; here is eighteen dollars," as Dad handed Jamie a wad of bills.

Jamie would come through the door about twenty times in the first hour. "Change for a twenty; here's your change."

Dad's shared that his skimming limit was $400 per night, no more. Dad took money at the door from the beginning and ramped up his skim as attendance grew so that the band members would not notice the dip, and there was no way for us to verify actual attendance. So, Dad walked out Friday nights with $100 as a thank you from the band and the $400 that Jamie collected. A total of $500 to a guy who made only $200 a week working in the factory for twenty years. And let's be honest; we had no way of knowing how much Jamie skimmed from Dad.

Dad thought it wasn't hurting anyone; he was taking from the rich and giving it to the poor. Dad was winning, even if he was winning ugly.

In addition to the Civic Auditorium performances, Those Guys also played two or three additional gigs per week. I was clearing over $1,000 a week in 1966, with Dad and I collectively pulling in over $1,500 weekly, in cash. No more hunger nor any unpaid bills in the Menard house; life was good.

REFLECTIONS

It was wrong. Didn't he realize he was also stealing from his son? I still feel a sense of embarrassment that my Dad stole from my friends and me.

My brothers all have their own May Avenue Stories about Dad and his "midnight discounts."

As I reflect on those years, I understand why he did it. He wasn't taking the money for drugs or alcohol; he was taking care of his family. Medical and dental care became available. There were real Christmas gifts under the tree for my siblings. Dad would even buy Mom a piece of jewelry from time to time.

He was happy to ride on the coattails of his children by that time. Even if he didn't see it that way.

# WHEN HOPE BETRAYS

## CHAPTER 19

"It's always something, to know you've done the most you could. But, don't leave off hoping, or it's of no use doing anything. Hope, hope to the last!"

– Charles Dickens

OUR MOM KNEW THE power and beauty of building hope in her children. Besides love, hope was often the only thing we had; it was enough to make all the difference.

Mom baked the theme of hope into every lesson and lived it out every day. She was filled with hope and faith. "Anything is possible." "Where there is a will, there is a way." She loved singing "Somewhere Over the Rainbow" as our bedtime song. She sang it better than Judy Garland. Her message was so evident. The idea is that pain and suffering aren't all there is. That somewhere is a better place. She made us believe that someday we could travel there and everything would be okay. It represented a warm place with as much food as we wanted. It meant having a bed, a pillow, and nice clothes. She made us believe it was all possible.

Hope fosters joy, and Mom was full of joy. She turned anything into fun. She loved rainstorms and told us it was God's way of washing the dirt off the roads and cleaning the dead leaves and twigs out of the trees. She waddled us out the door onto May Avenue in the middle of a downpour. Always barefoot, we followed her like baby ducks as she stomped and splashed, the water running down the curb gutters. I told her this could make us sick and catch a cold. We could count on her standard reply: "It'll be worth it."

Mom expected a rainbow to appear at the storm's end. When it did, she ensured we all went out to see it. She would make sure to tell us once again why God sent rainbows. She belted out the song "Somewhere over the Rainbow" and ended with the best part, the story about the pot of gold!

Mom told us that at the end of each rainbow was a pot of gold and the magic that made all dreams come true. She said the end of the rainbow is the enchanted land of lep-rechauns. Little Irish men in green suits guarded the pot of gold. You could steal the pot away from the leprechauns, but you had to be fast. I believed her. During one rainbow sighting, Mark Andrews from across the street loaned me his bike. I told my mom I would get the pot of gold, and she let me go. I rode off toward the south and the rainbow's end. I was afraid of the leprechauns but willing to face that fear to get the gold. I knew how to fight. The further I rode, the further the rainbow's end moved away from me until it disappeared. I made that trip many times until I realized I would never catch it. Yet, on each trip, I was filled with hope.

Hopes changed as we got older. From hoping for a BB gun to a twelve-gauge shotgun to hunt with Dad. From wishing for a pair of shoes to hoping for a suit jacket for the upcoming dance. From hoping for a bicycle to hoping for a motorcycle.

Motorcycles ran through my brothers' and my veins begin-ning around age ten. Uncle Babe, my dad's brother-in-law, Aunt Rita's husband, drove a huge Indian motorcycle with a leather helmet and goggles. Uncle Donny, my mom's youngest brother, looked and acted like Elvis Presley and drove a full dresser Harley. We were not allowed on Uncle Donny's Harley because, as a young man, Donny was crazy and reckless. He once dove headfirst off the Rock Creek cliffs into three feet of water and broke his back. He was always recovering from his last street fight, but to us boys, he was an idol.

One day, Donny talked me into meeting him down the street for a forbidden motorcycle ride. Uncle Donny and I headed into the Chicago Loop, more than an hour from Kankakee. Donny weaved in and out of the posts on Wacker Drive that held up the L-train. He got so close that the metal studs on his leather saddle bags created sparks, inches from my leg on the foot peg. It was exhilarating and forever cemented my commitment to have a Harley as soon as possible. As adults, all ten Menard boys rode big motorcycles. We still take annual cross-country bike rides together.

At fourteen, Jamie was the first to buy a motorcycle. He had his eye on a used 1955 Cushman scooter. The Cushman Eagle was the most desirable scooter in the US in the 1950s and 1960s. The designers at the American company had released a scooter that included all the design hallmarks of the big American motorcycles of the day built by Harley-Davidson and Indian. Jamie was as tough as they came, but he was a kind and generous brother. He referred to the Cushman he was saving for as "our bike," meaning it would be part mine. Jamie and I (as well as every red-blooded American teenage boy) laid awake at night dreaming of owning our own Cushman Eagle—with its contoured fenders, teardrop fuel tank, sprung saddle, wide handlebars, tubular steel frame, air-cooled flathead engine. And most importantly of all, a beautiful girl on the back.

Dad was as excited about having that Cushman in the family as Jamie and I were, and Mom reluctantly gave her nod of approval. Hope was alive that this was going to happen. Dad, Jamie, and I found the 1955 Cushman for sale for $250. To put that in perspective, $250 in 1962 is equivalent in purchasing power to $2,525 as of the publishing of this book in 2024.

Jamie was highly industrious when he was motivated,

cutting lawns, collecting glass soft drink bottles for the two cents deposit, and stacking newspapers onto the trucks at the *Daily Journal*. He was a working fool.

In the 1960s, it was common for children to have their own savings accounts. They were called passbook saving accounts. You took your cash to the bank, went to the teller window, and handed her the cash and your small blue passbook. The teller counted the money in front of you and entered the amount of the deposit and the date onto the next available line on the page. Occasionally, the teller entered the accumulated interest on your savings, usually pennies.

It was Mom's job to deposit Jamie's earnings into his passbook savings account. Jamie was in a panic to save up the $250 before someone else bought the red 1955 Cushman. Jamie and I would ask Mom to look at the passbook to see the progress. It took Jamie only six weeks to save up the $250.

The big day arrived. Dad, Jamie, and I agreed to keep the date a secret so as not to cause a stir with the other boys waiting for their first ride. Dad worked the second shift, so the three of us would go to the bank, make the withdrawal Friday morning, and make the purchase. We were giddy and filled with anticipation and excitement on our way to the bank.

We walked into the Credit Union, where Mom and Dad did their banking. Dad was proud of his son and that we had that much money. Dad approached the teller, handed her Jamie's passbook, and said, "We would like to make a withdrawal."

The teller looked as if she was already joining in the excitement. "How much would you like to withdraw?"

Jamie stepped forward, gently pushed me aside, and quickly replied, "All of it."

She smiled and stepped away to get the money. After what seemed like a lengthy five minutes, the teller returned and told us there was only eight dollars in the account and that the other entries into the passbook were made by someone else, not by anyone at the Credit Union. Dad's shoulders dropped.

Yes, hope is a powerful emotion. However, hope lost or destroyed can be devastating. Once lost, it takes heavy lifting to get it back. There would be no motorcycle.

When we got home, Dad explained what had just happened. To this day, that moment remains a sad memory. Mom was dressed in her old, dirty house dress. She wept with her elbows on the table and face in her hands. She attempted to explain and apologize. It was pitiful. And the worst possible had happened to Dad: public humiliation.

The word spread quickly to the younger children. They consolidated their change, went down to Lola's, and bought Jamie a small bag of penny candy. They offered it to him while he sat sadly on the swing in the backyard.

Over the next few days, the story unfolded. Of course, Mom didn't use the money for herself. There was never enough money to even keep food on the table, so she took Jamie's money and bought food, then made the passbook entries herself. It was Mom's responsibility to file Dad's annual taxes. He typically received around $500. The money was earmarked and used to catch up on some pressing bills, make a payment to the corner grocery store, or get some seriously overdue dental work for her children. Mom planned to repay Jamie's bank account before he accumulated the $250 for the Cushman. Jamie beat all expectations.

Shortly after, Mom and Dad came up with the money, and Jamie bought the Cushman. Mom ended up not being defeated and did the work to restore Jamie's faith in her and hope in us all.

REFLECTIONS

To this day, I stop and smile at the sight of a rainbow and think of Mom and those days on May Avenue.

Mom taught all her children that hope was the most powerful of all emotions. Hope is what carried me through my childhood. It was my greatest human persuader, inciting a sense of purpose and ambition during my most desperate times. At times hope lay sleeping until its incredible strength was awakened in me, delivering a strong belief that I would overcome, I would persevere, and I will endure anything that came my way.

The greater the gap between where you are and where you want to be, the greater the power of hope. Hope grows from need, sadness, unfulfillment, or physical or emotional pain—a profound longing to be better and believe it will be.

This story tells about the time Mom caused us to lose hope. It's the only time in my childhood that anything like that happened. My childhood is full of memories of Mom building hope in me and my siblings. Hope is what kept us going and kept us believing that something better was just around the corner. Today, my siblings and I remain so beautifully full of hope.

# BLOODSTAINED STREETS

## CHAPTER 20

"Darkness cannot drive out darkness; only light can do that. Hate cannot drive out hate; only love can do that."

– Martin Luther King, Jr.

IN 1985, I WAS forty-four years old and the Director of Engineering at the Johnson & Johnson company in Skillman, New Jersey. Based on my position, I was offered wonderful opportunities for self-improvement and advanced training.

My boss was Dr. Phil Stevenson, who had white hair and a white mustache that he stroked when thinking. Dr. Stevenson was one of the original Johnson & Johnson gentlemen who built the corporation through the sixties and seventies. Dr. Stevenson was kind, gentle, and wise, much like King Solomon. He called me "young Michael."

Dr. Stevenson was responsible for innovating and developing new products, and reporting to Dr. Stevenson was Dennis Holtman, Director of Research and Development. Dennis was the head of the department that brought new products to reality; I was the head of the department that designed and built the machinery and shipped those machines to factories around the Johnson & Johnson world. Dennis and I couldn't get along; we had an open and long-standing feud that got in the way of getting things done. At the heart of the problem was my passion and talent for innovation. I would develop a product idea, file a patent application, and then hand the product idea to Dennis. Dennis believed it was *his* job to innovate new products and didn't appreciate the head of engineering upstaging him. Getting my new products through the research and development process (called R&D for short) became agonizing.

Dr. Stevenson called Dennis and me to a late morning meeting. "Your childish backbiting is getting in the way of getting things done. I don't care who is to blame; I say both of you might be wrong. Here's twenty dollars. Please go to lunch, work it out, and then see me so you can tell me the war is over. If you can't do that, I'll fire both of you."

We had a great lunch and an honest talk. We emptied our suitcases of shit on each other and agreed to be best friends. We walked into Dr. Stevenson's office after lunch, holding hands. Dr. Stevenson broke out in the open mouth, panic-stricken laugh he was known for. It worked.

During my annual performance reviews, Dr. Stevenson heaped praise on me. "You are a superstar, young Michael. You make work disappear as soon as I give it to you." He gave me the highest raise and bonus possible.

Yet one review wasn't so enjoyable. "I need you to work on something for me. When you engage in a disagreement, I know that you are always right, and you know you are right, or you wouldn't engage in the fight. You always win because you are always right. But winning isn't enough for you; you aren't happy until you destroy your opponent. It would be best if you stopped once you've won. Here is Gert's phone number; she is a psychiatrist and trainer specializing in assertiveness training. She will teach you the difference between aggression and assertiveness; it will do wonders for your career."

I met with Gert every Wednesday for six weeks in downtown Manhattan. Gert developed a series of workshops and lessons; it was an excellent experience. I graduated with honors; never again would I go for the jugular.

Gert reinforced what my dad had taught me when I was twelve, "When you are angry, you will flail and swing wildly. Your anger will blind you." Gert taught me that calm in the storm is power and phrases like, "Be that as it may..." "Here's how I feel when you say things like that..."

She videotaped us while we role-played. She gave me homework, I was engaged. I needed this training because it helped unknot my dad's teachings. "In the fight, don't stop until you are sure they won't get back off the ground."

Gert's training and coaching made me an even stronger fighter; words replaced my fists.

Assertiveness training was the most impactful education of all the classes I took from Johnson & Johnson over my twenty-five-year career. Gert and I became great friends. I was so impressed with Gert and my newfound tools that I worked with her to develop a three-day class approved by the Johnson & Johnson University. This group organized adult learning classes on a wide variety of topics. I made the training mandatory for the 200 engineers in my department. Word spread, and the program became popular. Gert knew that women benefited more than men from the training, and she created a second course, Assertiveness Training for Women. The classes were taught on-site at the Johnson & Johnson headquarters twice a year. I had lunch with Gert whenever she was in town.

In the 1980s, a few megatrends swept through large, progressive corporations like Johnson & Johnson—quality, safety, and diversity. Diversity at Johnson & Johnson meant the practice of ensuring the inclusion and involvement of people from a range of different social and ethnic backgrounds and different genders. Johnson & Johnson took the subject of diversity seriously and did a great job raising honest awareness and training. I was required to take a three-day advanced course on diversity. It was a rewarding and beneficial course for me. To this day, I'm thankful for having had the opportunity to participate in that eye-opening training.

The setting for day one of the training was ten executives in a circle, like musical chairs. The group included an equal mix of women and men, black and white. I knew all participants well— the instructors were all black. My prejudice and racism kicked in —I mistakenly believed I knew where this was heading. For the first exercise, we worked alone. Each given a flip chart and markers, we were asked by the instructors to make a drawing that depicted our first memory of an encounter with a person of the opposite color. Make the drawing as detailed as possible. We had an hour to complete the drawing. After the hour, we spent the day presenting our drawings and telling our stories. After each participant explained their drawing, the instructors facilitated an open discussion. The goal was to raise awareness about our personal, early experiences with the other race. The exercise was transformational. Each story brought tears and laughter. There was no defensiveness, excuses, or game-playing. It was all very real.

Dr. Al Mays volunteered to go first. Al was vice president of a large J&J division, black, and my boss at the time. We traveled the world together and developed a close friendship. I trusted and loved Al Mays.

Al was a highly educated and accomplished scientist but a lousy artist. Al's drawing included two parallel, vertical lines. Between the lines were three stick figures, one man, one woman, and a child standing beside the woman. Al explained his drawing.

The lines represented the aisle in a grocery store. The man was Al; he had just entered the aisle looking for an item his mother had asked him to find. He was alone in the aisle when a white mother and her young daughter entered the opposite end of Al's aisle. When the mother and child saw Al, they hurried to the next aisle. Al knew they were avoiding him because he was black.

One of the instructors asked, "To my white friends in the room, can you put yourself in Al's shoes?"

I could. I was immediately ashamed of myself and sad for my friend Al. *How many times had I turned away to avoid a black person?* The discussion in the room was rich, as were all the discussions around each drawing. I was next. My drawing included a stick figure of a man lying on the ground with blood spilling from him. Around the bleeding figure where ten large stick figure men holding sticks.

The mid-to-late 1960s was a time of extreme racial tension. Chronic and pent-up frustration exploded in poor African American neighborhoods and cities across America. Unconcealed forms of racial discrimination converged to propel violent upheaval in the streets, ruthless policing, a faulty justice system, dishonest consumer credit practices, poor or inadequate housing, high unemployment, and voter suppression.

In 1967, riot-related deaths were reported nationwide: forty-three in Detroit, twenty-six in Newark, and thirty-four in LA. Uncontrolled crowds were burning, damaging property, looting, and creating chaos. Kankakee was no exception. I remember a day when riots broke out at my high school. Whites were attacking blacks, and blacks were attacking whites. I was home sick in bed when Mom woke me with the news. My sister Polly was at the high school; I had to get her to safety. Most cops knew all the Menards (for the wrong reasons), and I got into the building to retrieve my sister. I walked through the halls amid fistfights and school destruction. I played football with primarily blacks; we were friends, and they let me through the hallways unharmed. I found Polly in her classroom with barricades against the inside door. I got her out, and we found the nearest exit.

Kankakee residents and law enforcement suffered

appallingly indiscriminate injuries and deaths. In 1967, I was sixteen and was a victim of the race riots. In the fall, a bonfire was held at the high school on Thursdays before the Friday night football game. It was a pep rally with the presentation of the players, cheerleaders cheering, and a motivational speech from the coach. The bonfire raged high into the night sky. In retrospect, the fire seemed senseless, given that cities burned across the country.

I explained my drawing to my colleagues:

On the way back to my car after the bonfire, a large group of black guys jumped me. It wasn't a fight; it was a beating. All I could do was cover my head. I didn't recognize any of them, and none of them spoke my name. I was beaten unconscious and taken to the St. Mary's Hospital emergency room. I was surrounded by Dad, and my Uncles Babe, Sam, and Donny when I came to.

My dad wasn't a white supremacist or a vigilante; he was an ignorant bigot who hated black people. He wasn't an isolated case; racism ran deep among most white men when I was a child. He did his best to bestow his hate of blacks onto his children, but our mom was constantly working to unravel the knot of racism in her home. She taught that we are all truly equal in the eyes of God. She believed and explained that the white man was responsible for the death and destruction caused by the race riots of the '60s.

Many years later, my sweet daughter Jenna, seven at the time, picked out a small statue of a black boy as her Christmas gift to Grandpa Menard. I tried to discourage that selection by telling Jenna that Grandpa didn't like black people and would probably throw the statue down and step on it, which I honestly believed. No changing Jenna's mind—what I said made no sense to her. My dad loved all his grandchildren and expressed that love in a way his children never experienced. When he opened Jenna's gift, he placed it gently on the ground and stepped lightly on the statue. Dad saw the immediate panic on Jenna's beautiful little face. He reached down and collected the statue, put Jenna on his lap, and told her how much he loved her gift. Jenna gave me her signature face with one eye half closed, which said it all. *I told you Grandpa would like it.*

As my dad and uncles huddled around my bed in the emergency room, it was clear they were not there to see if I was okay. They were shelling me with questions to help determine who did it—who was responsible? It was as if they were putting on Indian war paint and bandanas. They left my bedside swiftly once they determined I couldn't help them.

At dawn the following day, my dad and three uncles returned to the emergency room to inform me they had taken care of it. All four had blood on their clothes and hands. They had visited every black bar in Kankakee and Pembroke, an all-black neighborhood outside the city. They broke arms, heads, and teeth all night long. They sent a message: never touch another Menard.

As my mom tended to the healing of my wounds over the following weeks, she constantly sermonized on one of her favorite beliefs, the power of forgiveness.

REFLECTIONS

I knew I was beaten by men who didn't know me. They did it because I was white, and my dad and his uncles didn't know the men they hurt that night, and they were beaten because they were black—all senseless acts of ignorance and hatred. My story was fertile ground for the instructors of the class. They spent the first day using my story as a springboard for their class content.

# BEYOND CRUELTY

## CHAPTER 21

"Trauma is not the story of something that happened back then, but the current imprint of that pain, horror, and fear living inside people."

– Dr. van der Kolk

DAVID IS A FASCINATING guy. He is full of passion and information about his interests: his grandchildren, fishing, his lawn, motorcycles, and buying and selling cars. Without trying, David is hilarious.

David has the most negative memories of our dad, and for good reason. Dad was harder on a few of his sons: Patrick, Adam, and David. We don't know why. Ironically, David looks and acts most like our dad. Like Dad, he is tough as nails, quiet, and a bit narrow-minded. Also, David can build and fix anything. David's feelings and problems with Dad are valid.

Dad's teachings and examples were confusing and downright criminal at worst. Dad openly encouraged us to cheat and steal. He saw himself as a kind of Robin Hood, taking from the rich and giving to the poor. It was all okay, but don't get caught.

When David was twelve, he was caught and arrested for driving Mark Andrews' car without a license. The cop brought David to the police station and put him in jail. His bail was set at fifty dollars.

"Let him sit in jail a few days," Dad ordered.

Dad said that because he didn't have fifty dollars, but I did and would not let twelve-year-old David sit in jail. I bailed him out and brought him home. Dad wasn't happy with me. Dad was angry because David got caught and ordered us not to get David out. Also, I'm sure Dad was embarrassed and frustrated that he didn't have fifty dollars to his name.

Not long after being bailed out for underage driving, Mom got a call from the police. David was caught shoplifting at Bell Scott, one of the first department stores in Kankakee. Ricky Stone, an older neighbor boy from down the street, had dared David to steal a chrome gas cap for Ricky's car. David took the dare. He didn't even make it out the door with the cap. David technically didn't steal the cap, but it was in his pocket, and David was heading out the door. The police brought David to the station to scare him, mainly because David was a Menard.

This time, Dad went to collect David. Dad somehow talked the officer out of charging David. When they got home, Dad ordered everyone into the kitchen. He explained that David had been caught shoplifting, and he had embarrassed the family.

Dad called David over to his side and asked, "What hand did you use to steal that gas cap?"

David raised his right hand. Dad grabbed David's right hand and forced it onto the stove burner which was set on high. David screamed as Dad left his hand in the fire way too long. Mom took David to the emergency room at Saint Mary's Hospital. David had third-degree burns across his hand and wrist. Mom told the hospital that David had tripped and fallen into the open oven, which was open to provide heat to the house. That day, David received two scars. One on his hand, the other on his heart.

This was the same father who taught us how to win ugly. This was the same father who taught and encouraged me to steal steaks and silverware from my job at Yesteryear Restaurant. What was the difference? David got caught. It was all so messed up.

It's impossible to make excuses for what Dad did to David. It was child abuse; it was sad, tragic, and criminal.

### REFLECTIONS

---

"And once the storm is over, you won't remember how you made it through, how you managed to survive. You won't even be sure, whether the storm is really over. But one thing is certain. When you come out of the storm, you won't be the same person who walked in. That's what this storm's all about."

– Haruki Murakami

---

This is one chapter I did not want to write. It was never included in what became known as the May Avenue Stories. It happened; I was there. When I told my siblings I was finally writing the May Avenue book, they were all in. They approved the list of stories and agreed to let me "name names."

Jamie told me confidentially that there were three stories I could not tell, stories Jamie said he and I had to take to our graves—I agreed. Then, one day, David reminded me of the gas cap story. He told me it was okay to include it in the May Avenue Stories. It was more than okay with David; he *wanted* his story to be told. The recollection of that story brought immediate sadness. It was the worst of all my memories as a child.

Complex childhood trauma, precisely like the adverse childhood experience David had when our father burned his hand, creates post-traumatic stress disorder. The symptoms of PTSD range from unhappiness to adult dysfunctional relationships and can cause serious health problems later in life. If healing does not occur, the sufferer lives out a lifelong sentence that robs them of the joy God intended for them.

Observe David from a distance, and you see an impressive man, and he is. A beautiful family surrounding him, a long-term career at Armstrong Flooring, a charming home with no mortgage. A master angler, bass king, and a world-class comedian without even trying. Look a little closer, and you will see a guy who isn't as happy as he deserves to be.

I have told him more than once, "Brother, you have the world by the ass; I wish I had your life." I wasn't saying *you need to be happier* or *you need to celebrate your life* or *you need to smile more.*

David experienced more trauma than what is shared within these pages. He experienced neglect, mental abuse, and brutal physical abuse. His childhood experiences did create grit, toughness, and work ethic, but at what cost?

David tells me he has, but I'm not convinced that David has forgiven our father for that viciousness. Even if he has forgiven Dad, big black marks remain on the books.

This was the worst childhood trauma that I know of that took place at 118 South May Avenue. I know Patrick and Adam experienced trauma at the hands of our dad, and they didn't survive. David survived, but how much trauma continues to hurt David today?

David is retired, surrounded by a loving wife and family, and has the most beautiful lawn I have ever seen. Still, we can all see a shadow of sadness across David's face.

I'm not a psychologist or a therapist. However, based on the knowledge I gained while researching the subject of complex childhood trauma for this book, I'm convinced David never really healed from the trauma he experienced. I sent the following letter to David a few days ago and received his permission to print it here.

DEAR BROTHER DAVID,

IT IS SO DIFFICULT TO FORGIVE WHAT YOU CAN'T FORGET. WHAT DAD DID TO YOU WAS THE WORST THING THAT HAPPENED TO ANY OF US. THERE IS A HANDFUL OF STORIES WE AGREED SHOULD NOT BE TOLD, THINGS WE THOUGHT BEST TO TAKE SECRETLY TO OUR GRAVES. DAD BURNING YOUR HAND WAS ONE SUCH STORY. I ADMIRE YOUR COURAGE IN REQUESTING YOUR STORY BE TOLD. HEARING YOUR STORY AND WITNESSING YOUR SURVIVAL AND REDEMPTION HAS THE POTENTIAL TO HELP MANY IN NEED.

YOU HAVE TOLD ME YOU HAVE FORGIVEN DAD. AND WHILE I BELIEVE WHAT YOU SAY, BROTHER, I FEAR YOU HAVE NOT FORGIVEN HIM COMPLETELY. I FEAR THE PAIN AND RESENTMENT OF WHAT HAPPENED ARE STILL WITH YOU; I CAN STILL SEE IT IN YOUR FACE; I HEAR IT IN YOUR VOICE. I'M WRITING TO ENCOURAGE YOU TO OFFER FULL FORGIVENESS, NOT FOR HIM, BUT FOR YOU. TO NO LONGER ALLOW THE ONE WHO HURT TO STEAL ANY JOY FROM YOUR AWESOME LIFE. TO NO LONGER LET HIM LABEL YOU OR TELL YOU LIES THAT HE BELIEVED ABOUT HIMSELF.

I'M NOT TRYING TO MAKE EXCUSES FOR HIM, BUT I BELIEVE THAT AS A CHILD, DAD GOT HURT. HURT VERY BADLY. I KNOW IT IS INCONSISTENT, BUT I DON'T BELIEVE DAD WAS A BAD MAN. I BELIEVE HE WAS AN UNHEALED MAN. AND I'M CONFIDENT OUR DAD NEVER forgave those who hurt him; you and all of us saw the burden Dad carried his entire life.

I have forgiven Dad for what he did to you. I have forgiven Mom for allowing it to happen. And I know how strange this must sound, but I have also had to forgive God for not stopping this bad thing from happening to you. You and I share our faith in God, but we also know there are many things that go beyond our understanding.

You know that your family and I love you deeply. You are an amazing man. You have broken the generational sadness of childhood trauma by being a wonderful husband, father, grandfather, and brother.

If you haven't forgiven Dad, then do it now and do it completely. I want you to be the happiest and most thankful man possible.

I love you, brother,

Mike

the scent of the rose stays on the hand of the giver

# GOD BLESS THE CHILD

## CHAPTER 22

"The best lightning rod for your protection is your own spine."

– Ralph Waldo Emerson

WE WELCOMED OUR BEDTIME ritual. Our days were filled with action and commotion. We prepared and ate meals in shifts to accommodate six people sitting and eating at a time. The bedtime ritual orchestrated by Mom was something we looked forward to.

Once we were upstairs and the jabber tapered off, Mom went to her chair at the bottom of the stairs and would begin to sing. She had the voice of an angel. Mom sang solos in the church choir and performed for weddings and funerals. Mom snuck me into the choir loft when she sang for funeral masses. Only me. She understood my love of music. Her singing voice stayed beautiful and clear right up to her death. Her repertoire included old-time gospel hymns, classics like "Ave Maria" and "Our Father," and popular ballads from movie soundtracks. She welcomed requests. Mom regularly weaved in lessons reinforced with scripture during her bedtime singing. Mom sang and taught until we fell asleep. The day's friction and joys, victories, and disappointments ended peacefully with a message of thankfulness and hope.

Mom and Dad's philosophies on parenting were juxtaposed, and they lived their beliefs daily. Dad's philosophies...

"This is a great day because it's another day I can tell someone to kiss my ass."

"Hit first and hit hard."

"If you want it, take it... just don't get caught."

"Don't trust a priest."

"Winning isn't enough; you must destroy your opponent."

"Fuck them all."

Hurt leads to bitterness, and bitterness and anger hurts others. Dad shouldered the burden of resentment and anger his entire life.

Mom's outlook on life...

"Love thy neighbor."

"What you carry in your heart will determine what you see."

"To be kind, you must love people more than they deserve to be loved."

"Remember that it is always better to give than receive."

"The scent of the rose stays on the hand of the giver."

"Jesus loves a thankful heart."

Mom filled her children with love and hope. *Amen!*

Mom's parenting was magnificent. She rarely disciplined, but taught by love, kindness, and example. One masterclass she conducted with me:

"Michael, it's your turn to clean the basement. You know what clean means: declutter, organize into piles, sweep, and wash the concrete. When you are finished, you can go to the pool."

I was anxious to get to the pool with my brothers, so I gave the basement a lick and a promise and called Mom down for the inspection. I knew the second Mom's feet hit the ground that I was guilty and it would never pass the inspection. Mom took her time inspecting the basement, occasionally gently pushing something on the floor with her foot and signaling that it should have been in a pile.

Finally, she spoke with her hands clasped behind her.

"Now, if I had asked Tommy across the street to clean the basement, this is what I would expect to see. But I asked Michael Joseph Menard to clean this basement. I know how good a job Michael Joseph Menard can do; he is my son. I'm going to go upstairs and make you a nice lunch, and when I come back down, you will show me the type of work Michael Joseph Menard can do."

*Didn't I feel like a shit?* She didn't embarrass, criticize, or punish me. I heard and believed that I was special, better than others, and could do more because I was more. I was the son of Arletta Marie Menard.

While most of our relatives treated us like we had leprosy, they did have an impact on our growth and development. Our family included lots of aunts, uncles, and cousins. Mom was from a family of seven: four girls and three boys. Dad was from a family of eight: five boys and three girls. I loved my aunts and uncles. Like most people, our aunts and uncles played a crucial role in our lives. Uncle Bob and Aunt Rose were my godparents. They never missed a gift or money card on birthdays and Christmas. For my First Communion, they took me shopping and bought me a white suit. They did their best to fill in the gaps.

Uncle Sam and Aunt Dolly lived on the south side of Chicago, about an hour from Kankakee. Aunt Dolly was my dad's older sister. She married Uncle Sam, an Italian guy from Chicago. It was a rumor, or maybe a family secret, that Uncle Sam was a mafia member and had done prison time for shooting a man. Uncle Sam was one of our favorites; he was as Italian as one could be. He believed there were only three types of people: Italians, those close to an Italian, and those who wanted to be Italian. Aunt Dolly became an Italian immediately after marrying Uncle Sam. Uncle Sam taught her how to cook, and oh my, what a great cook she was.

My dad's sister, Aunt Pauline, also married an Italian, Uncle Tony. Aunt Pauline always seemed angry and looked like my dad, but Uncle Tony was warm and loving. Like Aunt Dolly, Aunt Pauline also converted to Italianism and became an excellent Italian cook.

While I loved all my aunts and uncles, Aunt Dolly, Uncle Sam, Aunt Pauline, and Uncle Tony were the only relatives I recall playing an active role in our lives. While the other aunts and uncles kept their distance and rarely invited us to their homes for a meal, the Mantukas and Africanos regularly invited us for dinner, all sixteen of us. Those meals were feasts: salad with green olives, garlic bread, pasta with gravy (what Italians called red sauce), meatballs, and sausage. As much food, soda, and milk as we wanted. We felt welcomed and loved. Each of us left dinner with a few quarters in our pockets. Maybe it was an Italian thing.

Uncle Sam and Uncle Tony shared common Italian traits. These traits were essential values and aspects of the Italian lifestyle, including spending time with family and religion, maintaining Catholic traditions, and the pleasure of watching guests eat meals prepared with love and dedication. Uncle Sam and Uncle Tony made me want to be Italian.

On the other hand, some aunts and uncles made my siblings and me feel unwanted and unwelcome.

My mom's sister, Aunt Rosemary, was a charming woman. She was still a beautiful woman through her eighties when she passed away. All of us boys had crushes on Aunt Rosemary. As an adult, I visited Aunt Rosemary in her home in San Diego just before she died. During lunch at her swanky country club, I asked Aunt Rosemary her secret for maintaining her beauty. She attributed it to staying thin, "The thinner you are, the less there is to sag."

Aunt Rosemary visited us more than all our aunts and uncles. A striking contrast to my mom, Aunt Rosemary was barren. She often joked about the unfairness of her sister having fourteen children while she had none. She regularly offered to adopt a few of Mom's children. She was dead serious.

Aunt Rosemary married Uncle Bill, the son of a wealthy landowner from Peotone, a small farm town ten minutes north of Kankakee. Uncle Bill was a stockbroker with little in common with Aunt Rosemary's relatives. We saw Aunt Rosemary and Uncle Bill as super wealthy. On the rare occasion when Uncle Bill joined Aunt Rosemary on a visit to our home, it was made clear by Uncle Bill that he was uncomfortable. Wealthy people can feel uncomfortable around poor people. Uncle Bill constantly chewed gum and talked fast between his rapid chewing. Uncle Bill had noticeably oversized muscles on each side of his forehead, near his temples. His bald head and these bulging muscles made Uncle Bill a bit Martian-like. Yet another reason for us to poke fun and not like him.

Unexpectedly, Aunt Rosemary invited our family to a cookout. While we always welcomed free food, this was an outing none of us looked forward to. It would be our first visit to their home. Mom lectured us for days leading up to the visit. "Don't talk too loudly, don't run in the house, say 'please' and 'thank you', don't pee on the floor around the toilet." Mom was nervous, and Dad just didn't want us to go.

We drove up the driveway and were speechless when we saw their home. It was all brick with a sizeable chalet-like section off to the right. Three stories of glass revealed a majestic stone fireplace. We entered the house, walking on eggshells.

Uncle Bill was rich and tightfisted. Maybe that was the secret to getting rich. There was a small dish out with a few pieces of carrots and celery—not even enough for one piece for each visitor. Uncle Bill was nervous, and we could tell he wanted to get the visit over with and us out of there. He quickly took our orders and wrote them down, "Hot dog or hamburger?" We could get one hot dog *or* one hamburger, not both.

To drink, there was a stack of small plastic cups and one two-liter bottle of Coke. That's sixty-seven ounces for eighteen people. Do the math; that's less than four ounces per person.

Uncle Bill said, "Help yourself."

I did just that by pouring myself a full cup.

"Whoa, whoa, whoa!" cried Uncle Bill. "Don't take too much; leave some for your brothers and sisters." Mom nervously grabbed my cup and poured half of it into another as she gave me the stink eye.

We ate, and then Dad got us out of there. Mom was embarrassed for herself, her children, and Aunt Rosemary, who looked like a victim. Dad was pissed and quiet. We were never invited to Aunt Rosemary's house again.

During the winding down ritual that night, something was off. Something wasn't right, but it wasn't to be discussed. With the light relocated to the attic and the dirt scraped off our feet, we settled into the mattress and waited for Mom to sing. Instead of hearing a song, we listened to the rumbling of Mom trying to calm Dad. He was pissed and couldn't let Bill's rudeness go. We heard Dad telling Mom what he wished he would have said to Uncle Bill and how he should have just "busted him."

Once Mom had Dad settled, she sang one of our favorites, "God Bless the Child." Mom sang this song with a mix of blues and jazz. Mom loved telling us how Billie Holiday wrote and recorded the song in 1941 and how it became a type of anthem for all black people in response to Judy Garland's "Somewhere Over the Rainbow," recorded in 1939 as the theme song to *The Wizard of Oz.*

Mom tied the lyrics to what she believed was the lesson and, of course, jumped on any opportunity to connect the words to scripture.

*Them that's got shall get*

*Them that's not shall lose*
*So the Bible said, and it still is news...*

Mom explained this referred to Matthew 25:29: "For unto everyone that hath shall be given, and he shall have abundance: but from him that hath not shall be taken away even that which he hath."

*You can help yourself*
*But don't take so much...*

This was Mom telling us to take control of our lives without depending on the kindness of strangers and even relatives. Don't count on handouts. On this night, Mom sang with a nodding-off voice filled with resentment and a hint of courage and possibility.

Two weeks later, Aunt Rosemary invited Mom and Dad out to dinner. This was a rare occasion, Mom and Dad on a date. Mom was tickled and so looking forward to dinner out with her sister. We found out later that Aunt Rosemary prompted the date to get Uncle Bill to apologize for treating us so poorly at the cookout. Uncle Bill never got around to the apology. Jamie, David, and I sat on the front stoop when Uncle Bill pulled up to drop off Mom and Dad. After a few minutes of talking, Dad quickly jumped out of the back door, opened Uncle Bill's driver's door, and pulled Uncle Bill out by grabbing and twisting the top of his shirt as Dad blasted Uncle Bill in the face with three fast and powerful left arm jabs. With Aunt Rosemary and Mom screaming, Dad released Uncle Bill, and he fell limp onto the street.

It took us a few days to get the backstory. Uncle Bill and Dad were heatedly discussing an upcoming local election. Dad was confident the pro-union candidate would win. Bill was in a violent disagreement.

"I'll bet you a dollar the union will win," offered Dad.

"A dollar?" Bill sniggered, "Why not a hundred dollars? Do you have a hundred dollars, Paul?" That was all it took.

That night, Aunt Rosemary threw Uncle Bill out of his own house and told him not to come back until he apologized and gave Dad one hundred dollars. Three days later, Uncle Bill came and apologized and paid Dad a hundred bucks. To celebrate Dad's victory that night, we loaded up in our 1955 Chevy Carryall with the top cut off and took a field trip one hour north to the corner of Route 45 and Cicero Avenue, the closest White Castle restaurant to Kankakee. We could have as many hamburgers as we wanted. In 1960, the small square White Castle hamburgers cooked in sautéed onions cost five cents each. Dad started with an order of sixty hamburgers and went back three more times. I ate eight, and Jamie ate a dozen.

God bless the child that has his own, and God bless Uncle Bill!

### REFLECTIONS

I grew up with the gift of being seen through the eyes of someone who loved me dearly and unconditionally. Such power was given to her children by knowing their mother believed in them and taught them self-reliance.

We experienced beauty and ugliness at 118 South May Avenue. This story is full of goodness.

The amalgam of hate and love, grudges and forgiveness, hope and desperation, anger and peace shaped the lives of my thirteen siblings and me. We are unique, beautiful people. I grew up believing anything was possible and that I was a remarkable man, destined for greatness. I fear no man and no opponent is tough enough.

My siblings and I have achieved uncommon success. Their children, my nieces and nephews, continue to demonstrate distinctive achievements and are delightful people. At family gatherings, I see our mother in each family member.

# UNQUENCHABLE WRATH

## CHAPTER 23

"Revenge can only be found on the road to self-destruction."

– Wayne Gerard Trotman

ONE OF DAD'S LEGACIES was his talented predisposition to get even.

Mom took every opportunity to explain and indoctrinate us about the grace and beauty of forgiveness and the ugliness of unforgiveness and resentment. Her foundation always came from scripture. She also reinforced the message with her own powerful words. She was so balanced and practical in everything she taught. She told us that while forgiveness was never easy, it was essential. It was important because God said so and required it for our well-being. We healed and transformed with forgiveness, but resentment would eat us up inside. She taught us that resentment was like taking poison and hoping it would kill someone else.

Dad always saw it as getting even, settling the score. It all fits with Dad's persona. In the years of my childhood, he was bitter, angry, and unhappy.

"It's a great day because it's another day I can tell someone to kiss my ass" was one of Dad's favorite maxims, and he lived it. While sitting on his front stoop, he waved his hand "hello" to everyone driving by. He waved enthusiastically at friends and strangers alike, but a closer look revealed that he had his middle finger flying at everyone he waved to. Dad had a great sense of humor mixed in with bitterness and sarcasm. When he knew death was days away, he told his sons that he wanted to be laid to rest with both middle fingers on his chest, crossed like two six guns. He was serious. We conveyed Dad's wish to the undertaker, who knew Dad well. Mr. Clancy smiled and said, "I can only do that with your mother's approval." Mom was always the spoilsport.

Dad came alive at any opportunity to get back, to get even. Forgiveness was not in his vocabulary. If someone wronged Dad or any of his family, he would not sleep until he had justice, until the offender felt pain. Justice to Dad was more than getting even; it was punishment. The deeper the offense, the greater the penalty. The only scripture Dad knew, understood, and lived was "An eye for an eye." Dad taught through example. We have a long list of his May Avenue displays of revenge. Some amusing, some revolting.

When Dad was forced to retire because of his health, going for coffee was his favorite pastime. Whether at McDonald's, Hardee's, or Dunkin' Donuts, Dad had a group of friends to join for coffee. Dad loved to have one of his children join him for coffee. He never said it, but it was apparent that Dad was proud of his children.

When Dad introduced one of us to his friends, he made sure he gave a little advertisement, "This is my second son, Michael; he's visiting from out east. He's the one from Johnson & Johnson."

After Dad's death, I often heard my siblings say to each other, "I wish I could have just one more talk with Dad over coffee."

Growing up, it was rare to talk with Dad; he just wasn't there. He was either working, sleeping, or with his pigeons. So, the talks over coffee with Dad are our best memories with him. We sat for hours and talked. We recognized that no talks were private because he wanted his friends to hear the conversation. When Dad did speak, he had plenty to say. He was a thinker and a fascinating man once you got him talking.

During one coffee talk, I tried to weave in some advice. Dad gave me the illusion he was listening, but it was futile when trying to provide Dad with any suggestions that might improve his life. He was very opinionated and had the answer for everything. I tried to get Dad to better understand his desire and practice of getting even. The conversation went something like this:

"You know, Dad, your resentment toward others and your need to get even may not be the best thing for you."

"What do you mean?"

"When you try to settle a score and punish someone, it may hurt you more than your enemy."

"No, trust me, my enemy will hurt much more than me."

"Maybe try forgiveness as opposed to revenge."

"Forgiveness works for your mother; it doesn't work for me."

"What about karma? Don't you worry about karma?"

"Fuck karma! What's karma?"

My earliest memory of Dad exacting revenge was when I was five and Jamie was seven. For Christmas in 1956, Jamie got what he had hoped for, a double-barrel air pop gun. It was also called a cork gun. Cock the gun, and when you pulled the trigger, a strong puff of air discharged. The gun came with a few cork plugs. Wedge the cork plug at the end of the barrel, and the air propelled the cork maybe twenty feet. Jamie quickly discovered the trick of sticking the barrel tip in the dirt making it a shotgun, spraying the dirt in a broad pattern.

Franky was our next-door neighbor and one of those characters who stuck in the minds of Jamie and me. He was old, mean, and scary. He was cartoonish, with oversized jeans too long for his short legs and big clown shoes. Franky had a hole in his throat just below Adam's apple and had to put his fingers over the hole to talk. When he did speak, his voice was robot-like, gruff, and scratchy. We thought it was some trick Franky employed to make his voice sound scary. Franky was always pissed off and rarely said anything to us. He walked through our front yard many times each day. I remember Franky's house set back much further than our house. I was afraid of Franky, but Jamie wasn't.

Franky walked down the sidewalk like he was pissed off. Head down, quick, short steps with his stubby arms swinging at double time. With his eyes on Franky, Jamie slowly cocked his gun and stuck the barrel in the dirt to reload, all in one smooth motion. I knew what was going to happen.

As Franky approached us, he had his hand at his throat and mumbled some unpleasantries. Jamie couldn't help himself. He raised the double barrels, pointed them at Franky's face, and pulled the trigger. The dirt buckshot sprayed Franky's face and eyes. Franky mouthed obscenities as he tried to clear the dirt from his eyes, but no sound came out. Franky snatched the gun from Jamie and smashed the stock on the curb. He beat the curb until the gun was in pieces.

We waited for Dad to come home from the factory around midnight. Jamie told the story and showed Dad the pieces. Of course, Jamie was only defending himself and his brother. Franky threatened Jamie and me and was about to attack us when Jamie shot Franky in the face. There was no discussion about who was right and who was wrong; Franky was guilty.

"We will take care of this in the morning," Dad said tiredly.

Dad was awake and dressed when Jamie and I woke up and rushed downstairs to hear Dad's plan.

Dad picked up the gun pieces and said, "Let's go."

It was on. Dad banged loudly with three fist pounds. When Franky opened the door and saw Dad holding the broken gun parts, fear fell over Franky's face. Franky said nothing, just stared at Dad.

When we were a little older, Dad taught us to stare at our

opponent before the fight began. "Let fear build in them; fear will disable the fighter."

After what seemed like an hour, Dad said, "You broke my son's gun; you owe him twenty dollars for a new gun."

Franky attempted to tell my dad what happened, but Dad would not have any of it. "Give my boy his twenty dollars, or I will break this gun over your head."

Jamie and I hoped that Franky would refuse to pay so we could watch Dad whip the tar out of him. But Franky quickly pulled out his wallet, gave Dad a twenty, and closed the door. That day, we went to the sporting goods store and bought Jamie an even better pop gun.

But getting paid back wasn't getting even—Dad still needed to punish Franky. After a few days, Dad had a plan. On Friday morning, Dad quietly told Jamie and me not to poop that day and to wait up for Dad until he got home from his shift.

Dad walked in, dropped his lunch box off, and said, "Let's go."

In the darkness, Dad led us to Franky's front porch. He signaled us to be quiet with his finger over his lips. Dad unbuckled his belt, dropped his work pants, and pooped right on Franky's porch. He signaled for us to do the same. I could not believe it, our dad letting us, encouraging us to shit on a neighbor's porch. We did it, and it was great. Franky got off easy.

We had two types of neighbors: those who loved us and those who didn't. Those who didn't love us disliked us. It was no secret that we were a nuisance to some neighbors, and even worse to others.

Mrs. Philips, two doors down, was like our third grandma. She loved the Menards and always brought us food, vegetables from her garden, and little holiday gifts. Mr. and Mrs. Philips lived in a beautiful two-story home with a vast garage. Mrs. Philips always invited me in for some treat. I tasted my first banana cream pie at Mrs. Philip's kitchen table. It was indescribable. My joy encouraged her to make the pie more often; she always saved a piece or two for me. During one of my frequent bouts with strep throat, Mrs. Philips heard from my mom that my throat was so swollen that I couldn't eat. Mrs. Philips brought down two oversized banana cream pies to ensure everyone in the house had a piece. I heard her instruct Mom, "Make sure Mike gets a piece as soon as he feels better."

Mr. and Mrs. Gwenn lived across Court Street, down one block, next to the Illinois Central train tracks. Mrs. Gwenn always had her famous chocolate cookies available and handed them out anytime the neighbor kids were near her home. They had two daughters, Barb and Carol. They were beauties and a few years older than Jamie and me. The day we moved into May Avenue, Mrs. Gwenn sent Barb and Carol to walk Jamie and me down to the Dairy Queen at the corner of Station and Wall Streets, their treat. It became a regular thing. The ice cream was great, but the real treat was being with these two older girls. Jamie and I had our first crushes on the Gwenn girls. They grew up to be beautiful women whom we occasionally run into, and we tell the stories of their kindness and thank them again.

Then we had those neighbors who wished we lived somewhere else. I understand; what neighbor would want to live near a family with fourteen kids? Grass couldn't survive in our yard; there was too much traffic. Toys and stuff were strewn across the front and back yards, and we ran amuck. The neighbors treated their homes for cockroaches and mice, but the overflow visitors from the Menard house were a constant threat, and just imagine the noise.

Mrs. Dione was our chief adversary; she lived directly across the alley from us on Alma Avenue. She lived with her adult son, who also didn't want anything to do with the Menards. We thought that Mrs. Dione living with her adult son was weird. She had a picture-perfect garden where she spent most of her summer. Every vegetable imaginable, with half of her garden just tomatoes. Her house and garage were spotless, pure white with forest green trim. Her home had a wrap-around porch.

We were told by Mrs. Dione that walking in her yard was trespassing, and she would call the police if we stepped a foot on her grass. She must have counted her tomatoes each afternoon because she knew exactly how many tomatoes we stole from her. Whenever she was sure we had stolen her tomatoes, she stomped up our back porch steps, knocked on the door, and complained to Mom. Mom always defended us and said that her children don't steal. Of course, we were always the suspects; a family with fourteen hungry kids would steal.

One day, David cut through Mrs. Dione's backyard to get to our house. Mrs. Dione was in her yard uprooting dandelions with a long steel shaft. It had a sharp end split like a snake's tongue. Stick the sharp edge in front of the dandelion and then pry up the root. Mrs. Dione spotted David, and the chase was on. For an old lady, Mrs. Dione could move. She poked David in the butt with the dandelion tool and ripped a patch from David's pants.

Mom marched right over to Mrs. Dione's yard and bitched her out. "Never touch one of my children again, or I'll call the police on *you* for a change!"

Mrs. Dione called the police on the Menards at the drop of a hat, for any reason at all. One time, she called the police and claimed that my dad's pigeons pooped on her laundry while it dried on her clothesline. The police were obliged to come to our house and register the complaint. My dad explained it was impossible for this to happen because pigeons do not poop while in flight and also would never land in a neighbor's yard. The police reported back to Mrs. Dione. That day, Mrs. Dione screamed at my dad from across the alley about his pigeons.

Dad told Jamie, David, and me to collect all the tomatoes we could find, including all those from Mrs. Dione's garden. The next night, just after midnight, when Dad arrived home from his shift, the four of us pelted Mrs. Dione's garage until it turned from white to red. The following day, we saw an ambulance pull up to Mrs. Dione's house with the sirens on and lights flashing. When Mrs. Dione saw her garage redecorated, she had a nervous breakdown. She recovered, returned home, and never again complained about the Menards. *Mission accomplished.*

After graduating high school, I moved out to a third-floor attic apartment. It was small, hot, and had many outside stairs, but it was mine. The first time I invited my girlfriend for dinner, I saw someone standing near my door like they were listening. I saw the person's shoes when I looked under the door. It was creepy and a little scary. It became a regular occurrence; the person stayed there for about fifteen minutes and then walked away. By this time, my dad was forced to retire due to heart disease, and he had plenty of time on his hands. He had retired from the factory, but not from revenge taking.

I told my dad about the creeper and asked for some advice. Dad heard the story; he looked like the cat who swallowed the canary. Dad knew my landlord but never liked him, and Dad believed he was the prime suspect. Dad had a plan.

Dad went to my apartment in the morning and stayed there all day. Such determination. No trips in or out. He fixed himself lunch and dinner. He told me to bring my girlfriend to the apartment around dusk; we followed his instructions. He told us to talk naturally while waiting for the creeper's arrival, but Dad would stay silent. As we expected and hoped for, the eavesdropper appeared at my door. Dad, in his stocking feet, crept to the door, pulled out a handgun, and put his finger over his lips. Dad opened the door with his right hand and, with his left, shoved the gun deep into the stomach of the creep and shot three fast shots. My heart sank. My dad would never have done that. My mind screamed, and my girlfriend was in shock.

The villain, now victim, was my landlord, Mr. Landry. As Mr. Landry fell to the floor, soon to be dead I was sure, Dad said,

"Landry, oh shit, I didn't know it was you!" Also in shock, Mr. Landry recovered to his feet while holding his stomach with both hands. Dad had used blanks in his handgun. He used the starting gun for track meet races. "Sorry, Landry, I didn't know it was you. Some guy has been creeping around when my son comes home with his girlfriend, and I wanted to catch the guy and scare the hell out of him." Still in shock, Landry staggered down the stairs.

There was no air conditioning in that attic apartment. Three windows had those expandable screens, helping to make it barely sleepable. That night, Dad brought a large squeeze bottle of wood glue. He took the screens out, laid a thick bead of glue along the inside of the sash of each window, and closed the window. Those windows would never open again. I moved out the following day.

Dad believed others thought he was a loser. Dead end job, too many children, his inability to provide even the basics for his family; all rational for the chip on his shoulder. Dad had voluntarily relinquished leadership and control of the family to Mom. The job was just too big for Dad. Mom always stepped up. Yes, Dad emerged when it was time for a real butt-whooping, but he had little he felt in control of. So, Dad demonstrated his value by inflicting pain upon others in the name of punishment and his need to win, even if it meant winning ugly.

Dad didn't always need to win ugly; he did win clean before we knew him as Dad. He was a standout high school basketball and football champion. Dad never talked about it to us, but we heard from some of Dad's old friends and our aunts and uncles. "Your dad was one hell of an athlete," we heard. "He could have played college ball if he hadn't entered the Navy."

Uncle Bob said Dad scored all fifty-six points in a 56-0 championship football game in 1942. Dad was the fullback and middle linebacker. We asked Dad if that story was true.

Dad said, in his matter-of-fact tone, "Yes."

"No way," said Jamie.

Dad replied, "Let's go."

Jamie, David, and I, not knowing where we were going, loaded in the Carryall with Dad behind the wheel. In silent excitement, Dad drove us to the office of the *Daily Journal* in downtown Kankakee. *Where could Dad be taking us?* At the front desk, Dad said he wanted to search old newspapers. We were led to a large room in the basement where Dad received instructions on how to find a particular article. After Dad fuddled with pieces that looked like photograph negatives, Dad loaded one of the films into a microfiche reader. He pulled up the front page of a newspaper dated October 1942 with the headline *MENARD RUNS AWAY WITH CHAMPIONSHIP GAME 56-0*. Jamie read that Dad did make all fifty-six points and set a Bradley High School record. Dad said nothing further on the subject.

Dad was also a gifted boxer, winning every Golden Glove match until he left for the Navy. Dad was the Navy boxing champion in his first year in the Navy. He went on to box in the Army-Navy championship, losing to the Army.

Maybe Dad didn't always have to win ugly. As *we* knew our dad, if there was a competition he was involved in, he had to win, even if it meant cheating, even if it meant winning ugly.

Football was Dad's favorite sport. We were all required to play high school football. Dad could not make many of our games, but we could do nothing right when he could be there. Never a compliment; it was always about what we could have done better, what we should have done.

Once Dad retired, he dove right into coaching. In 1972, he volunteered to coach the Kankakee Pop Warner Midget Football team of boys ages twelve to fifteen. Brothers Tim and Warren played on Dad's team. The Kankakee team had a long losing streak. Dad announced at the first parent meeting that his team would play in the December Titusville Florida National Pop

Warner game. He wasn't promoting a goal; he told the parents they had better start saving up for the airline tickets.

The first order of business for Dad as the new coach was recruitment, which was against the Pop Warner rules. The Pop Warner team played at the Bird Park football field, built expressly for the Pop Warner league. Bird Park was in the all-white section of Kankakee, so the entire team was white. While Dad was a racist through and through, he knew black athletes were superior. His reference point was the black high schools up north near Chicago, which dominated when they played against the primarily white Kankakee High team.

In 1970, segregation was illegal but prevalent. There was an all-black neighborhood in east Kankakee; Dad started hanging out and scouting in the black part of town. He explained to the black parents with boys between the ages of twelve to fifteen that their children were missing the opportunity to play football at an early age. Dad morphed from a bigot to a philanthropic hero.

I don't know where he got the money, but Dad paid the team membership and insurance fees for the boys he recruited. Most of the new black boys on the team couldn't get a ride across town to the Bird Park field, so Dad picked them up and dropped them off after practice. He became a father figure and best friend to his team.

Dad was a coach who focused on training and loyalty. Early on, Dad indoctrinated his players to have blind loyalty. If Coach Paul said it, then we believed it. For Dad, it wasn't about building character, it was about winning. Dad's pre-game warm-up was a spectacle. With precision, the black captain led the team in a series of drills; you would think you were watching Knute Rockne and his Notre Dame team on the field.

In his first season as coach, Dad's team was undefeated. They won big. Dad assembled a team of the best players and taught them to play dirty and win ugly.

If Dad's team was winning decisively, there was no need for

any foul play trickery. However, if he were in danger of losing, Dad gave secret signals that instructed his players to employ different levels of travesty. The first level was focusing on the other team's best players and attempting to injure them unfairly.

"Try to get your fingers through the guy's helmet. Go for their mouth and eyes. Push into their eyes, get them out of the game. Don't let the refs see you; do it on a pile-up." I heard Dad say many times.

Dad's players followed his instructions devotedly. If sidelining the opponent's team members wasn't enough, Dad signaled to use the hat pins hidden in the thigh pads. When in a pile, Dad's team members pulled out the hat pins and jabbed them into someone on the other team, creating a subliminal fear of being in a pile-up. Was it a bee? There was no blood or evidence; the pins were dropped to the ground and never discovered.

Dad used his most offensive tactic if the opposing team were primarily white. The target was typically the quarterback or a star running back. After a pile-up, one of Dad's black players jumped off the pile and yelled, "That quarterback just called me n----r!" In the racially-charged seventies, the umpire had to eject the player from the game.

Dad's team won the regional, district, and state playoffs ugly. He fulfilled his promise to Kankakee and brought his team to the national championship game in Titusville, Florida. With money raised by the Kankakee Chamber of Commerce, Dad chartered a plane and flew his team and their parents to the championship. He lost the game but remained proud of that season.

Dad coached seven seasons of Pop Warner Football. At his funeral, many of the black boys, now men, filed by Dad's casket to show their respects for their coach. Many cried openly at their loss as they told how Dad had changed their lives.

There was a sweet side to Dad's winning ugly. Dad and all his sons took a fishing trip during a long weekend in Little Rock,

Arkansas. We rented a large condo; it was a once-in-a-lifetime trip. We rented a pontoon boat to go out on the lake. On our first morning, we were loading up the boat when Dad announced the challenge for the day. We each put fifty dollars into the pot, and Dad would hold the $550. The rules: the one who caught the first fish of the trip won half of the pot, and the one who caught the smallest fish of the day got the other half. Everyone agreed.

After the pot was in Dad's pocket, he yelled, "First fish!" as he raised a minnow-sized fish over the boat railing. He had rolled up ten feet of fishing line with the tiniest fishhook on one end. He put a small piece of rolled-up bread on the hook and lowered it alongside the boat while still sitting at the dock. As we pulled into the dock after a great day of fishing, Dad shouted, "Smallest fish!" as he laughed hysterically. Dad had won ugly once again.

At dinner that evening, with Dad at the head of the table, he stood up, got the entire restaurant's attention, and said, "I want to thank you all for coming tonight. For those who don't know, we just completed a national fishing tournament here in Little Rock. I was lucky enough to win the tournament, so I will take my prize money and buy dinner for all those who participated in the Paul Menard Annual Fishing Tournament."

The entire restaurant applauded.

## REFLECTIONS

Growing up with opposite parents created an alchemy that explains how my siblings and I survived and thrived. Mom taught us that all truth was in the Bible, but Dad believed all truth was in his fists. Mom taught that we were all so blessed, but Dad thought he was under some curse. Mom taught us to be colorblind, that God made all of us equal in His image, and Dad taught us that everything wrong in America came from black men. It's not an embellishment that the actual differences between Mom and Dad were between good and evil, or fairer to say right and wrong. I have often said that we all grew up with an angel on one shoulder and the devil on the other. The most significant difference between Mom and Dad was their philosophy and beliefs on revenge and forgiveness.

These stories had to be told for completeness, but as I wrote the stories in this chapter, I felt a heavy burden: the weight of betraying Dad by revealing his weaknesses. Feeling bad for him choosing to live the way he did. He felt the need to cheat to win; there was no way winning the way he did felt good. Didn't it all just make things worse? Why couldn't Dad understand that he was enough, more than enough?

Winning ugly is the other side of the resentment coin.

As Dad aged, he mellowed. He became a grandpa loved dearly by his grandchildren. His meanness subsided, and his sense of humor grew. I never remember hearing Dad laugh when I was a child, but as a grandpa, he roared with laughter until his side hurt. His winning ugly turned into practical jokes and games he invented.

One of Dad's favorite games to play with his in-laws and grandchildren was his version of "Pin the Tail on the Donkey." Dad always needed an audience. The victim was seated in a kitchen chair and then blindfolded. Dad explained that he held an imaginary donkey and named a part of the donkey's body. The contestant would then point to the part on the imaginary donkey.

"Okay, now point to the donkey's ear."

The player pointed, and Dad would say in a winning voice, "Yes, perfect, that's his ear."

After correctly pointing out four or five body parts, Dad said, "You have a perfect score. One last try, point to the donkey's butt."

As the player raised their finger to point, Dad lifted an open jar of peanut butter and stuck it over the person's finger.

Everyone would burst into laughter, and the person would pull off their blindfold to see a finger full of brown, runny donkey-doo.

I still too often channel my dad when there is an opportunity to get even or get back at someone. I have inherited his devious mind and internal drive for revenge. When I share my diabolic plans with my wife Emilie, she gently guides me toward forgiveness, almost like Emilie is channeling my mom.

Until his death, I often turned to my dad to help formulate payback plans for any unfairness. I, too, found pleasure in getting even. The last time I conspired with my dad for retaliation was when I worked as an engineer for Johnson & Johnson at a location about thirty minutes north of Kankakee. I was a machinery engineer who designed and built machines that produced many consumer products. The parts I designed would be fabricated at several machine shops across the Chicagoland area. I assembled bid packages, sent them out to three vendors, and selected the vendor with the best price and delivery. Johnson & Johnson spent millions each year on machinery parts.

The head of my department was Don Babcock. He was the Director of Engineering at the time and a longtime employee. He was challenging and demanding. Don announced one day that he had selected one machine shop to produce all the machine parts, Bob Blask's machine shop. Don said Bob Blask had agreed to give us a thirty percent discount in consideration of Johnson & Johnson giving Bob all our machinery work. Bob Blask was a hard-working machinist who did good work. We were also promised faster deliveries.

I was testing out a high-speed machine when a critical metal shaft broke. I brought the post to Bob Blask's shop and asked that he make a replacement as fast as possible.

His workers made the part while I waited. All the engineers had a budget, and we were responsible for our spending. When the bill for that rushed part came in, I was shocked at the price:

$3,000. A few months earlier, I received a bid from Bob for that same part; it was $300. There had to be a mistake. I went to Bob's place with the invoice and the previous quote in hand. I needed an explanation.

Bob sat with his head down and said nothing for a few minutes; I waited.

"I don't know what to say, Mike," Bob said sadly. "I'm just going to give it to you straight, Mike, but you must promise me you won't tell anyone. Promise?"

I gave Bob my word.

"Don Babcock is on the take. He sets the price, which is always jacked up, and once he gets paid, I must pay him a fifty percent kickback. That's why he has told all the engineers to bring the work to me. If you tell Don Babcock, he will get you fired, Mike."

The next day, I had the opportunity to talk with Don, and I told him that Bob Blask was ripping us off and showed the invoice for $3,000. Don brushed it off and explained that Bob was getting greedy. Don would talk with Bob.

Business continued as usual. Engineers began complaining about Bob's prices, but Bob kept getting the work. Of course, I knew what was happening but said nothing to anyone except my dad. I explained to Dad what was happening and wanted a plan to rat out Don without anyone knowing it was me. Dad was concerned that the pilfering might be happening at the higher levels of the organization and that it would be too dangerous to try and go above Don. It took a few days for Dad to develop his master plan.

Dad was a distinguished-looking man. A well-kept beard with just the right touches of gray. He always dressed well: tweed jacket, a button-up sweater vest, and a button-down collar. Dad told me he would walk into my office. It was easy to find because everyone sat in office cubicles, including Don. When Dad approached me, I was to stand up, and Dad would pretend to whisper to me. Don was a vigilant man, always looking over his shoulder. Once I saw Don stand up and look at me, as I was sure he would do, I was to shake my head three times, count to ten, and then point directly at Don. Dad would turn to make sure Don saw him. As soon as Don saw Dad, Dad left the office in a pathway, ensuring there was no opportunity for Don to get to Dad.

The plan worked exactly as designed. Exactly. Within one minute, Don was at my cubicle, and I knew what to say.

Don inquired, "Who was just at your desk?"

"I don't know who he is."

"What did he want?"

"I don't know."

"Well, what did he say?"

"He wanted to know if I was Mike Menard."

"What did you say?"

"Well, of course, I said yes, I am Mike Menard."

"Why did you point him to me?"

"He asked me if I knew you, Don Babcock. I said yes. Then he asked where you sat, so I pointed to you. He just shook his head and said 'okay,' and then he left."

Dad explained that we had to plant the thought that someone was on to Don. Dad knew that once someone did something wrong, they would be constantly worried about being caught, and in Don's case, being caught meant losing his job and going to jail. Dad knew that Don would immediately assume Dad was from either the Johnson & Johnson internal auditors, the police, the FBI, or the IRS. This would lead Don to believe he was busted.

Don soon promoted me with a big raise and began treating me like I was his son. Don asked me regularly, "Has anyone talked with you about me?"

Bob Blask told me that Don believed he was being investigated and that his phone was tapped. Don stopped taking payments from Bob. Almost overnight, Don's jet-black hair turned white. He became paranoid and strange. He began losing his eyesight and, within a year, was blind. He retired and wasted away in his beautiful house in Palos Heights. Two years later, he died. Just bad luck? I don't think so.

We all know what guilt feels like, how debilitating and draining it can be. Don's guilt consumed him, robbed him of peace, and decayed his health.

Even though I had become a successful engineer in a world class organization, looking back I realize how my upbringing still allowed me to solve things the Paul Menard way. Wouldn't it had been better for me to simply inform leadership of Bob's stealing? Instead, I got pulled into being a winged monkey and playing Dad's game of getting even. I still find myself thinking to get even by "hitting first and hitting hard."

# FLIGHT OF THE MONKEYS

## CHAPTER 24

---

"The worst lies were the lies I told myself about the lies others told me."

– Alice Little

---

APPROXIMATELY EVERY TWELVE TO fourteen months, like clockwork, a new baby arrived at 118 South May Avenue. It was a welcome, exciting ritual. Part of that routine was farming us children out to our aunts and uncles, a logistics challenge for sure. These outings are some of my most vivid memories.

From ages six to twelve, I wet the bed most nights. No one wanted me as a house guest. I don't know what negotiations went on behind the scenes, but most of my aunts did not welcome me for these week-long stays. I didn't care where I would stay as long as Jamie was with me.

Aunt Edna was one of my favorites. She was severe but kind and regularly willing to help Mom. Aunt Edna married my Uncle Bob, my dad's brother. Uncle Bob had a successful cabinet-building business in Limestone, three miles west of Kankakee. Aunt Edna and Uncle Bob had six children: four girls and two boys. They had a beautiful stone home with plenty of room and food. They routinely took in two to three of us during Mom's deliveries.

When Billy, number seven, was born, Jamie and I went to Aunt Edna's. There were negatives and positives about staying at

Aunt Edna's. My girl cousins, Nancy, Becky, Mary Beth, and Julie, were all beautiful, blonde, blue-eyed, and were kind to Jamie and me. In addition, the food was good, and Jamie and I got our own room with a bed, and we both had a pillow. On the downside, the oldest cousin, Bobby-Lee, didn't want us around. He didn't want us to ask him if we could drive his go-cart or play with his things. He never said yes. Also, Aunt Edna was tough. She rarely smiled and she ran a tight ship.

To the Paul Menard family, Aunt Edna and Uncle Bob were rich. They had a lovely house and a nice car, and Bobby-Lee had an extreme go-cart that he raced on the weekends at a track near the fairgrounds. His go-cart had twin Briggs and Stratton engines and real tires, not stolen wagon wheels like we had on our go-cart. Dad took Jamie and me to Bobby-Lee's races a few times; we always got a banana-flavored snow cone from the concession stand. Bobby-Lee regularly took first place and brought home another tall, shiny trophy with a go-cart teetering on top.

Denny was Aunt Edna's second son, and he was Jamie's age. Denny was like his sisters, kind and happy all the time. Denny was stricken with polio at a young age, and his health declined rapidly. Denny couldn't breathe because his lung muscles were paralyzed by polio. When Jamie and I stayed at Aunt Edna's, Denny was kept alive by a coffin-like cabinet respirator with legs, better known as an iron lung. The cabinet enclosed Denny's body except for his head. While lying flat on his back, the air pressure in the confined space varied to stimulate Denny's breathing. The machine made a strange and loud 'whooshing' sound. Dad took Jamie and me to visit with Denny for about fifteen minutes at a time. We sat near Denny's head and talked with him. He was always happy to see us. So, when staying with Aunt Edna, we visited with Denny all day. Maybe Denny's condition was why Aunt Edna was always so serious.

On the first night of the sleepover, I was determined not to fall asleep. If I didn't sleep, I wouldn't wet the bed. I could not bear the thought of the embarrassment should Nancy discover that I wet the bed. Sometime in the middle of that night, I lost the battle, fell asleep, and immediately wet the bed. Like always, I woke when the warm wet turned to cold wet. There was no way I would stick around and face Aunt Edna's wrath. I got dressed and headed to 118 South May Avenue.

I knew the way home, and I arrived at daylight. Dad cleaned me up and put me to bed. Before his shift started at three, Dad brought me back to Aunt Edna's. She wasn't happy. When I walked by the crime scene, the bed was stripped to the mattress to expose the plate-size stain. There were two fans blowing on the stain. Everybody in the house knew what I had done. Aunt Edna might as well have given me a tee shirt with a giant *P* on the front. The next night, I felt the crinkle of plastic under my sheet. *Why hadn't she done this from the beginning?*

When Allen, number eight, was born, I stayed with Jamie and David at my favorite guest house: Aunt Rita and Uncle Babe's. They lived on a farm outside of Herscher. They were as poor as us, so we felt right at home. The three of us slept on the floor in the living room, and we each had a pillow. Aunt Rita was Dad's sister, and Uncle Babe was my dad's best friend. Uncle Babe farmed for a living and could fix anything. He talked so fast that we hardly understood him. He was a big guy with a big heart, always smiling. Uncle Babe listened intently to people. To make sure you knew he was listening, after every sentence, Uncle Babe said, "da heck," which we understood as "you don't say."

The O'Connor farm had horses, pigs, cows, and chickens. We used the horse trough as a swimming pool in the summer. Uncle Babe let us take turns riding his huge John Deere tractor with him while he plowed his farm. On one of my rides, I saw Uncle Babe push the earth and disrupt a thousand black snakes. I got so excited that I fell off the tractor, onto the plow, and right into the nest of snakes. In the fall, I gashed open my shin. Back at the house, Aunt Rita bandaged my leg and gave me a double serving of her warm fudge.

Aunt Rita made many desserts: brownies, cookies, and cakes. My cousin Linda introduced me to pouring milk over my cake. When I'm served ice cream and cake today, I let the ice cream melt into the cake and recall my stays at the O'Connor farm.

The big bonus of staying at the O'Connor farm was their television. Not all homes had TVs; we didn't have one on May Avenue. Aunt Rita and Uncle Babe had a big black and white TV, one of the original home TVs with tubes that had to be tested and replaced regularly.

It was a Saturday evening, and Dad visited us at his relative's home. It was a special night: the annual showing of *The Wizard of Oz*. Our cousins had seen it a year earlier and talked about it like it was magical. Aunt Rita made a jumbo batch of buttered popcorn. Dad stayed in the kitchen with Uncle Babe and his own bowl of popcorn, and all the kids went in to watch the movie.

I was full of excitement and expectation as the movie began. It was not what I expected. Like generations of children who witnessed the movie for the first time, I was traumatized. A witch smashed by a house, a green witch out to kill Dorothy, a group of small people with high-pitched voices whose appearance was odd at best, and the friendly Scarecrow having his limbs pulled off. But the scariest part of all was the monkeys with wings doing the bidding of the Wicked Witch. When David saw the winged monkeys, he cried and jumped into Dad's lap.

David recalls Dad pushing him off his lap while saying, "Look at your girl cousins, do you see them crying like babies? Get back in there and watch the movie."

David went back into the room with eyes closed and ears covered. When recalling those memories with David while writing this book, we both had a good laugh and then David told me he still has nightmares about those "fucking blue monkeys with wings." So do I.

## REFLECTIONS

I have watched *The Wizard of Oz* thirty or more times since. It's a beautiful movie full of positive messages. As an adult, I saw more in the film. I saw clinical syndromes in the Scarecrow, Tinman, and Cowardly Lion of depression, low self-esteem, and anxiety. What I saw most clearly in the movie as an adult was what my siblings and I had in common with those winged monkeys.

Like those monkeys, some of my siblings and I were under Dad's spell, compelled to do his evil bidding. Stealing for his benefit, hurting others with our fists, and damaging property in the name of revenge. Some flying monkeys are victims themselves, trapped by the lies and deception of the witch, not caring about the damage they are doing to themselves and others.

As flying monkeys, with the help of our mother, we began to realize that we were participants in our dad's evil plots as his true colors were revealed. We all had our metaphorical moment when *ding dong*, the Wicked Witch was dead.

There are incomprehensible things Dad did to and through some of us. Things that were wrong, hurtful, and even evil. Things that can be forgiven but never forgotten or explained away. The damage done by our dad varies in each child. It isn't easy to measure, but we know it's there.

When Jamie delivered Mom's eulogy, he said she taught her children many things, including mercy and receiving forgiveness that we didn't ask for or deserve. Most of Dad's children have reconciled with him through mercy and grace.

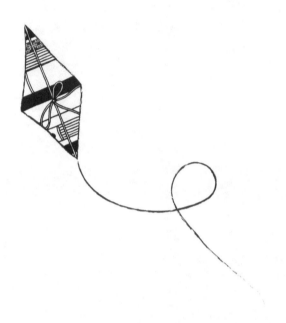

# AFTERWORD

A kite that can't fly can win first prize. A child who has experienced complex childhood trauma can become a happy, successful adult and can stand up straight with their shoulders back.

It is my opinion that Jordan B. Peterson has emerged as one of the most influential intellectuals in the world today. His recent book, *12 Rules of Life: An Antidote to Chaos*, has sold over five million copies. Rule #1: Stand up straight with your shoulders back. Peterson uses lobsters to make his main point. He tells his readers that scientists have been able to map the brain circuitry of lobsters. This work has helped us understand the brain's structure and function in more complex animals like humans. As it turns out, we have more in common with lobsters than anyone could have imagined.

Based on this research and Peterson's creative explanation, a loser lobster's brain is different from that of a winner lobster, and that chemistry correlates with the lobster's posture. A loser lobster cowers and shrinks, while a winner lobster stands tall. The winning lobster has high serotonin levels, stands erect, and struts his stuff. He will win almost every fight, get the best food and real estate, and always gets the girl. If you give a lobster who has just lost a fight an injection of serotonin, he will stand more erect and even pick a fight with the lobster that just beat his ass.

Peterson transfers the lobster logic to humans. Standing up straight with your shoulders back physically represents standing up mentally. He believes standing tall physically and metaphysically will cause your nervous system to respond differently. You will respond to a challenge versus bracing for a disaster. You will see the pot of gold at the end of the rainbow rather than fearing those combative leprechauns. You will take a step forward to take your place in the dominance hierarchy, occupy your territory, defend it, and transform it. In his book, Peterson writes that standing tall with your shoulders back "means that you willingly undertake the sacrifices necessary to generate a productive and meaningful reality."

I will not use loser or winner; it is simply too judgmental. But I will generalize and translate Peterson's description of "productive and meaningful" to have a high level of well-being and a general state of happiness.

As adults, my siblings and I stand tall and have uncommonly high levels of well-being, happiness, and success. My brother Mark, number twelve, and I were recently discussing how we Menards are so lucky, always land on our feet, and get the best jobs. We continue to be amazed at how our brother Warren undeservingly ended up with his remarkable wife, Lori. Mark explained, "I think the Menards are just a little smarter than the average bear." I think it is more than intelligence. I think we are outliers.

Malcolm Gladwell's best-seller, *Outliers: The Story of Success*, deals with exceptional people, especially those who are intelligent, rich, and successful, and those who operate on the extreme outer edge of what is statistically plausible. Gladwell's thesis argues that the idea of the rugged, individual success is inaccurate and that the "self-made man" is a myth. He makes the compelling case that people become successful based on circumstances that just happened to be in their favor. Those unlikely and hidden advantages and sometimes extraordinary opportunities allow the person to learn and work hard to make sense of the world in ways others cannot.

Gladwell believes success results from cumulative advantage and that seemingly unrelated benefits appear. Those early advantages lead to an opportunity, which makes the difference a little bigger, and that edge leads to another chance, which makes the difference more significant still—until that person becomes an outlier. Gladwell uses the Beatles' success as a great example. Most believe the Beatles were a group of gifted musicians. Well, they certainly had talent. But what most don't know about the Beatles' success is that it was born out of their early experience as a band.

Around the shipping docks in Homberg, Germany, the bars were open twenty-four-seven, and all the bars had live music. If you were a band lucky enough to get one of these gigs, you had to play twelve-hour shifts, seven days a week. The Beatles landed one of these gigs. Over the years that they performed at that bar, they played over 10,000 hours of live music. Running out of cover songs to play, Paul, George, and John began writing their own songs, perfecting them by practicing and refining the songs at the bar. They were not overnight wonders; they worked in the trenches playing twelve hours a day for two and a half years to perfect their music. Practice makes perfect.

My siblings and I didn't start as outliers; we were born into an unusual environment, one that included circumstances which would traditionally generate failure as opposed to success. As you will discover in the epilogue, my siblings and their children are outliers, successful by any measure.

I hope you agree that the dynamics and synergy of Mom, Dad, and fourteen children in a tiny house on May Avenue generated some interesting stories. But there is more than just entertainment here; there are "acres of diamonds" below the surface in the backyard at 118 South May Avenue.

If you had met my siblings, if you knew them, you would see what I know. My siblings are extraordinary people. This may be bloodline bias; however, I believe it to be real. You could not help but be drawn in by them. You would see joy and excitement in their eyes and hear it in their voices. If you see them together, you'll know they are part of a club you wish you were in, a club they would welcome you into.

You would see our mom's teachings come through. Teachings of unconditional love, faith, grace, mercy, patience, gratitude, hope, and love thy neighbor. You would see the Pygmalion effect in practice—believing will make it so. While many of our father's lessons were taught the wrong way, you would see the badassery embedded in each of us by him. You would have to dig a little deeper to uncover their success stories. Stories of unlikely success, leadership, creativity, tenacity, and unparalleled work ethic. Our Dad taught us different lessons, maybe taught in the wrong way, but just as universal. *Stand up for yourself. Don't fight, but if you must, hit first and hit hard. There is always a best way to do anything. Keep your head and chin up. You are a Menard.*

You would notice their posture, standing tall with their shoulders back, head and chin up. You may misread it as cockiness, but you'll soon discover it's confidence. These are winning lobsters.

I see personal strength when I see my siblings. Maybe the world becomes a less scary place after someone has experienced growth after childhood trauma. I've heard more than one of my siblings say, "If I survived my childhood, I can survive anything," and "Nothing can stop me now."

The May Avenue Stories are about what happened to us, but I must acknowledge what didn't happen. Brother Mark, told me, "As a child, I felt invisible like no one knew I was there."

What attention, nurturing, reassuring touch—fundamentally, what *love*—didn't Mark and my siblings get? Dr. Bruce Perry, MD, PhD, child psychiatrist and neuroscientist, believes neglect is as toxic as any childhood trauma.

It's easy to glamorize growing up in such a large family. Great memories and stories. Tales of love, endurance, and survival. While I have no regrets or resentment, I would be negligent to dismiss and overlook the sad side of growing up as one of fourteen children.

Our mother believed she had enough love for all her children. However, we each received one-fourteenth of her love. Was one-fourteenth enough? Our dad was absent and rough on us but rougher on some. What each of us experienced growing up in such a large family can be simplified as neglect and a form of parental abandonment. The psychological consequences can manifest as educational difficulties, low self-esteem, depression, and trouble forming and maintaining relationships. Some of us made out better than others. Patrick and Adam died of drug overdoses after years of struggling with addictions and mental illness. The dysfunctional environment of their youth had a foundational impact on their ending.

Was there more positive than negative in our childhoods? Is there something to be learned and applied? It's time for closing arguments.

Life is full of paradoxes. Abhysheq Shukla said, "It takes sadness to know what happiness is, noise to appreciate silence, and absence to value presence."

While there isn't much written on the paradox of complex childhood trauma, it's real. Within our family, childhood trauma created post-traumatic growth on one side of the spectrum and post-traumatic stress disorder on the other: growth and disorder. When I think about the Arletta and Paul Menard family, my heart swells with pride and joy. My heart is heavy when I think about losing Patrick and Adam to addiction, and when I recall other stories not included in this book. I know the childhood trauma we experienced created pain and scars in all of us. Regret sets in. Could I have done more to change the trajectory of Patrick's and Adam's lives? Could I have intervened and stopped some of the bad?

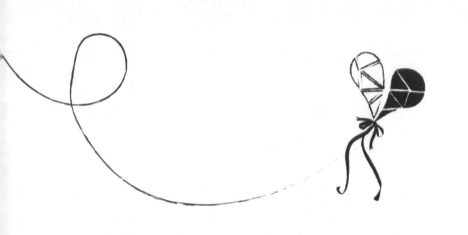

# THE PARADOX OF COMPLEX CHILDHOOD TRAUMA

"I believe not only that trauma is curable, but that the healing process can be a catalyst for profound awakening."

– Peter A. Levine, PhD

In addition to my successes, I researched many stories of fascinating people who had experienced complex childhood trauma. I was interested in people like my siblings who were committed to growing far beyond where they came from, transcending their childhood trauma and moving on to post-traumatic growth. They somehow saw trauma and adversity as possibilities for transformation, wisdom, and growth. They not only thought through and processed what had happened to them and recovered from it, but also enriched their lives. They more than survived; some emerged with a new understanding of life, a deeper connection to others, and an awareness of their divine purpose.

Complex childhood trauma is tragic, problematic, and knotty. Post-traumatic growth isn't automatic; it's challenging work. Experiencing post-traumatic growth is real; unfortunately, based on the stack of books listed in the Resources section of this book, it's the exception and not the norm. Complex childhood trauma can generate rocket fuel for post-traumatic growth, but it is also the fuel to power mental and physical disorders. This is the paradox of complex childhood trauma. It has the power to transform and to destroy.

I have witnessed this paradox in my family. Some siblings have achieved success and happiness beyond all expectations, while others experienced addiction and death. Some remain healthy, while others face diabetes, obesity, heart disease, high blood pressure, depression, and anxiety. Some have wobbled under the load, others have collapsed. No one knows why some collapse and others do not.

Here is the great news: suffering from complex childhood trauma does not have to be a life sentence. With awareness, love, and healing mental health treatment, those who have experienced childhood trauma can acknowledge their past and move on to a beautiful future.

*The Kite That Couldn't Fly: and Other May Avenue Stories* is not a "how to" self-help book to heal, grow, or transform. It simply demonstrates that it is possible. It can be a vehicle to ignite awareness and hope in readers who have experienced childhood trauma and adversity, or in anyone the reader might know, who are suffering from such past trauma.

For those who desire to know more about childhood trauma, with Kristin's help, I have included several books that have helped me understand the disorders and the possibility of healing. The book I recommend as a starter is *The Adverse Childhood*

*Experiences Recovery Workbook* by Glenn R. Schiraldi, PhD. It's written in everyday language and offers background and a guide on how to heal the hidden wounds from childhood trauma that affect adult mental and physical health. If a disorder is disrupting the well-being of the person affected, professional mental health treatment should be pursued.

Our oldest sibling, Jamie, has undoubtedly experienced post-traumatic growth as an adult. A success by all measures: a fantastic wife and children, a master's degree, a school principal, an entrepreneur, and a man of deep faith. However, experiencing post-traumatic growth doesn't always include a free pass on the disorders that come from childhood trauma. While writing this book, Jamie realized he had experienced uneasiness for years. Read Jamie's recovery story in the epilogue; it is intriguing and enlightening.

With the juxtaposed teaching principles of Mom and Dad, something almost magical happened. Dad did and said things that can only be explained as wrong, but some brilliance was mixed in with that wrong. I don't believe it was part of their parenting plan, but what played out in our lives might be explained by Carl Jung's belief:

"No tree, it is said, can grow to heaven unless its roots reach down to hell."

Jung was not discussing hell, and he was not talking about heaven. Instead, he made an analogy of light opposing darkness, that every high must have a corresponding low. Maybe we needed the bad and tough lessons as something to push against to reach up.

It's a fact that storms and wind are required for the roots of a tree to grow bigger and stronger. If you prevent a tree from being moved by the wind, the roots won't grow as strong or deep, increasing the probability of the tree toppling and preventing the tree from reaching its ultimate height. Adversity is necessary for the tree to strengthen, allowing it to withstand even more harsh conditions. Did the adversity in our lives make us stronger?

Would I have been better off if I could remove all the bad from my childhood? Maybe, but I fear all the happiness would be wiped out if I did. I'm proud of all my life experiences and will forever hold my uniqueness high in the air, just as I held the trophy I won with the kite that couldn't fly.

"The most beautiful people we have known are those who have known defeat, known suffering, known struggle, known loss, and have found their way out of the depths. These persons have an appreciation, a sensitivity, and an understanding of life that fills them with compassion, gentleness, and a deep loving concern. Beautiful people do not just happen."

– Elisabeth Kübler-Ross

# EPILOGUE

IN 1966, there was a significant migration for those living at 118 South May Avenue. Mom's father died, and we bought his house —six bedrooms, two bathrooms, and a big front porch. In June, we moved into the house at 389 South Washington, just across the river, the same distance to Bird Park. Dad converted the one-car garage in the alley into a pigeon coop. The May Avenue era had ended.

In 1970, Dad had a heart attack. The heart murmur he developed from rheumatic fever while in the Navy had destroyed three of his four valves. He had five open-heart surgeries and three artificial valves implanted. Dad couldn't work after his first surgery. Through Mom's tenacity, the VA deemed Dad 100 percent disabled due to his wartime illness. Dad began receiving monthly disability checks three times the amount Dad brought home from the factory. The amount of disability was calculated using the number of dependent children in the home. Those siblings over eighteen also received a monthly check, assuming they were in college. For the first time, Dad viewed having fourteen children as a blessing. He was rich.

The older seven siblings remember a different childhood and

dad than the younger seven. Many of my younger siblings find the May Avenue Stories unbelievable. They come to Dad's defense.

I hope one of my younger siblings will write the Menard family sequel. The South Washington Stories will be as rich as the May Avenue Stories. You won't read about poverty and hunger or the scarcity of lightbulbs, but you will continue to read about the alchemy of a tough and tender childhood.

## MOM

Mom continued to love, preach, and teach her children, in-laws, grandchildren, and everyone she encountered until her death at eighty in 2008. She died in the new home her children had bought for her. Mom had fourteen children, forty-five grandchildren, and fifty-five great-grandchildren as of the writing of this book.

Four months before her death, still beautiful with incredible skin, no wrinkles, and natural color in her hair, Mom was diagnosed with stage four uterine cancer. The siblings created a schedule; a team of two siblings would be with Mom in her home twenty-four-seven. One would tend to Mom. The other would run the house, cooking, cleaning, and telling Mom's visitors their time was up. In addition to the two siblings, there was always a group of Mom's children and grandchildren visiting with her during the day and joining in for dinner.

Mom was a blessing right up to her final breath.

Of course, mothers and grandmothers should be remembered in the very best light. As so it is with our mom, but it's different with us. Mom's children, grandchildren, and friends remember Mom almost as a legend. When my daughters talk about their Grandma Menard, they tear up even with the happy stories.

I hope these few May Avenue Stories provided a glimpse into the life of Arletta Menard.

## DAD

I must start with a retraction. Throughout the May Avenue Stories, I have called Dad a devil and even inferred he was evil. He was not. Dad was a victim of childhood trauma. He was limited and took on a Herculean job as the father of fourteen children. Throughout the book, I have contrasted Mom and Dad as good versus evil. The more accurate analogy would be right versus wrong.

After Dad's forced retirement due to his heart disease, Dad was a different man. His forty-five grandchildren adored him. He always had a new story, a joke or a wooden toy he made for them. Dad would make up hand signs and teach them to his grandchildren; each gesture would be connected to a swear word. He would make the grandchildren promise not to tell Mom and Dad; Grandpa Menard's secret. He was a rock star to his grandchildren.

At one of Mom and Dad's visits to New Hope, Pennsylvania, I invited Dad to come with me to a new product launch at Johnson & Johnson. I was the keynote speaker at the event. After my speech, I sat next to Dad.

He leaned over and asked, "Where did you learn to talk like that?"

"From you."

After a life of non-believing, Dad turned to Christ a year before he died. Mom's constant dripping on Dad finally paid off. He even became a eucharistic minister at Saint Martin's Church. I was so proud of Dad's transformation until Maria recently gave me insight into Dad's possible motivation for becoming a guy who delivered the communion host to the churchgoers.

In the Catholic Church, at every Mass, the ritual and one of the seven sacraments is for the priest, or as in Dad's case, the eucharistic minister, to administer the communion host to the parishioners. It's important to know that the Catholic Church believes the host is the Body of Christ. So, anyone who handles it must do so with respect and reverence.

After the consecration of the host by the priest, turning the bread into Jesus, those attending the Mass would walk piously up the center aisle with their hands clasped in prayer and wait in line to receive communion. When the person offering the communion, the priest or the eucharistic minister (Dad) would hold the host with one hand, between their thumb and index fingers at face level, and say, "The Body of Christ." The one receiving the host would respond "Amen" and then open their mouths and extend their tongue out. The one serving the host would then place the host onto the tongue of the receiver.

After Dad had given communion at a few masses, he told Maria and Adam to sit where they could watch Dad place the host onto the person's tongue. As they watched, with some parishioners, Dad would hold the host just an inch short of the person's tongue, causing the person receiving the host to lean in closer to Dad as Dad slowly pulled the host toward himself, causing the recipient to lean in even closer, until they had to step toward Dad. Only then would he place the host on to their tongues. Dad shared after that Mass that he only pulled that stunt on those he didn't care for. I felt silly thinking Dad had finally accepted God and became a eucharistic minister to secure a place in Heaven.

After five open-heart surgeries and continuous illness and recoveries from 1970 to 1996, Dad made the courageous decision to refuse a sixth surgery, a surgery the doctors said was required for Dad to live. He was given a fifty-fifty survival prognosis. He had had enough and forfeited the will to live. Dad died three weeks after he decided not to have that surgery. He had private talks with each of his fourteen children. He told us all the same thing at the end of each talk. "I wasn't a good dad, but I did my best."

Jamie, Polly, David, Warren, Maria, and Ellen inherited Dad's brilliant sense of humor. While sitting at Dad's bedside hours before his death, I was looking at the bank of monitors at the head of Dad's bed. I asked a stupid question, "Dad, what happens if one of those monitors stops working?" *Does a nurse come running in? Does it become a code blue?* With his matter-of-fact voice, Dad said, "There is a little speaker at the back of the monitor, and it will say, 'Goodbye, Paul.'"

While we will all challenge and dispute his parenting methods, there is no doubt of his positive influence. As Mom infused gratitude and forgiveness, Dad rooted us all in pride and did his best to help us overcome adversity in what, at times, was a dark setting. Like Guido, the father in the movie *Life Is Beautiful*, Dad used his creativity to make sad circumstances like a game.

One Christmas, when she was six years old and still believed in Santa, Maria asked Dad a tricky question: "Suzy across the street got a bicycle from Santa; I got pajamas. I've been a good girl, better than Suzy. Why didn't Santa give me a bike?"

Dad slowly looked over both shoulders to make sure no one else was listening while he came up with his answer. "Don't tell Suzy this, but Santa knows what children need. Suzy only has one brother. She isn't happy, so Santa gave her a bike to make her happy. But you, you have everything. You have thirteen brothers and sisters, you are happy, and you are a Menard. Suzy isn't a Menard, so she needs a bike to be happy."

Like Mom, Dad remains a legend among his children and grandchildren—the same, but different. His sons and daughters remember him as the king of badassery. His grandchildren remember him as a funny, loving grandpa with a bag full of tricks.

## JAMIE
### No. 1

Jamie's balloon has risen high in the sky.

After Jamie met and married Joanie, he experienced a life-long transformation.

Jamie and Joanie were immersed in the charismatic Jesus Movement of the '70s. They would admit they were "drunk" on God's milk. They still are. They both have been evangelists and living Christian lives their entire fifty-plus years of marriage. Jamie brought me to Christ when I was nineteen years old. He and Joanie continue to minister to us and to all they encounter.

Because of his poor high school grades, Jamie was rejected for admission into Southern Illinois University, where Joanie was enrolled. He attended a community college near Southern Illinois University for a few semesters, where he aced several freshman courses. He reapplied and was admitted to the university. Jamie received a bachelor's in Education with a minor in Special Education.

After graduation, Jamie and Joanie moved to Crawfordsville, Indiana, where they still live. They both landed teaching jobs; Jamie was teaching special education to a class of children with special needs.

Jamie invited me to join his class on a field trip to the Indianapolis Zoo. I rode the bus with Jamie and his class. Once we were all loaded in, Jamie said, "Let's pray." The entire class bowed their heads and pressed their hands together. After the prayer, Jamie asked if anyone had forgotten their lunch. Five of the twelve students raised their hands. Jamie had made extra lunches that morning; he knew some parents didn't have the money to pack a lunch.

I heard later that day from Jamie that he wasn't supposed to pray in the classroom, but he did. For some students, Jamie was their first exposure to prayer and faith.

Jamie went on to earn a master's in Education from Purdue University. He became a principal—true irony in real life.

After his educational career, Jamie founded several successful businesses.

Now retired, Jamie has three children and six grandchildren. All three of Jamie's children inherited his angelic voice. His daughter Rebecca is an opera singer and Luke was in the finals of *American Idol*, and performs daily in Branson, Missouri. Mark sings and plays the guitar, taking over Jamie's family business.

All my siblings met at Mary's home the Christmas after Mom's death. Jamie was the last sibling to arrive at Mary's. He walked in wearing a ten-gallon cowboy hat, chewing on a piece of straw. He closed the door behind him, stood with his hands in his jean pockets, and waited for the crowd to quiet.

With all of us looking at Jamie, he said, "There is a new sheriff in town."

Jamie remains our patriarch.

Towards the end of the book's writing, Jamie shared some very interesting developments in his life. I'll let Jamie tell his story.

*I HAVE KNOWN FOR YEARS THAT MIKE WAS COLLECTING MAY AVENUE STORIES FOR HIS BOOK. I HAD NO IDEA THE SOON-TO-BE-WRITTEN BOOK'S IMPACT ON MY LIFE. ABOUT SIX MONTHS AGO, MIKE TOLD US HE WAS PUTTING A SERIOUS EFFORT TOWARD PUBLISHING THE BOOK WITHIN THE YEAR. AS PART OF HIS RESEARCH AND PREP TO WRITE THE BOOK, MIKE ENLISTED THE OPINIONS OF THERAPISTS AND PSYCHOLO-GISTS. HE WAS DIGGING DEEP TO UNDERSTAND HOW AND WHY SOME OF US GREW AND EXCELLED IN LIFE DESPITE OUR CHILDHOOD AND WHY OTHERS DIDN'T. MIKE AND I WERE TALKING AND TEXTING ALMOST DAILY, AND WHAT*

HE WAS LEARNING AND SHARING WITH ME ABOUT CHILDHOOD TRAUMA BEGAN TO STIR MY INTEREST. MAYBE THERE WAS SOMETHING HERE FOR ME.

I'M CURRENTLY SEVENTY-FOUR. AT SIXTY-EIGHT, I EXPERIENCED SOME DAYS OF DEPRESSION. I HAD TROUBLE SLEEPING, AND I WAS DIAGNOSED BY MY PRIMARY PHYSICIAN WITH ADULT ADHD. I TOOK THE RECOMMENDED MEDICATION, BUT MY ISSUES PERSISTED. AFTER HEARING WHAT MIKE WAS LEARNING ABOUT CHILDHOOD TRAUMA, I MET WITH A PSYCHIATRIST TO SEEK HELP. THAT DOCTOR REFERRED ME TO A THERA-PIST WHOSE AREA OF FOCUS WAS TREATING PEOPLE WHO HAD EXPERIENCED ADVERSE CHILDHOOD EXPERI-ENCES. AFTER MY FIRST SESSION WITH MY THERAPIST, DEB HEWITT, SHE RECOMMENDED WE TRY EYE MOVE-MENT DESENSITIZATION AND REPROCESSING, OR EMDR THERAPY FOR SHORT.

AS MIKE RESEARCHED CHILDHOOD TRAUMA, I TOOK A DEEP DIVE INTO RESEARCHING EMDR AND DISCOVERED IT WAS DEVELOPED BY DR. FRANCINE SHAPIRO IN 1987. I READ DR. SHAPIRO'S BOOK AND SEVERAL OTHERS, INCLUDING STUDIES PROVING THE EFFICACY OF DR. SHAPIRO'S DISCOVERY.

ON THE SURFACE, EMDR SOUNDS A BIT STRANGE. THE THERAPY DOESN'T REQUIRE TALKING OR DRUG THERAPY. NO HOMEWORK OR JOURNALING. IT'S A PROCESS THAT UTILIZES EYE MOVEMENT TO TAKE THE TRAUMATIC MEMORY AND RE-PROCESS IT. IT DOESN'T REMOVE THE MEMORY; IT INSTEAD MOVES IT TO A DIFFERENT PART OF THE BRAIN AND REMOVES ITS DEVASTATING EFFECT ON THE PERSON'S WELL-BEING. MIKE HAD ALSO DONE INDEPENDENT RESEARCH ON

EMDR THAT REINFORCED MINE. WHILE REMAINING
SKEPTICAL, I DECIDED TO GIVE IT A TRY.

HERE IS AN EXPLANATION ABOUT EMDR AND MY
EXPERIENCE FROM MY THERAPIST, DEB HEWITT:

"EMDR, as with most therapy approaches, focuses on the individual's present concerns. The EMDR approach believes past emotionally charged experiences overly influence your present emotions, sensations, and thoughts about yourself. For example: 'Do you ever feel worthless although you know you are a worthwhile person?'

EMDR processing helps you break through the emotional blocks that keep you from living an adaptive, emotionally healthy life.

EMDR uses rapid eye movements to help you update disturbing experiences, much like when we sleep. We alternate between regular sleep and REM (rapid eye movement) during sleep. This sleep pattern alternates between sets of eye movements and brief reports about what you notice. This alternating process helps you update your memories to a healthier present perspective.

I had the privilege of working with Jamie Menard as his clinical therapist and provided EMDR Therapy. Jamie came in with a three-page list of memories from birth to present. Within four EMDR processing sessions, Jamie reviewed the initial list and realized the highest-level score on a scale of zero to ten (most disturbing), moved from eight, nine, and ten disturbing memories to zeros, only one memory a five. We plan to clear that memory at the next session."

OF COURSE, EVERYONE'S EXPERIENCE WITH CHILD-
HOOD TRAUMA IS DIFFERENT, AND I KNOW THERE IS NO

ONE-SIZE-FITS-ALL THERAPY. AS MIKE HAS WRITTEN, HIS BOOK IS NOT INTENDED TO BE A SELF-HELP BOOK. BUT WHAT I DO KNOW, AND CAN SAY WITH CONFIDENCE, IS THAT THE TRAUMA CAUSED BY CHILDHOOD NEGLECT AND ABUSE HAS THE POTENTIAL TO REAR ITS UGLY HEAD AND CAUSE DISORDER YEARS, EVEN DECADES AFTER THE TRAUMA TOOK PLACE.

I WISH I HAD KNOWN WHAT I KNOW NOW ABOUT THE ABILITY TO HEAL SOONER. IF YOU FEEL YOU MAY BE SUFFERING FROM CHILDHOOD TRAUMA, PLEASE TAKE THE FIRST STEPS TO SEEK THE HEALING YOU DESERVE. CHILDHOOD TRAUMA DOESN'T HAVE TO BE A LIFE SENTENCE.

– JAMIE MENARD

# MIKE
## No. 2

Mike lettered in football, basketball, and track in junior high school. In his freshman year, he was stricken with rheumatic fever, which ended his sports career.

In 1966, at fifteen, Mike moved out of 118 South May Avenue and into 389 South Washington Avenue. That same year, he joined a band, Those Guys, and met his first love, Ellen.

Ellen and her family exposed Mike to a whole new world. Ellen's father, Ed, took Mike under his wing and treated him like a son-in-law to be.

One day, Ed handed Mike a draftsman set of tools. Ed began his engineering career as a draftsman and suggested that Mike take a mechanical drawing course at school. "I think you would be good at this," Ed said. (And maybe you can support my daughter and her family.) That was one of life's defining moments for Mike.

Things didn't work out for Mike and Ellen, but he did take that class, which led to an apprenticeship at General Foods. He went to high school in the morning and worked at General Foods in the afternoon. Around that same time, based on his experience babysitting his younger siblings, Mike came up with the idea of disposable baby diapers with elasticized legs.

When Mike shared his diaper idea with Johnson & Johnson, he landed a job with them as a machine designer in Chicago. He attended night school for ten years and earned a bachelor's in Business Administration. That diaper idea led to his first US patent, and as of 2023, the worldwide market for disposable diapers was over $50 billion. Thirteen additional US patents later, at the end of his twenty-five-year career at Johnson & Johnson, Mike had become the first worldwide Vice President of Engineering for Johnson & Johnson. As his second career, Mike co-founded The GenSight Group, a leading global software corporation. During his work with GenSight, Mike became one of the original signatories of the United Nations Global Compact of Sustainability and Business Ethics. Mike remains the president of his company.

Mike is the author of *A Fish in Your Ear* and *The Kite That Couldn't Fly.*

Mike has five daughters and nine grandchildren and lives in College Grove, Tennessee, with his wife Emilie and their daughter Stella. Mike continues to take music lessons and plays his guitar most evenings.

Before Mike gave a keynote speech at The Coca-Cola Company in 2005, the Chief Innovation Officer at Coca-Cola, Danny Strickland, introduced Mike as, "The nicest and smartest person I have ever met."

## POLLY
## No. 3

Polly is now seventy years old. After high school, Polly put herself through nursing school and became a registered nurse. Our brother Allen changed Polly's nickname from "Bird Legs" to "Nurse." To this day, we call Polly Nurse.

Polly loved being a nurse. In addition to her full-time job, Polly had an almost full-time second job: tending to Dad. In 1971, Dad had his first heart attack, which began a continued decline in his health. Dad was a severe diabetic and was in and out of hospitals for twenty years until his death at age sixty-nine. Polly was by Dad's side twenty-four-seven. She was a great nurse and dedicated daughter. Polly treated our father as if he was the best dad in the world. Dad was always so thankful for Polly; they developed a beautiful bond, of which we were all a bit jealous.

Polly evolved to be a trauma nurse specialist. She has been in leadership roles in women's programs at her churches, volunteered for hospice, and serves as a eucharistic minister at church.

She was a role model who influenced our sister Mary, brother Tim, and countless nieces and nephews entering the healthcare profession.

Polly was always a bit crazy; she still is. When Mary brought Michael Kohl home (Michael became Mary's husband) to meet the family for the first time, Polly orchestrated an odd welcoming scene. She had all her ten younger siblings lie on their backs on the floor and impersonate dead frogs. To this day, Polly remains the class clown of the family. Sister Polly fought and won a hard battle with ovarian cancer.

Polly and Don have been married for forty years, and her focus today is her three sons and their families, which include six grandchildren.

Everyone loves Polly.

# DAVID
## NO. 4

David deserves his own book. When he tries to be, he is hilarious. When he isn't trying, he is even funnier.

When I was eighteen, David was fourteen. Jamie loaned us his brand-new Toyota Corolla and David and I took our first road trip. We drove through the night from Kankakee to St. Augustine, Florida, where we both saw the ocean for the first time. We traveled around Florida for a week, deep-sea fishing, swimming in the ocean, and enjoying fancy dinners. David and I regularly reminisce about our trip; it created a bond between us that has lasted a lifetime.

David had a rough start to life. You have read about the tragedy of having his hand burned as a child. In addition, Dad was more demanding on some, and David got an unfair dose of criticism and put-downs.

When a child who has experienced complex childhood trauma gets hit with trauma as an adult, the impact is many times worse. When David was sixteen, his prom date, Debbie, became pregnant. David quit school and took a job at the local corn processing factory. David and Debbie married soon after, and their first child was born. They had three children before they were twenty-one.

It was an unhappy marriage from the beginning. Debbie didn't take well to motherhood or housekeeping. After a twelve-hour shift at the mill, Debbie demanded that David clean half of the floor, even half of the toilet seat. Their marriage ended in an ugly divorce; David won full custody of his three daughters. I remember how difficult life was for David as a single father. Interestingly, David spoke on the Oprah Show years later about his single father experience. He spoke with pride and confidence.

David met Sue at the local drugstore while raising his young daughters. They married and became a blended family: Sue's young son and David's three daughters, and then one daughter together. Sue was and is the perfect partner for David. She sees everything good in David and continues to love him as if she is still trying to make up for the deficits he experienced earlier in his life.

David went on to have a thirty-five-year career at Armstrong Flooring Company, progressing from floor sweeper on the production line to quality control. I attended David's retirement party; the love and admiration for David as a friend and colleague was heartwarming. His co-workers lined up to tell me their favorite stories about David.

David is our go-to on many things: bargaining for a car or motorcycle, maintaining a perfect lawn, canning corn, and fishing. David has been a "master angler" his entire life; he has held the national record for the largest Northern Walleye Pike and still enjoys bass fishing with his cousin and best friend, Ricky Africano.

David has undoubtedly wobbled under the load of childhood and early adult trauma, but he has not buckled or collapsed. David is a beautiful example of the hidden gifts of childhood trauma. Since meeting Sue, David has been on a constant post-traumatic growth trajectory. I do not doubt that David still wobbles from that childhood trauma, but his wife, children, grandchildren, and siblings surround him with sustaining love.

## MARY
No. 5

Mary went on to have a beautiful life.

She became a Registered Nurse following high school and took nursing roles of increasing responsibility. Her specialty was operating room nursing, and I have heard glowing stories over the years about her proficiency and gifts in the OR. Mary continues to be a valuable source of advice and comfort to us all. I had open-heart surgery a few years back, and Mary and my nurse daughter, Anna, took twelve-hour shifts by my side in the hospital and my first week of recovery at home. What a fantastic team they were.

Mary married Michael Kohl, the love of her life, shortly after high school. They have three exceptional children and eleven grandchildren. After forty-five years of marriage, Michael is now gone, and Mary lives on the Kankakee River and is the Vice President of Clinical Services at Riverside Hospital.

Being the fifth oldest sibling, Mary was involved in or remembered all the May Avenue Stories. I recall Mom and Dad being unfairly watchful over Mary, unjustly accusatory and critical.

Like many of us, special people came into Mary's life as a young girl who helped direct and guide her and demonstrated that a better life is possible.

While some insecurities and painful memories remain from those May Avenue days, Mary is also an example of post-traumatic growth and beautiful redemption. She is a together, happy woman and always willing to help. While most of my siblings tend to exaggerate and cover the lily with gold (me included), we can always count on sister Mary to tell it like it is.

# TIM

## No. 6

While Tim was undoubtedly part of the May Avenue tribe, there are no stories specifically about him as a child. He was too young; he was nine when we moved out of 118 South May Avenue.

As a young man, I remember Tim as exceptionally handsome; he was an avid bodybuilder, which added to his beauty. With Dad as his coach, Tim was a standout athlete, playing in the Pop Warner Midget Football National Championship in 1972.

I remember Tim being highly sensitive, full of emotion, and would cry easily at anything happy or sad. He is still a very sensitive guy. Also, while I have some very bright siblings, I've always said Tim is the smartest of us all. He speaks with deep knowledge and authority on most subjects.

After high school, Tim became a registered nurse and quickly developed a passion for and expertise in emergency room practice. Tim said he thrived in the ER. But he wanted to do more, bigger things in medicine. Tim became a physician assistant; a licensed PA. Tim completed his internship and went on to practice his craft until a work-related accident ended his career.

Tim used his education and love for his family to provide a high level of care for our dad through twenty-two years of serious health issues. Tim was Dad's personal "doctor," and seemed to always be at his side. There is no doubt Tim extended our dad's life and covered Dad with a blanket of security and confidence. Tim provided that same loving care to our mom as she aged and during her short bout with cancer. Tim's siblings remain so thankful for the years of service to our parents. Tim continues to be a valued resource to all of us. He is still the first one I call when faced with anything medical.

At age sixty-six, Tim is living with serious health issues. Issues that are severely limiting his mobility and quality of life. Even in Tim's weakened position, he continues to help his siblings, their children, and close friends with his time and generosity. Tim has had open heart surgery, multiple strokes, has recently had a pacemaker installed, and suffers from diabetes, which has created neuropathy in his feet. A few months ago, Tim had another stroke, damaging his sight. The pain and imbalance caused by his diabetic neuropathy make it difficult to stand, let alone walk. And lately, the neuropathy has migrated to his hands. With all this going on, Tim is understandably experiencing episodes of depression and anger.

In preparation for this book, I asked Tim about his May Avenue memories. He said he had no memory of any adverse childhood experiences and no recollection of any childhood trauma. Hearing this, I replied, "Wow, I'm surprised, Tim, but I'm happy for you." However, I wasn't convinced.

I shared with Tim the findings from my research as part of the book project. It has been proven that those who have suffered complex childhood trauma have experienced severe health issues later in life. Tim didn't think that was the case for him.

"I'm just getting old, Mike; this is the shit that happens." And then Tim began to cry. "I want to stop now, Mike; I just don't like talking about this anymore." He wasn't mad, he was sad. He continued, "What should I do, Mike? Get a shovel and start digging until I find something from my past? And what if I can find something? Will it make my health issues go away or even get better?" I had obviously hit a nerve. What didn't I know about my brother Tim?

"No, Tim, it won't reverse any of the illnesses you are struggling with, but looking into your past just may help you spend the rest of the time you do have left happier, with less depression and anger," I replied. "And, Tim, I don't think you would have to dig very deeply."

I made a closing pitch about how professional mental health care has the potential to help him. Tim was quite adamant that it might also make things worse. I'm pretty sure Tim's shovel will stay in the garage.

## BILL
## NO. 7

What a joy Billy is. He was born William Vincent Menard after Sister Saint Vincent, the nun who helped deliver Billy in the hospital. His nickname became Vincent, which morphed into Vit-ent.

Billy was a good but hard child. He was stubborn and solid. He had Dad and Jamie's athleticism and muscles. At sixty-five his biceps are still hard as nails. Bill was a champion diver in high school; I loved watching Billy dive off the high dive at the Kankakee swimming pool.

Bill's athletics and schooling ended when his girlfriend Sue became pregnant at age sixteen. Sue was a loving new mother and loving wife. But like most teenage parents, they divorced a few years later. Billy now has five children and eight grandchildren.

Being the seventh sibling, Billy was at the end of the May Avenue era stories. He remembers doing without but has no dramatic May Avenue stories. I recall Billy being the tough brother.

I was babysitting Billy one day at May Avenue. I was maybe fourteen, Billy was seven. Billy was pestering Allen, so I ordered him to stop. He kept it up, so I gave him two swats on his bottom —hard swats. He didn't flinch. I hit him harder, no reaction. He stared at me with his face, saying, "Go ahead, I can take whatever you've got." I knew he would win this battle, so I walked away.

Bill began shining shoes at the local bar; Dad had made him and Patrick wooden shoe-shining boxes. He was a superstar salesman, and having money in his pocket on his first day of work transformed him. When talking about writing this book, Billy told me about that first day of work. "I got it immediately, how to make money. I knew I would never be hungry again."

Billy became a standout and award-winning salesman at his first job as an adult. He was driven and had a wife and a new baby to support. His garage began filling up with trophies and plaques, always Salesman of the Year. He had a gift; you can still witness his gift when talking with Billy. He says everything with a smile.

Billy, like several of his siblings, is a serial entrepreneur. Billy opened a thriving restaurant and bar and founded pest control and garment embroidery businesses that have bloomed into successful companies. He has interests and serious hobbies that consume him. He learned carpentry from our Dad and makes fine furniture. He is a gifted, self-taught musician who plays the cello, banjo, and saxophone. He could play any instrument he desired.

Like several of us, Billy has struggled with overeating and obesity. He has had open heart surgery, carotid artery surgery, and diabetes. I'm optimistic about Billy's future, though. He treats his health seriously, looks and feels great, and enjoys life with his loving wife, Karen, and their grandchildren.

## ALLEN
### No. 8

Allen was the best of us, and every sibling agrees. Not because he is gone. Billy recently shared a story when we were joking about Allen being Mom's favorite:

"We all knew Allen was Mom's favorite. Maybe it was because he was such a sickly child, always in and out of the hospital. Remember how Mom would wake all of us for school? She would scream at us and threaten to pour cold water on us if we didn't jump out of bed. Do you remember how Mom woke Allen?" Three of us began singing Mom's wake-up call for Allen in a syrupy melody, "Allen daden, bebop Allen, Allen daden." And I am not embellishing this story for effect.

Allen was number eight, smack in the middle of the fourteen. Mom took the longest break between Billy and Allen, three years. Maybe she was more ready for Allen; perhaps she caught her second wind.

Allen's magnetic personality and leadership qualities surfaced as a young boy. In his teenage years, Allen was no angel; he was always on the edge of doing wrong, but he never crossed the line. On graduation day, Allen rode his red Honda motorcycle right into the school and around all the halls.

Everyone knew and loved Allen. For his junior prom, Allen invited his cousin Wendy as his date. Wendy had a severe illness with her spine as a child and young woman. Her spine was severely curved, and she wore an apparent brace. She was a beautiful girl, but Wendy looked and walked differently. And being "different" in high school doesn't help with getting a prom date. Wendy continues to tell her Allen story with such tenderness.

Allen wasn't the best football player at McNamara High School but was the team captain and spirit leader. Upon Allen's death, his football jersey, #44, was retired. Allen's lucky number forty-four has become legendary within the extended Menard family. A family group text thread is named #44 and is used for the daily spotting of anything #44: the time, a highway sign, the temperature, a receipt number, and so on. The current group includes Allen's wife Diane, their five children, all siblings, in-laws, nieces and nephews, and even great nieces and nephews. Many in the group never had the opportunity to know Allen, but they all know *of* him. Because of who he was, his legend stays alive.

The love between Allen and his wife Diane remains a gold standard, a marriage everyone should strive to replicate. I recall something Allen shared: "When coming up our driveway, when I hit the garage door opener and see that Diane's car in there, I still get the same rush of emotion that I felt when seeing her walk down the aisle at our wedding."

If I could ask Allen about his childhood, I believe I would hear only good memories. Honestly, I think Allen escaped all possible childhood trauma. If he did experience any such trauma, he used it as rocket fuel for growth and success.

After receiving his bachelor's degree from Governors University, Allen became a superstar salesman, breaking all records and rapidly advancing in his company. Sales excellence wasn't enough; he went on to achieve an MBA from Northwestern's Kellogg School of Business, the most prestigious business school in the country at the time. Allen struggled with the courses, but he excelled.

Allen's knowledge of and faith in God grew steadily throughout his adult life. What an excellent example of a man in love with Jesus.

At the age of forty-four, Allen was diagnosed with Stage 4 colon cancer. His eighteen-month battle was his final demonstration of an exemplary life. Anyone and everyone could have benefited by knowing my brother Allen. The story of his life is deserving of its own book.

To get a glimpse of the best of us, I share a letter Diane, Allen's wife, recently wrote to Allen's five children, sixteen years after Allen's death:

JUNE 15, 1960

WHAT A DAY THAT WAS!

I WONDER IF GRANDMA KNEW WHEN SHE HELD DAD FOR THE FIRST TIME THAT HE WOULD HAVE SUCH A DYNAMIC, CONTAGIOUS LAUGH.

I WONDER IF SHE COULD TELL BY LOOKING INTO HIS EYES THAT HE WOULD BE SO PASSIONATE ABOUT WHAT ENERGIZED HIM AND THAT HE WOULD USE HIS EYES TO DRAW OTHERS IN AND CONNECT ON SUCH AN AMAZING LEVEL.

I WONDER IF SHE LOOKED AT HIS NINE-POUND BABY BUILD AND KNEW THAT HE WOULD FIGHT AND PROTECT THE ONES HE LOVED.

I WONDER IF SHE SAW HIS BIG HEAD AND KNEW IT WAS ALREADY FILLED WITH OUT-OF-THE-BOX INTELLI-GENCE THAT WOULD CHANGE MANY LIVES.

I WONDER AS SHE FELT HIS HEARTBEAT IF SHE KNEW HE HAD A HEART OF GOLD AND WOULD LOVE HIS WIFE AND KIDS SO PROFOUNDLY THAT THEY WOULD FEEL LIKE THE LUCKIEST PEOPLE ALIVE.

AS SHE WATCHED HIM BREATHE, I WONDER IF SHE KNEW EACH BREATH WAS A GIFT TO HUMANITY AND WOULD BE REMEMBERED AND CHERISHED LONG AFTER HE WAS GONE.

WHAT WOULD OUR LIVES BE LIKE WITH HIM STILL HERE?

BUT I DON'T HAVE TO WONDER FOR LONG.

I KNOW HE WOULD BE OUR BIGGEST ENCOURAGER.

I KNOW HE WOULD BE TOTALLY INVOLVED IN OUR BUSI-
NESS AND PERSONAL LIVES. HE WOULD HAVE BREAK-
FAST, LUNCH, COFFEE, AND DINNER DATES WITH US AS
OFTEN AS POSSIBLE. I KNOW HE WOULD BE DOING
CANNONBALLS IN THE POOL WITH HIS SONS AND
GETTING MANI/PEDIS AT THE NAIL SALON WITH HIS
CLAIRE. I KNOW HE WOULD BE TRAVELING THE WORLD
WITH ME AND ENJOYING EVERY SIGHT AND PERSON HE
CAME IN CONTACT WITH. I KNOW HE WOULD BE ON THE
PHONE WITH HIS SIBLINGS DAILY. I KNOW HE WOULD
RIDE HIS HARLEY DOWN CUTALOOSA ROAD AND STOP AT
YUM YUMS FOR DAILY DONUTS. I KNOW HE WOULD
WASH THE CARS AND BIKES IN THE DRIVE AND RELAX ON
THE PORCH SWING WITH A CUP OF BLACK COFFEE. I
KNOW HE WOULD BE LAUGHING UNTIL HIS BELLY HURT.
I KNOW HE WOULD BE AHEAD OF THE FASHION TRENDS
WITH HIS STYLE. I KNOW HE WOULD BE WEARING THE
SAME COLOGNE. HE WOULD BE RUNNING ASH MILL
ROAD EVEN IF HIS BACK HURT. I KNOW HE WOULD
SPEND EVERY MINUTE WITH US DOING WHAT WE LOVE
TO DO... EAT, LAUGH, TALK.

I KNOW IF HE HAD A CHOICE, HE WOULDN'T HAVE
LEFT.

ON THIS WOULD-BE SIXTY-THIRD BIRTHDAY, I WILL
CELEBRATE THE ONE WHO ROCKED OUR WORLDS AND
LOVED US LIKE NO OTHER!

HAPPY BIRTHDAY, ALLEN HENRY MENARD.

THE KITE THAT COULDN'T FLY

## PATRICK
## No. 9

Mom always said that Patrick was her prettiest baby. Mom was his greatest fan and understood and protected him more than any of her children. Dad was harder on some of his sons and the hardest on Patrick. From an early age, Patrick was a hustler. He wanted to make money and learned that shining shoes on Friday night in the local bars was a way to make a load of money for a twelve-year-old. It was then that we believe Patrick started drinking. He was an altar boy and got caught drinking the wine behind the altar. Those are my earliest memories of Patrick's troubles, and they followed him everywhere he went.

As a teenager, Patrick spent a lot of time at the local pool and ice arena. He was a fantastic speed skater. At age thirteen, he entered a few local competitions and would come in first place, even against seventeen and eighteen-year-olds. He caught the attention of a pre-Olympic program in Springfield, Illinois. The coaches met my parents and offered to take Pat to Springfield to live and train in speedskating. They believed his skating was Olympic-grade. Patrick was that good, with skates three times too big for him. He bought the skates from a local pawn shop with his shoeshine money.

Mom didn't want to give her son to strangers, and my dad said we didn't have the money to support him. That was a brutal hit for Patrick; he would have to wonder what could have been. Pat was good at everything he did. He didn't care about school and hated being in the classroom. His grades were awful in high school, and when my dad came down on him for it, he decided to show my dad that he could get straight A's if he wanted to. He did it. He had all A's the next semester and then quit high school. Some say he did it to piss my dad off; others say he was expelled for getting caught smoking cigarettes on school grounds for the last time. Patrick did go on to get his GED, and we were proud of him for following through.

Pat was labeled the black sheep early on and made terrible choices that got him into trouble repeatedly. There was one thing you could do to piss our dad off: embarrass him. Pat did this by having his name in the paper for being arrested for trying to outrun the police on his minibike. Getting into trouble at school or with the law became a pattern for Patrick as alcohol and drug addiction took over his life. My dad continued to come down hard on Patrick. That may have fueled Patrick's addiction. Patrick was in the local jail often as a young man. There was no money to bail him out of jail, and despite our dad wanting to leave him in there, Mom would somehow round up enough money to get him out.

Patrick was a good guy with a big heart. He was tough and afraid of no one. Patrick frequented the bars, and he often ended up in a fight. I'm sure he was antagonized because he had a reputation as a Menard, and that meant you were tough and couldn't be beaten. In everyday life, that meant people didn't mess with you; in a bar scene, you better be ready to prove yourself. Patrick had no problem proving how tough he was. We used to get calls to the house from local bar owners warning us to get Patrick before he got killed. Maria remembers getting the calls and running to the older boys' rooms to wake them in the wee hours of the morning to help Pat.

Patrick moved to Texas to work in the construction boom that was happening. We hoped the move would straighten him out, but he found trouble with the law there and his drug use continued, so he ended up coming back home. He was in and out of rehab, always trying to stay clean. He did want to be clean. He met a girl and fell in love; she made it her mission to get Patrick clean and sober. She managed to do it. They bought a house and had a son, and while it was hard, Pat stayed clean for years. He worked as a coffee machine serviceman for the Tri-

State area and had an accident in his work truck during a winter storm where he broke his back in several places. After surgery, Patrick quickly became addicted to pain medication, and he spiraled. He divorced his wife and went from job to job, working construction and trying to stay clean. He remarried and had two more sons. Patrick continued using drugs and alcohol and eventually did time in the county jail.

After his release, Patrick worked construction and continued his alcohol and drug abuse. During that time, Patrick had united with his first son, who was from a brief relationship in high school. He was a grandfather and was introduced to his grandson. Patrick was looking forward to making up time with his son and grandson, but he continued to struggle with pain med addiction when an overdose took his life at age fifty.

Patrick loved his boys, and while they knew their father struggled with addiction, they also saw the awesome guy he was when sober. Patrick's memory lives on in his boys. His two older boys are strong and hard-working men with children of their own and are excellent fathers. His two younger boys still live with their mother.

Patrick was fun and a favorite uncle to many of the grandkids. He will be remembered and respected for his kind soul, strong work ethic, fantastic carpentry skills, and love for family and fishing.

## WARREN
No. 10

Warren is a wonder. He is a crazy but awesome man.

There are no May Avenue stories involving Warren; he was just a baby when we moved to Washington Avenue.

Warren's nickname is Bones; when he was a young boy, he was so skinny his hand-me-down tighty-whities had to be held up.

Warren was a star basketball player. He was always a goofball and was so funny that he should have been a stand-up comic. Warren draws a crowd whenever we can goad him into dancing —he could make Prince walk off the dance floor. His grandchildren, nieces, and nephews surround him, always waiting for the next performance.

Warren married Lori, and some thirty-seven years later, she still laughs at his jokes and capers. After marrying Lori, she gently guided Warren to college, and he became an occupational therapist, work he still does today. Warren has four children and eight grandchildren. His grandchildren adore him, maybe because he is one of them.

There is no evidence of any childhood trauma in Warren today.

Warren's view of May Avenue is this:

> I HAVE HAD THE PRIVILEGE OF GROWING UP WITH THIRTEEN BROTHERS AND SISTERS AND WONDERFUL PARENTS. BEING THE TENTH, I HAVE BEEN A PART OF THE BEST FAMILY ANYONE COULD HAVE; SO MANY STORIES TO TELL, GOOD AND BAD. I HAVE WORKED IN THE SAME FIELD FOR THIRTY-SIX YEARS, AND OVER THOSE YEARS, I HAVE BEEN TOLD MANY TIMES BY MY PATIENTS AND FAMILY MEMBERS ABOUT A FALLING OUT

WITH A BROTHER/SISTER/FATHER/MOTHER, WHICH HAS ALWAYS LEFT ME NOT ONLY HEARTBROKEN TO HEAR IT, BUT ALWAYS WONDERING HOW THIS COULD HAPPEN TO FAMILY MEMBERS. IT'S BECAUSE OF HOW I WAS RAISED. UNTIL THIS DAY, MY BROTHERS AND SISTERS ARE THE CLOSEST PEOPLE I KNOW. WE HAVE A BOND THAT WILL NEVER BE BROKEN, NO MATTER WHAT. THIS IS A BLESSING BEYOND BLESSINGS. MY LIFE HAS BEEN TRULY BLESSED, AND I OWE IT TO MY PARENTS/BROTHERS/SISTERS, MY WIFE, CHILDREN/GRANDCHILDREN, AND LARGE EXTENDED FAMILY.

## MARIA

NO. 11

Maria is someone we all love to be around.

She has no May Avenue memories but is filled with childhood stories that took place on Washington Avenue. Maria shares her childhood stories, with an excitement that pulls the listener in.

Maria was as cute as they come growing up—she still is. I was grown and gone when Maria was young, but I often watched her ice skate. She was fantastic; she reminded me of Dorothy Hamill even sporting that famous haircut. Maria was one of the popular girls in high school, making homecoming court.

After high school, Maria attended the local community college to become a nurse. She didn't want to do it, but our dad told her that's what she would be. It made sense; her mom, two older sisters, and a brother were all nurses or physician assistants. It didn't take long for Maria to realize this was not what she wanted to do. Between feeling lost and having a recent breakup with a boyfriend, I talked Maria into coming to live with me, my wife, and our four young daughters in Doylestown, Pennsylvania. It was just what she needed. I helped her get her first job, car, and apartment. Forty years later, Maria still lives in Pennsylvania. A Father's Day doesn't go by without hearing from her, and always with a thank you.

After an early failed first marriage, Maria found Michael and has been more than happily married for twenty-four years. Maria and Michael have two daughters and live near the Pennsylvania Pocono Mountains.

Maria remains one of the siblings who are the glue that holds our family together. Maria is the family communicator and storyteller. I typically need more patience for long, intricate stories. With Maria, I can't wait for her next story.

Early in her life out east, Maria landed a dream job at Polo

Ralph Lauren. She worked at the office in New York City where the celebrities ordered their high-end clothes. One day, as I walked into Maria's office, Tom Selleck walked out. Yeah, Maria knew Tom Selleck, among other stars, and helped them build their wardrobes and have custom suits made. She wasn't starstruck; she was a colleague. After a successful fourteen-year career with Ralph Lauren, she decided to stay home to raise her daughters full-time, and she did that for the next twenty years. Today, Maria owns an environmental consulting company she runs with her husband.

Maria talks with such pride about her siblings and her childhood. From Maria's perspective, as she would put it, "It wasn't all good, but overall, it was a great childhood. Maybe I live in denial at some level, but it works for me."

When Maria talks of her childhood, she speaks of the "pack," the six youngest, and how they spent the summers at the Kankakee swimming pool and the winters at the Ice Arena blocks from home. Maria focuses on the good, much like our mother did. She sees the glass not only as half full but overflowing. She has a family pride that can't be shaken and is very protective of the Menard name. She realizes there was dysfunction in the family dynamics, especially with our dad and the boys —he was hard on them. However, she quickly follows it up with what she calls the "Menard Factor." How did Mom and Dad raise such awesome people? The combination of their strengths and weaknesses melted into each one of us, she believes, is what creates great people—troubles and all.

Maria shared that one of her favorite places is a hotel breakfast with her siblings after a family get together. It's all story time and laughter. Outside of her husband and daughters, being born into this family with her siblings is what she considers her greatest blessing.

# MARK

## No. 12

No May Avenue stories about Mark; he was a baby when we moved to the Washington Avenue house. For some reason, I have the most vivid memories of Mark of all my younger siblings.

Mark had earlier challenges than most of the Menards.

At age three, Mom found a bump on Mark's forehead. After a visit to Dr. Zaroff, our family doctor, Mark was immediately taken to the Chicago Children's Hospital. Dr. Zaroff didn't know what the bump was, but he knew it was serious.

The bump was a brain tumor. Exploratory surgery revealed that the tumor had spread across most of the top of Mark's brain, and the tentacles of the tumor had already embedded its roots into Mark's frontal lobe. The prognosis was not good. A quarter of Mark's skull was removed because the cancer had weakened it. Children's Hospital used an experimental type of surgery; they cut out what was possible and then used suction to remove the roots of the tumor's network. They replaced Mark's scalp with a synthetic material that would theoretically compress over time with the growth of Mark's skull. Only time would tell about Mark's recovery.

Mark has a calm and confident demeanor today at fifty-six. That same personality shone through even as a three-year-old as he sat for weeks recovering from his surgery.

Children's Hospital was in the middle of Chicago, a sixty-mile ride from Kankakee. Mom visited often, but it was difficult for her; she had a gang of little ones at home to mother. At the time, I was working at an office in downtown Chicago, minutes from Mark. After work, I'd head over to Mark and stay with him until he fell asleep for the night. He was always happy to see me, and he never cried.

A year following surgery, Mark had another medical emergency. A neighbor's large German shepherd broke his chain and headed to the Menard house. Mark, now four years old, was standing in the front yard. The dog, being playful, not hurtful, wound himself and that chain around and through Mark's legs, wrapping the chain around Mark's right leg. When the owner called the dog, it took off with just enough slack in the chain to give the dog a running start. The chain pulled Mark's leg out of its socket as the dog dragged Mark four doors down. The only thing keeping Mark's leg connected to his little body was a thin tube of skin. All tendons and nerves had been severed.

At the emergency room, they talked about amputation. Mom pleaded, "Please do your best to reconnect his leg."

With confidence and expectation, Mom stayed in prayer through Mark's recovery. The probability of Mark walking again was low. Now, some fifty years later, Mark is thriving. He had two miraculous recoveries, two more examples of the power of prayer—Mom's prayer.

I love all my siblings equally, but I have always had a special connection with Mark. I relate more closely to him. Even though we are sixteen years apart, we look alike, have the same passion for music, and I like to think we have similar personalities.

Mark is more intelligent than the average bear. During high school, Mark became a Rotary exchange student to Brazil. It was a great experience, and Mark came home an even more mature, confident man. Mark's college entrance exams earned him the right to attend the university of his choice. He picked the University of Illinois and graduated with honors with a communications major and a business minor.

Mark is a gifted salesman. He has excelled in selling large fuel tanker trucks, always at the top of his game. Mark has four adult children and lives alone with his two rescue dogs, Lady and Big Girl.

Other than his medical traumas, I didn't know of any of

Mark's adverse childhood experiences. I was wrong. I asked Mark what it was like growing up on Washington Avenue.

He said in his calm, confident voice, "I felt invisible, like no one knew I existed. I was the fat kid always at the bottom of the pile."

Neglect is a harsh form of childhood trauma, but somehow, like many of his siblings, Mark has emerged as an excellent, successful, and happy man. Mark may have excelled not despite his childhood, but because of it.

Mark casually mentioned that his Washington Avenue Stories would make my May Avenue Stories pale like that one light bulb. Mark, I throw down the gauntlet—start writing!

## ADAM
No. 13

Not only was Adam good-looking, but he was modest, unaware of how good-looking he was. Adam second-guessed everything about himself. He didn't second-guess anyone else, only his decisions and confidence. We constantly teased him about it. He would get overly stressed about the most minor things. He was obsessive about silly things, like how many bricks were on the side of a building, so Mom would stop and make us all count until we knew so that Adam would have the answer.

My younger siblings told me that growing up with Adam was easy and fun. He never started trouble with anyone, and he was non-confrontational. He was funny, a great team player, and always made us laugh. He never had an enemy; people lit up when they saw Adam. He had girls chasing him, but he preferred a steady girl over dating around. Adam was known as the most organized and tidiest brother.

Being the youngest of ten boys meant that he got a lot of ribbing. In our family, it was about how tough you were and the pecking order. So, Adam would always be last. Dad was a little more lenient with Adam than the other boys. Adam got to take Dad's moped when he wanted, which made the older boys refer to him as spoiled. But Adam's lack of confidence and inability to "fix anything" made Dad harp on him.

He was the baby, and unlike his brothers, Adam was not a fighter. He didn't feel the need to prove his masculinity like most of his brothers. He could hold his own in a fight but tried to avoid physical confrontation. He was more a lover than a fighter, not a mean bone in his body. Adam chose peace over a fight any day. He had a great deal of compassion and knew when he was needed. He never turned anyone down when asked to lend a helping hand.

Adam always had a job and money. He saved better than all

of us. He invested, owned nice cars, and his clothes were washed, ironed, and hanging in the closet. He was well-manicured and as handsome as they come.

I can't think about Adam without considering how he loved his son. He loved his boy more than anything else and wasn't shy, telling everyone who would listen how talented his son was. He showed us his three-year-old's artwork and pointed out the talent in a crayon drawing or a painting. Even at a young age, he saw something exceptional in his son's art. He once came to a family reunion and brought what looked like a professional portfolio of his son's artwork. He had his son show us all his drawings, and Adam explained the medium used (paint, chalk, or pencil.) I wish Adam could see his son now and the creative talent he became. It's amazing how he saw this in his son at such an early age.

We think Adam had ADHD. He told me he couldn't fall asleep without biking twenty miles or running five miles that day. I believe he was never diagnosed or treated for ADHD and suffered because of it. Therefore, he self-medicated. That was where his drug use began—he was always seeking something to "calm him down." Adam once checked himself into a three-month rehabilitation center. He didn't want his addiction to ruin his marriage and career. He also said that he knew his son was getting older, and he didn't want him to have a dad with an addiction. It was during that time that Adam and his wife divorced. Adam took it hard but continued in the program, determined to graduate. He moved in with our mom while the divorce details were worked out, but three months later, Adam relapsed and overdosed.

He was only forty years old when he died. Adam's son was seven. His son went on to become the fantastic and talented artist that Adam saw in him at three, and I know how proud he would be of him.

Adam's life left me with compassion for those who have an

addiction. I have a better understanding that it's an illness, no different from cancer. No one wants it; no one chooses it. Our brother Mark, who was a year older than Adam, gave Adam's eulogy. Mark struggled with how to address the fact that Adam had passed away from an accidental overdose. How could he do Adam's life justice when he was sure everyone would be thinking about how he died? Mark did a fantastic job. We had lost our brother Allen after a battle with colon cancer just six months before Adam's passing. Mark said that Adam's death was no different than Allen's. Allen had cancer and sought treatment, but it didn't work, and God called him home. Adam had the disease of addiction; he sought treatment, but it didn't work, and God called him home.

Adam will always be remembered for his good looks, quick and witty sense of humor, ability to connect with people easily, and his love for his son. After Adam's passing, his prayer diary was found. Adam had an enormous amount of faith and prayed daily, which brings us all a sense of peace.

## ELLEN
### No. 14

Baby Ellen. Baby Ell.

There is something special about the baby of the family.

According to a new study conducted by Brigham Young University's School of Family Life, the family's youngest sibling tends to be Mom and Dad's favorite child because of perception. If the younger sibling feels like they're the favorite child, their bond with their parents is strengthened, and the entire family begins to perceive the youngest sibling as the favorite. So, because they are perceived to be the favorite—they become the favorite by default.

Imagine being the baby of fourteen!

Ellen is the only sibling who did not live on May Avenue. The book has no stories about Ellen, and I barely remember her childhood. Ellen is eighteen years younger than me; I was out of the house during Ellen's first year of life.

Being the youngest of fourteen had its benefits, but I'm sure it came with its detriments. While there were many built-in play-mates and protectors, getting a word in edgewise or being heard was undoubtedly complex. Ellen learned at a young age that she had to work hard to be heard, and to find where she brought value. These lessons have served her well in her life.

Dad had his first open heart surgery when Ellen was two years old. He had four open heart surgeries in his life, and when he passed, Ellen was twenty-six years old. Our Dad was weak, usually ill, and going into surgery or recovering from his last surgery during Ellen's time with him. If you asked Ellen, she'd say her life was seeing the best of Mom and Dad. Ellen witnessed the care and love of our mother for our father while caring for all of the children. Ellen also witnessed our strong mother returning to college to become a nurse when Ellen was in first grade.

After high school, Ellen put herself through college, receiving a Business and Speech Communications degree from Eastern Illinois University. Starting with her first job at a major pharmaceutical company, Ellen catapulted into senior management at some of the most prestigious companies in the world. Today, Ellen is a senior vice president at a major pharmaceutical company.

I observe with joy Ellen's two daughters, who both reflect some aspect of their mother's unique gifts and personality, both destined for favorable futures.

I advise senior executives from Fortune 50 companies. One day, I received a phone call from one of my clients, a top executive at a global medical device company. He told me he had someone sitting next to him who knew me and wanted to say hi, and then he put my sister Ellen on the phone. What are the odds that the baby of fourteen siblings got a seat at the table at the top of corporate America? It was a fantastic moment for me. (And I think for her, too.)

Ellen's childhood experiences were filled with more time with our parents and a different father than I experienced as a child. Our dad seemed more patient and was there for her. He undoubtedly learned to be a better father as he aged. Ellen also possesses a solid Christian faith that she gained from our mother's example and influence.

Ellen is no runt of the litter. She is a strong woman with the highest confidence, assertiveness, and ambition. Like all of us Menards, Ellen has her quirks, flaws, and insecurities, but she knows who she is and what she wants.

# COMPLEX CHILDHOOD TRAUMA

## Kristin Trudeau

"The effects of unresolved trauma can be devastating. It can affect our habits and outlook on life, leading to addictions and poor decision-making. It can take a toll on our family life and interpersonal relationships. It can trigger real physical pain, symptoms, and disease. And it can lead to a range of self-destructive behaviors."

– Peter A. Levine

Let's talk about Adverse Childhood Experiences (ACEs) and complex childhood trauma briefly. As a reminder, this is not a self-help book. More than anything, I want you to know that you are not alone.

ACEs are possible traumatic events that occur from birth through adolescence (zero to seventeen years of age.) ACEs came to fruition through a study by Dr. Vincent Felitti and Dr. Robert Anda to identify negative critical conditions a child may experience and their lasting impacts. Dr. Felitti, the head of Kaiser Permanente's Department of Preventive Medicine in San Diego, along with Dr. Anda, a researcher for the Centers for Disease Control and Prevention, set out to conduct a study between 1995-1997 with the hypothesis that childhood trauma is relational to poor physical and mental health in adults. The two doctors collected survey data from 17,000 patients (gathered during their physical exams.) The adverse childhood experience survey had ten questions to identify traumas and neglect. The ACEs were identified as neglect, abuse (sexual, emotional, and physical), and household dysfunctions (including aspects such as parental divorce or separation due to incarceration, substance abuse and addiction, mental health problems, and witnessing violence.)

The results of the study were shocking; there was a direct connection between a child experiencing ACEs and poor mental and physical well-being as an adult. The Centers for Disease Control and Prevention (CDC) reports that the ACE study confirmed that sixty-four percent of adults had experienced at least one ACE before age eighteen. What is more alarming is that almost one in six adults has an ACE score of four or more. It was the first time there was hard evidence that trauma may be directly linked to negative adult circumstances.

The National Institute for Children's Health Quality (NICHQ) reports that 34.8 million children are subjected to adverse childhood experiences. Research has shown that the higher the ACE score, the higher the risk of chronic medical disorders, mental health disorders, substance use, as well as engagement in risky behavior. What exactly are we talking about here? Carrying an ACE score of four or more puts you at a higher risk for long-lasting health concerns like diabetes, heart disease, cancer, drug abuse, suicidality, risky sexual behaviors, struggles with finances, job security, and maintaining relationships (just to name a few.) The saddest piece of information—the effects can be passed down to our children, which only continues the cycle. For those with an ACE score of six or more, research has shown these individuals may live twenty years less than those with a lesser ACE score.

There are two criteria used to define complex childhood trauma. The first is when a child has experienced multiple ACEs before the age of eighteen. The second criterion is when the child's trauma comes directly from their caregiver, or they are in a position where their caregiver does not protect them. Individuals who endure childhood complex trauma may be diagnosed with complex post-traumatic stress disorder (C-PTSD) by a trained trauma-informed professional. The Georgetown University Center for Child and Human Development explains that complex trauma is chronic, begins in childhood, and occurs within the primary caregiving environment. Typically, complex trauma includes an occurrence of trauma one after the other or a cluster of events co-occurring within the realm of sexual, emotional, and physical abuse, witnessing violence, and neglect.

The good news—we can heal. There is hope.

Some people are aware of how trauma and adverse experiences have impacted their lives, realizing how it may negatively shape their beliefs and behaviors daily. Others may have no idea or are in extreme denial, so they continue in the vicious generational cycle. Each person's journey through their trauma is different; there is no "one size fits all." As a therapist, I am biased and believe that anyone can benefit from engaging in a therapeutic relationship with a trained professional. However, I also recognize that is a very privileged stance and appreciate that not everyone is comfortable seeking help outside their comfort zone, nor is quality mental health care always accessible and affordable. For that reason, it's so crucial that you know that a simple relationship may be transformative and helpful in your trauma journey.

If you feel those internal strings pulling saying, "This could be me," consider your options. The hardest step is asking for help —the journey of processing trauma can be difficult and scary. I encourage you to start when you are ready. Maybe it's by continuing to read about trauma and its effects; see the resources section of this book. Maybe it's by opening up to someone you trust, or perhaps you're ready to find a professional who can walk with you, step by step, through your recovery. Regardless, know you are not alone. You are worthy of healing, and there is hope.

– Kristin Trudeau, M.A., LPC-MHSP, LADAC, CFRCI

# RESOURCES

I hope this book has prompted you to think about and understand yourself and others around you. We are all born into the stories that make us. I have touched ever so briefly on the topic of childhood trauma, an area that is wide and deep with profound implications for all. Kristin and I have assembled a list of good places to start if you want to learn more.

*The Adverse Childhood Experiences Recovery Workbook*
    Glenn R. Schiraldi, PhD
    Powerful new strategies to help heal the hidden wounds from childhood affecting your adult mental and physical health.

*The Unexpected Gift of Trauma: The Path to Posttraumatic Growth*
    Dr. Edith Shiro
    A groundbreaking approach to healing from trauma and experiencing posttraumatic growth from a leading psychologist, featuring a powerful, five-stage framework to help readers not just recover but thrive and transform.

*What Happened To You? Conversations on Trauma, Resilience, and Healing*
  Bruce D. Perry, MD, PhD
  Oprah Winfrey
  Our earliest experiences shape our lives far down the road. This book provides powerful scientific and emotional insights into behavioral patterns that many of us struggle to understand.

*Own Your Past, Change Your Future*
  Dr. John Delony
  We are all carrying the weight of our trauma based on our stories—and those stories are like bricks in a backpack that keeps us from being happy and healthy. In his book, Dr. Delony provides a clear, five-step path to being well.

*GRIT: The Power of Passion and Perseverance*
  Angela Duckworth
  Learn that the secret to outstanding achievement is not talent but a unique blend of passion and persistence that Angela Duckworth calls "GRIT."

*What My Bones Know: A Memoir of Healing from Complex Trauma*
  Stephanie Foo
  A memoir of reckoning and healing from the investigation of the little-understood science behind complex PTSD and how it shaped the author's life.

## HELPFUL WEBSITES:
  Center for Disease Control - CDC.gov
  National Child Traumatic Stress Network - NCTSN.org
  Early Childhood Mental Health Consultation - ECMHC.org
  National Institute for Children's Health Quality - NICHQ.org

# ACKNOWLEDGMENTS

Thank you to all my siblings who went on this ride with me. Thank you for your vulnerability and willingness to have your stories told and for your whole-hearted cheerleading along the way. A special thank you to brother Jamie for his daily talks and texts during the writing, and for allowing me to tell his stories. A special thank you to my niece and nephews from my departed brothers Allen, Patrick, and Adam for helping me tell who they were.

Writing a book and getting it to readers takes a monumental effort. During the writing, I was totally absorbed. Thank you to my wife Emilie, who allowed me that freedom, and more importantly, for serving as my editor, advisor, and constant champion.

Thank you to my daughters Laura, Jenna, Melissa, Anna, and Stella for your love and inspiration. For relistening to all the stories and offering new insights and guidance. Thank you for the feedback, "No, Dad, you cannot write that!"

My thanks and appreciation to Svetlana for her contribution as cover designer and illustrator of the chapter headings. And beyond her artwork, Svetlana offered invaluable counsel.

I am grateful for the editorial commentary provided by my long-time trusted friend, Dr. Jim Murray.

I must thank Dr. Aschanti Abarca Selva who actually saved my life in 2019. She remains my guardian angel.

My appreciation and thanks to Kristin, the mental-health contributor for the book. I interviewed several therapists, psychologists, and psychiatrists during my search for a mental health professional to help with the book. All the others wanted to focus on the complex childhood trauma aspects of the book. They were obsessed with what they believed to be our hidden disorders. They all wanted to "treat" me versus collaborate with me. Kristin was different. She kept coming back to the beauty of the May Avenue Stories. She acknowledged the trauma and the disorders, but she was more focused on and interested in the alchemy that produced the siblings I am so proud of.

# ABOUT THE AUTHOR

Michael Menard's journey from a childhood marked by complex trauma to a successful adult is a story of post-traumatic growth. As a teenager, he gained confidence and presentation skills as a member of a popular local rock band in Chicago. His early years were characterized by innovation, as seen in his creation of mouse-skin gloves at age twelve and his idea for a disposable diaper with elastic legs at age nineteen, leading to his first US patent.

Without formal education beyond high school, Michael's inventiveness caught the attention of Johnson & Johnson, where he eventually became the Worldwide Vice President of Engineering, earning a total of fourteen patents that revolutionized the absorbent products industry. His inventions are now responsible for over $50 billion in annual sales.

Michael later co-founded The GenSight Group, a consulting and software company, advising major corporations like Coca-Cola, NASA, and the United Nations. He is the author of two best-selling business books and remains the President of GenSight. Living in Tennessee with his wife, Emilie, Michael is a proud father of five daughters and nine grandchildren.

**Learn more at www.TheKiteThatCouldntFly.com**